eir
hands small books which they say are
feminaries.

MONIQUE WITTIG

Words unspoken fester inside us.

Goliarda Sapienza

Drawn & Quarterly would like to thank Sofia Jansson and
Rights & Brands.

drawnandquarterly.com
978-1-77046-345-5
First edition: January 2019
Printed in China
10 9 8 7 6 5 4 3 2 1
Cataloguing data available from Library and Archives
Canada.
Published in the USA by Drawn & Quarterly, a client
publisher of Farrar, Straus and Giroux. Orders: 888.330.8477
Published in Canada by Drawn & Quarterly a client
publisher of Raincoast Books. Orders: 800.663.5714
Published in the United Kingdom by Drawn & Quarterly,
a client publisher of Publishers Group UK.
Orders: info@pguk.co.uk

Canadä Drawn and quarterly acknowledges the
support of the Government of Canada and
the Canada Council for the Arts for our publishing
program, and the National Translation Program for
Book Publishing, an initiative of the Roadmap for Canada's
Official Languages 2013-2019: Education, Immigration,
Communities, for our translation activities.

Drawn and Quarterly reconnaît l'aide financière du
gouvernement du Québec par l'entremise de la Société de
développement des entreprises culturelles (SODEC) pour
nos activités d'édition. Gouvernement du Québec —
Programme de crédit d'impôt pour l'édition de livres —
Gestion SODEC

This Woman's Work

julie delporte

Translated by
Aleshia Jensen and Helge Dascher

drawn & quarterly

Whenever anything
was poorly done,
my father would joke:

" must be a woman's
handiwork "

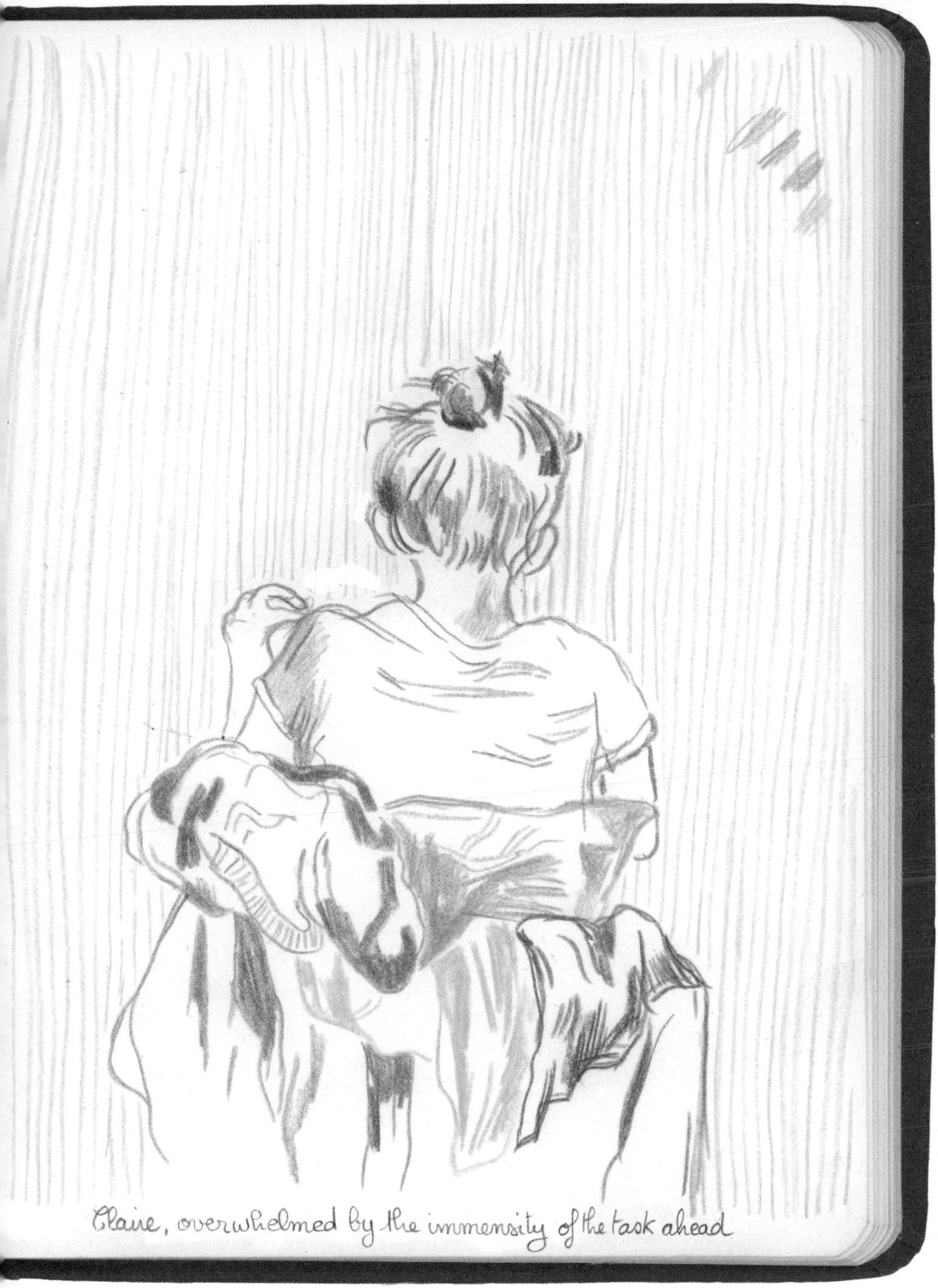

Claire, overwhelmed by the immensity of the task ahead

so why even bother
writing this book?

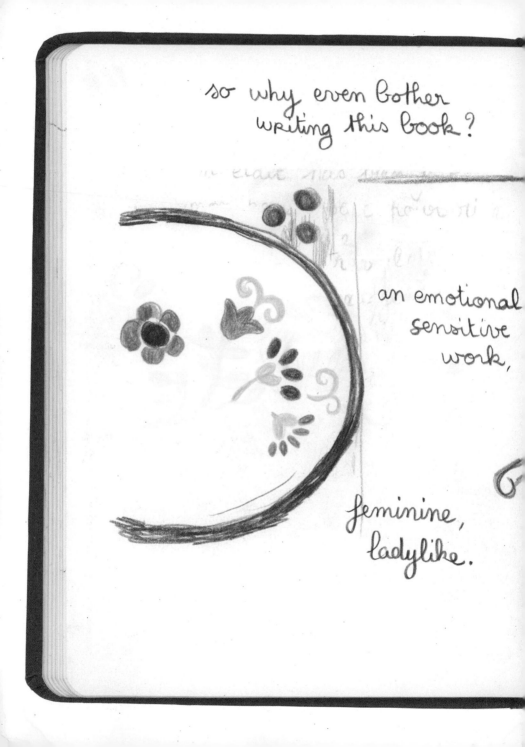

an emotional
sensitive
work,

feminine,
ladylike.

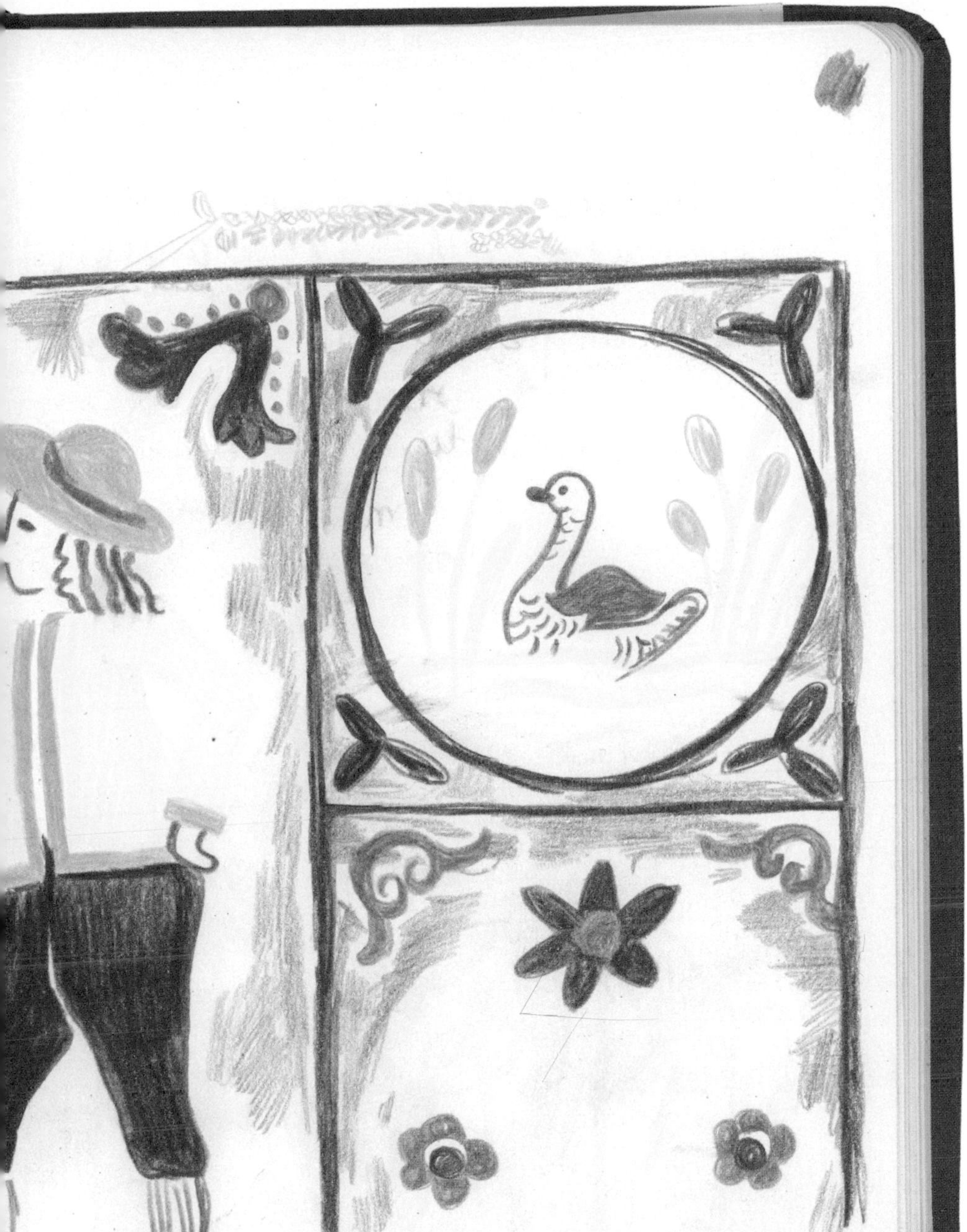

Brussels, September 2016
À ... avec br...

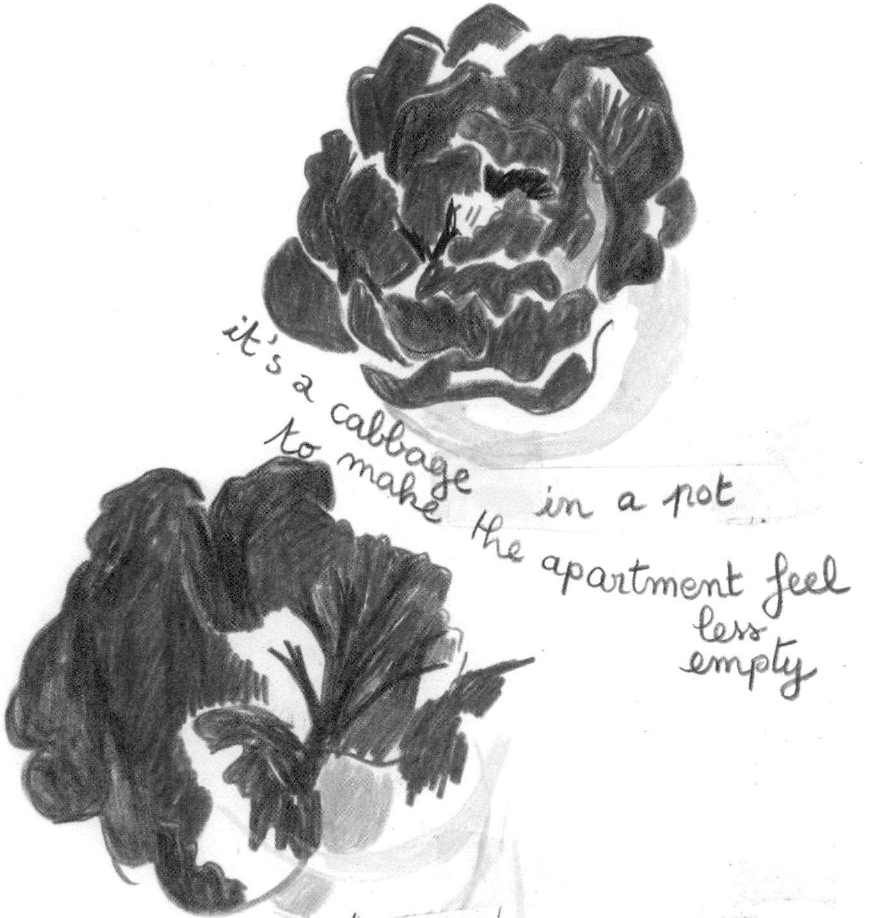
it's a cabbage in a pot
to make the apartment feel less empty
(I wouldn't have thought to buy roses.)

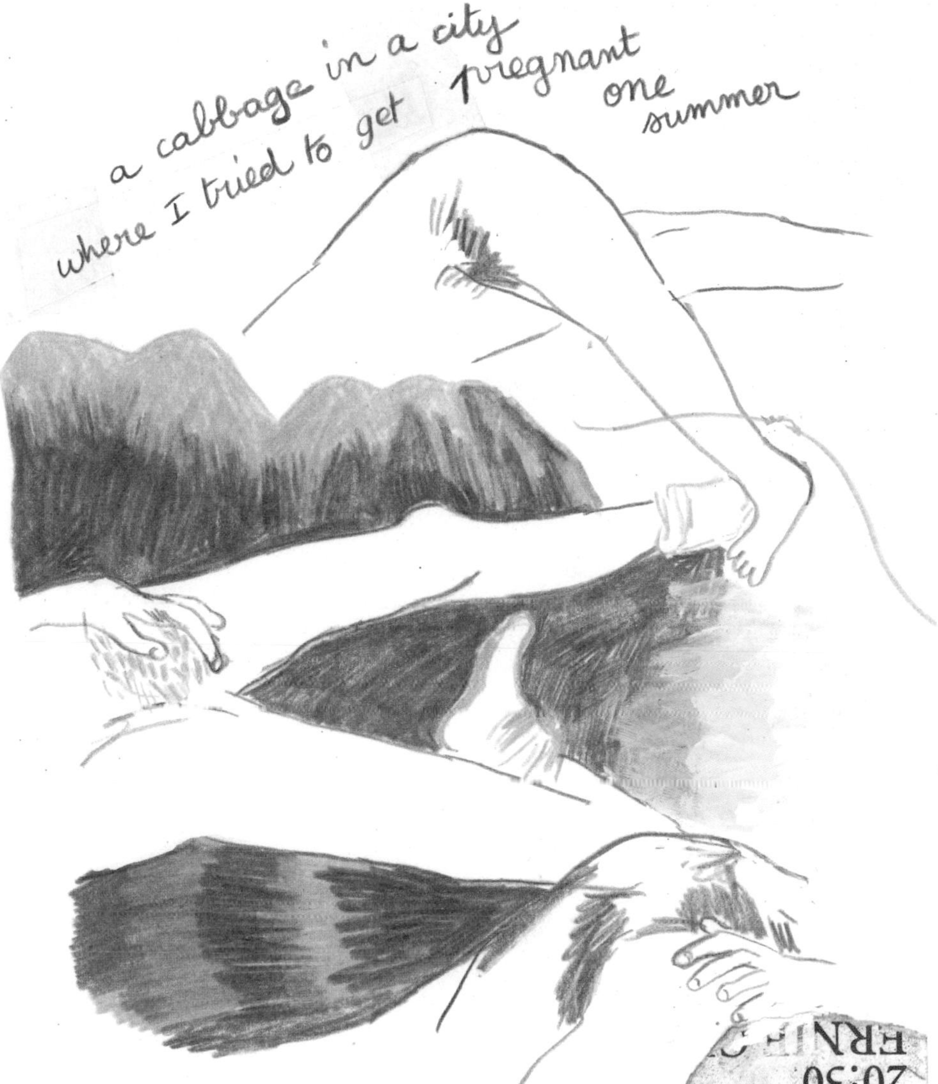
a cabbage in a city
where I tried to get pregnant
one
summer

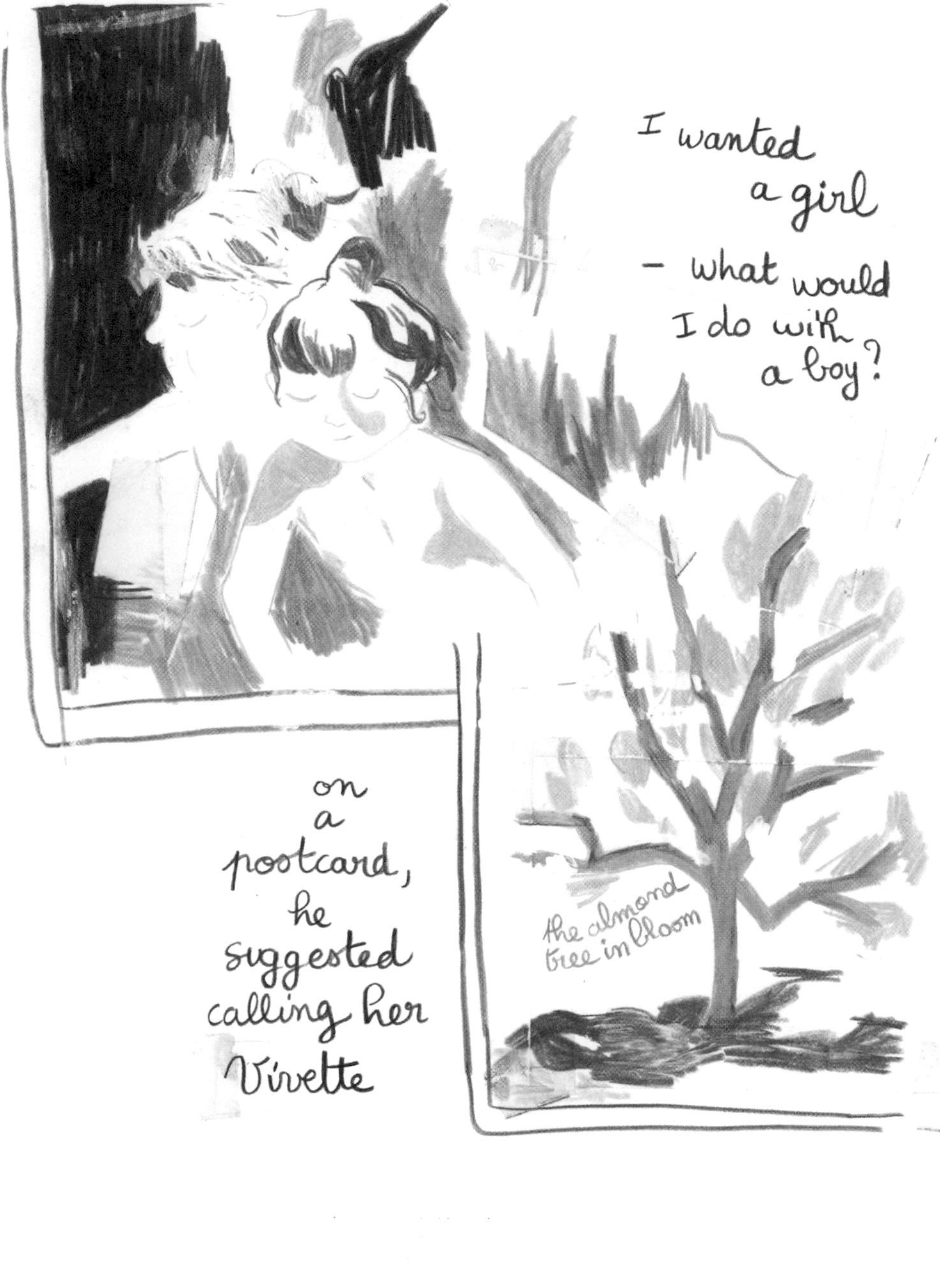
I wanted a girl – what would I do with a boy?
on a postcard, he suggested calling her Vivette
the almond tree in bloom

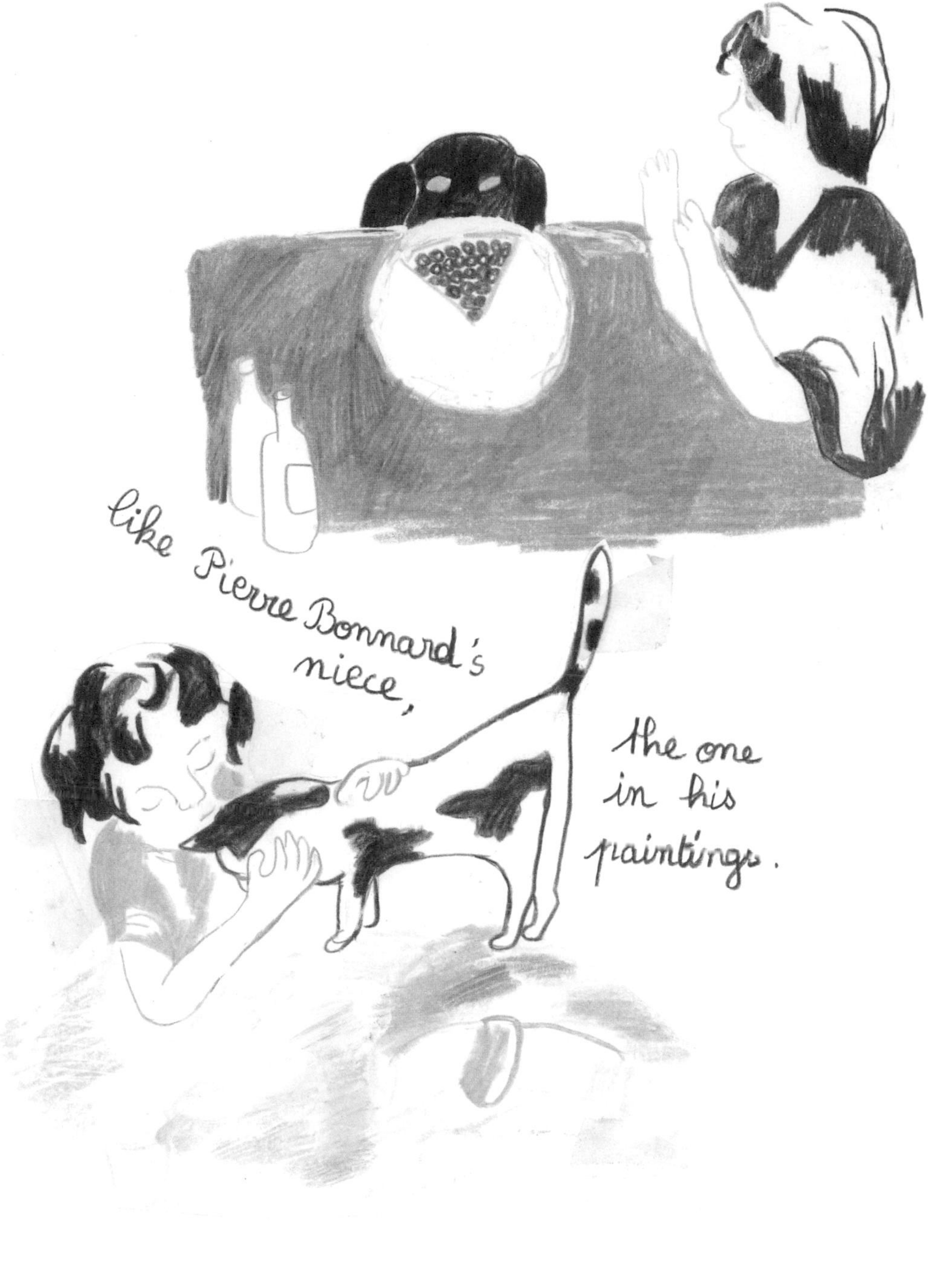
like Pierre Bonnard's niece,
the one in his paintings.

but
when he came inside me

a grey haze

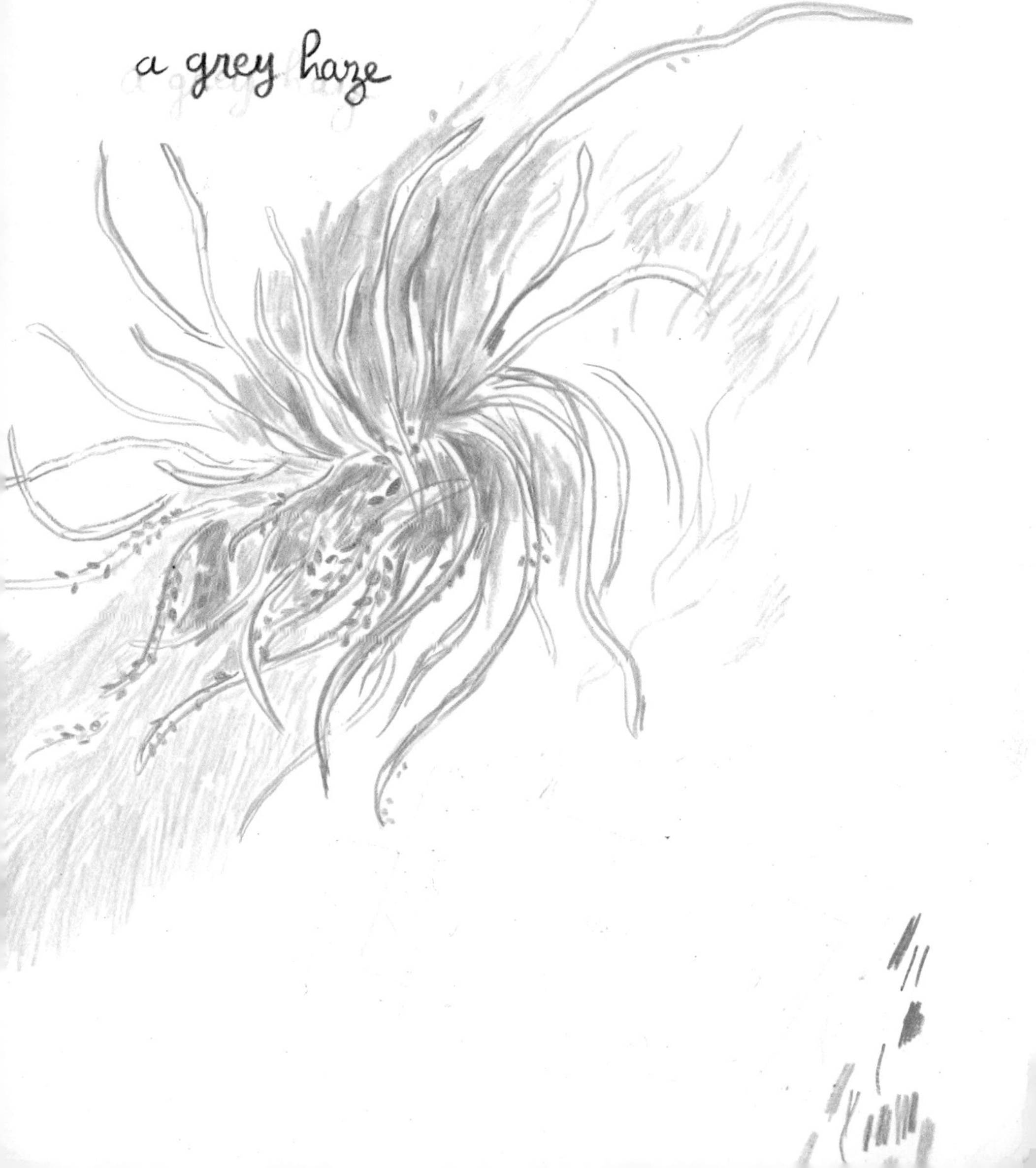

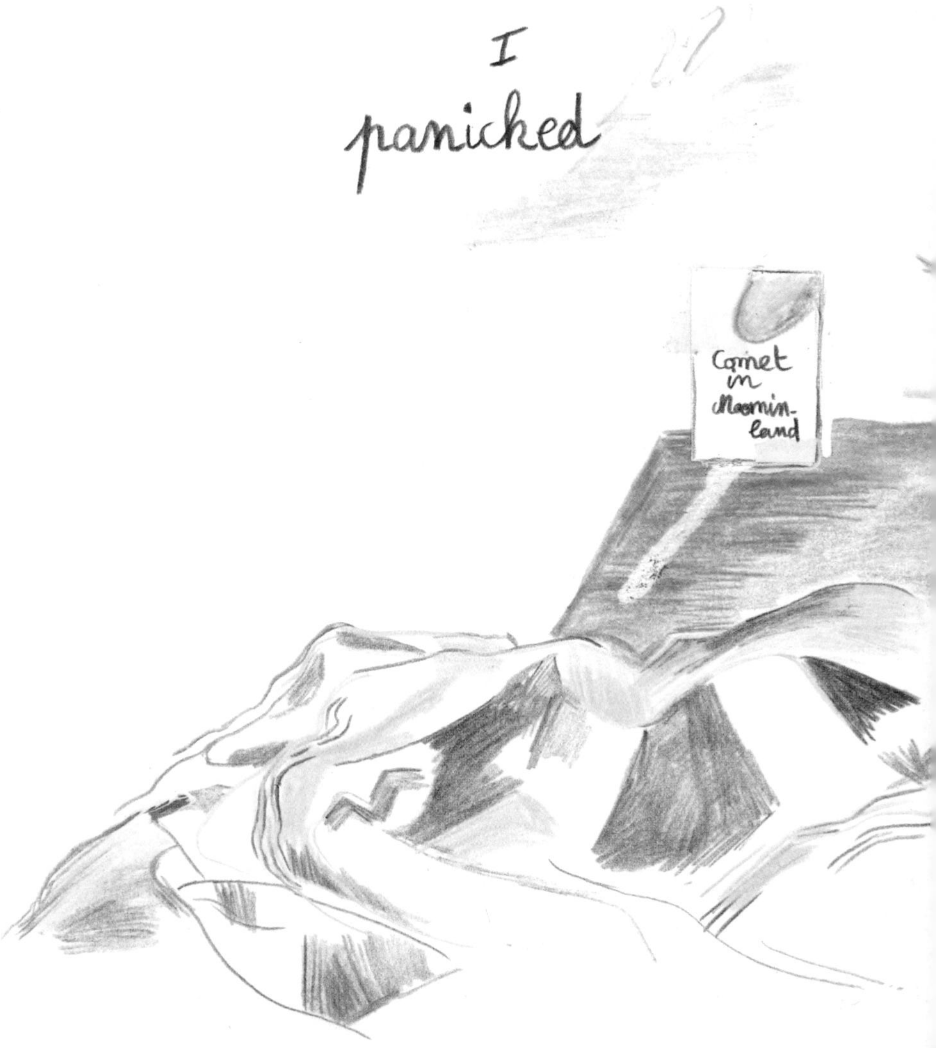
I
panicked
Comet
in
Moomin-
land

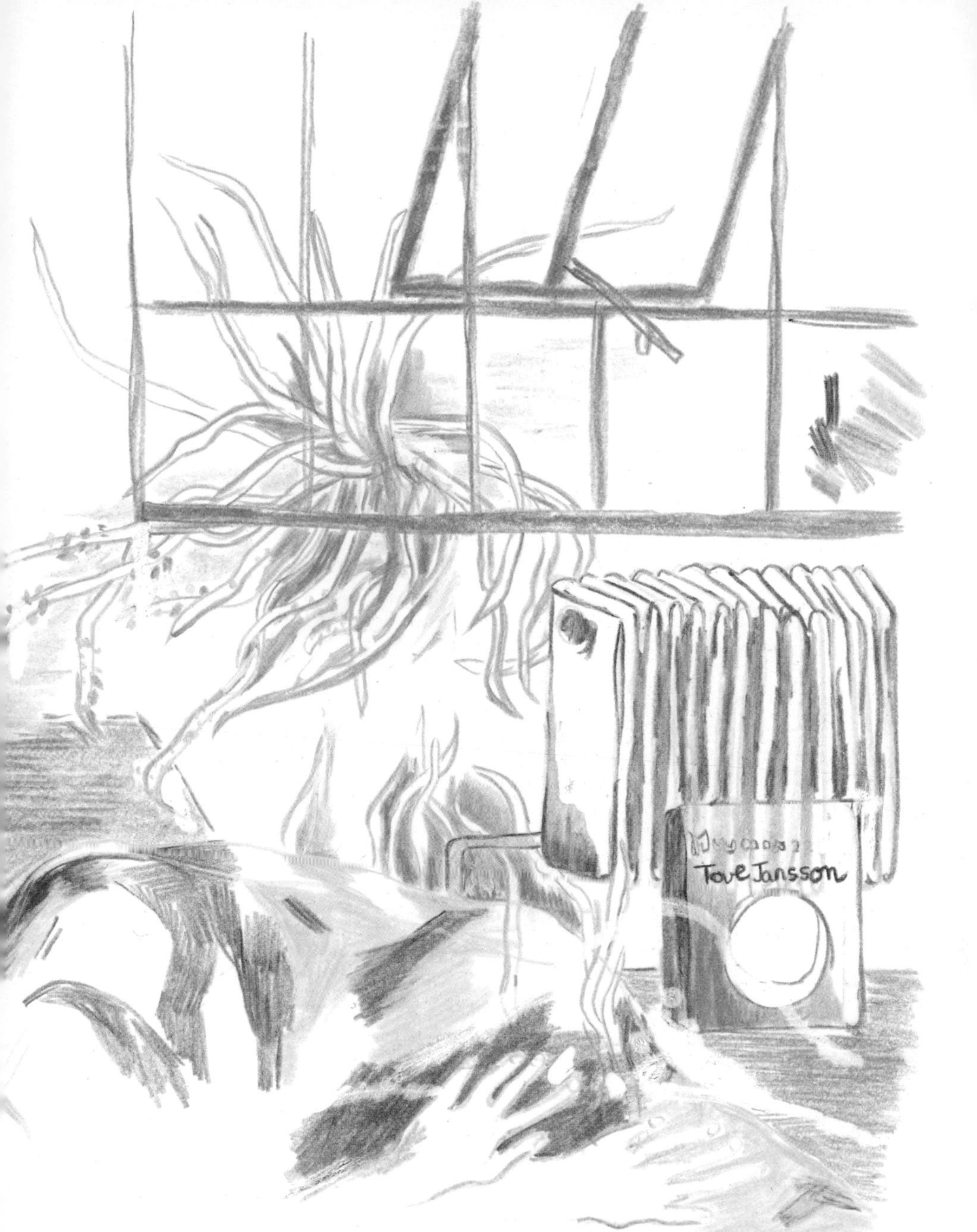
Tove Jansson

I would have liked him to say

I'll take care of her
you'll be able to draw
I'll change the diapers
I'll even nurse her

(Grégoire Colin
in Nénette and Boni, ⟶
by Claire Denis)

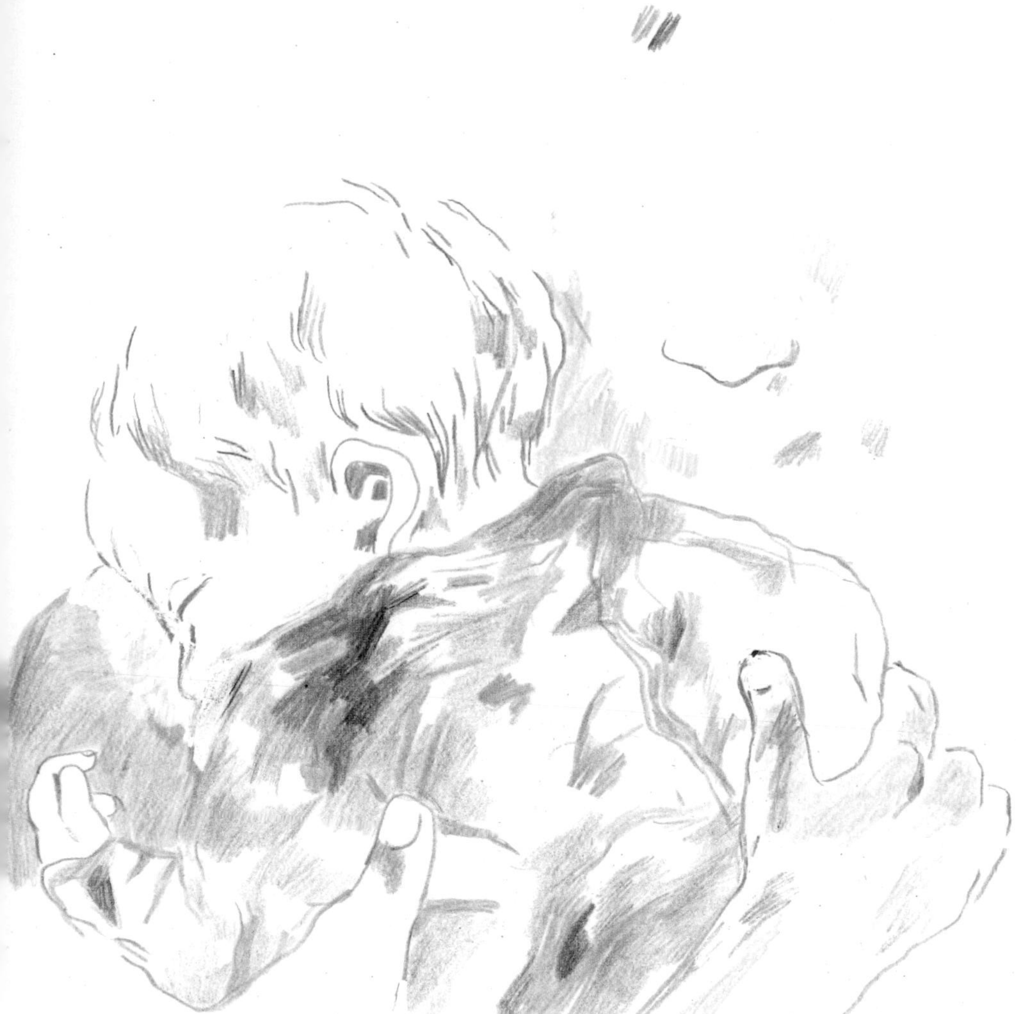

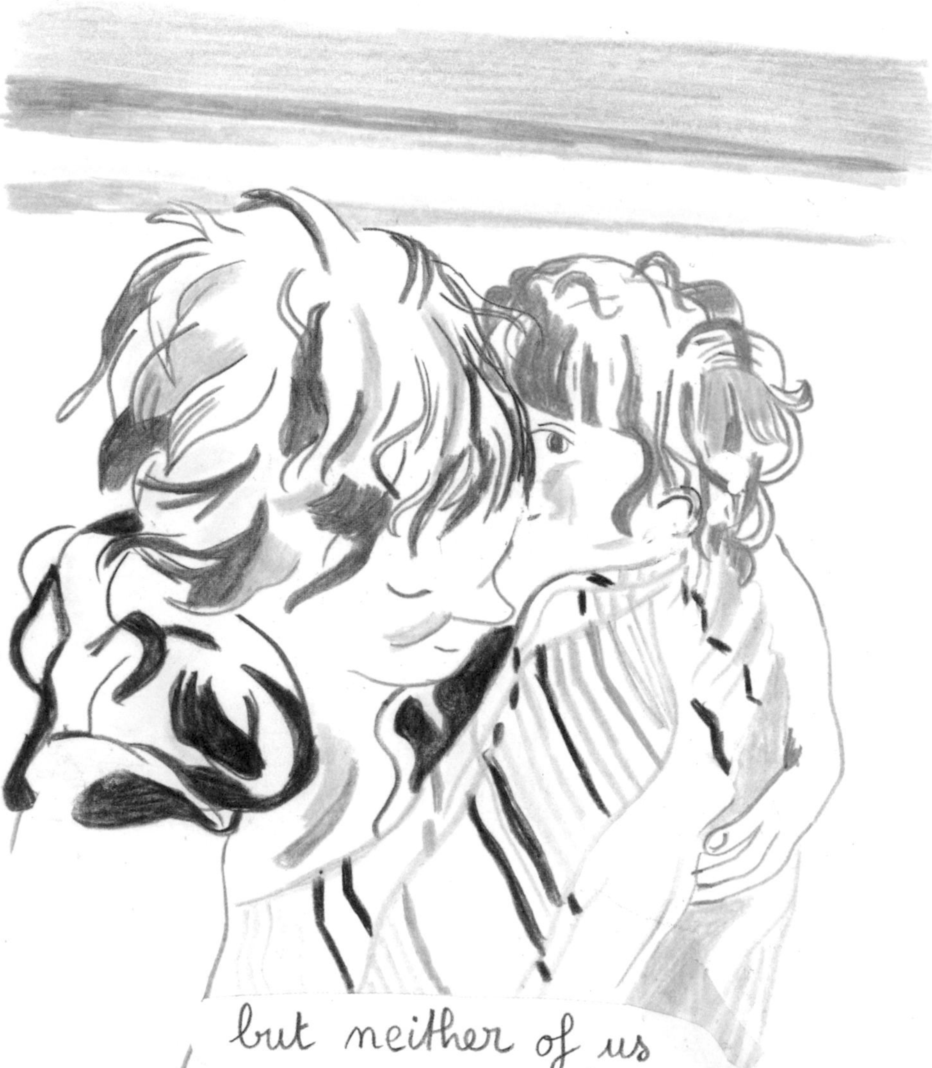
but neither of us
said anything

and when he came, I felt

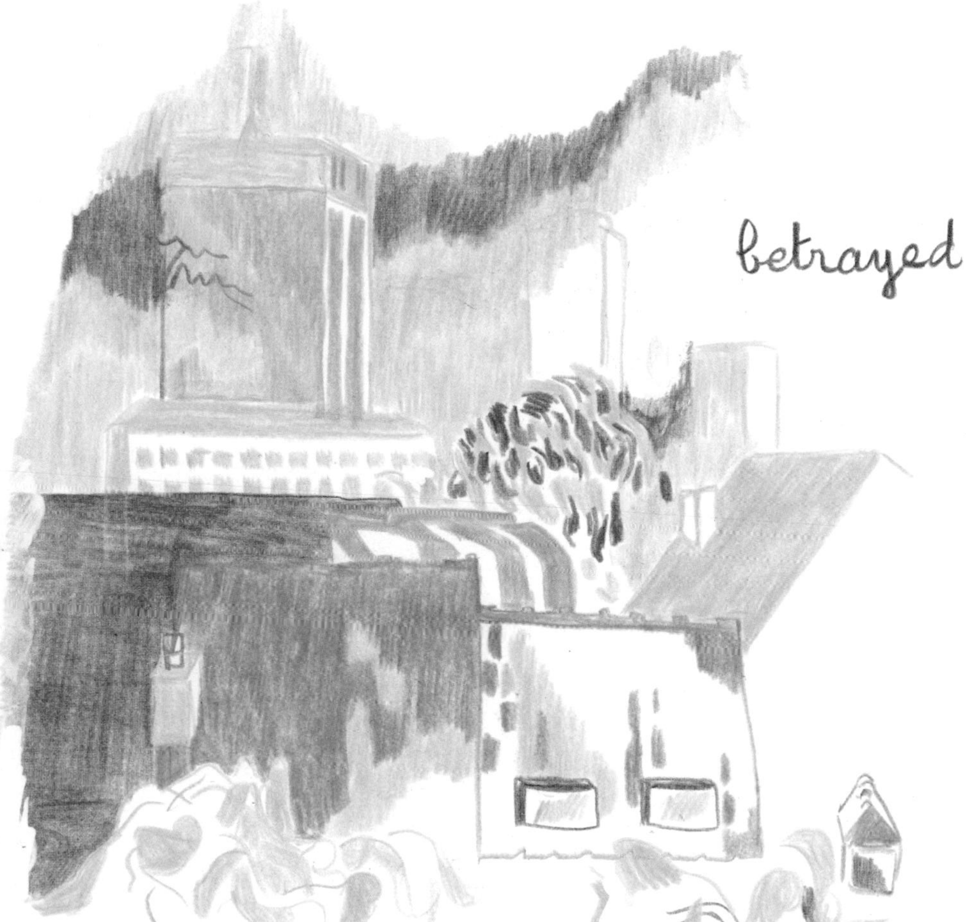
betrayed

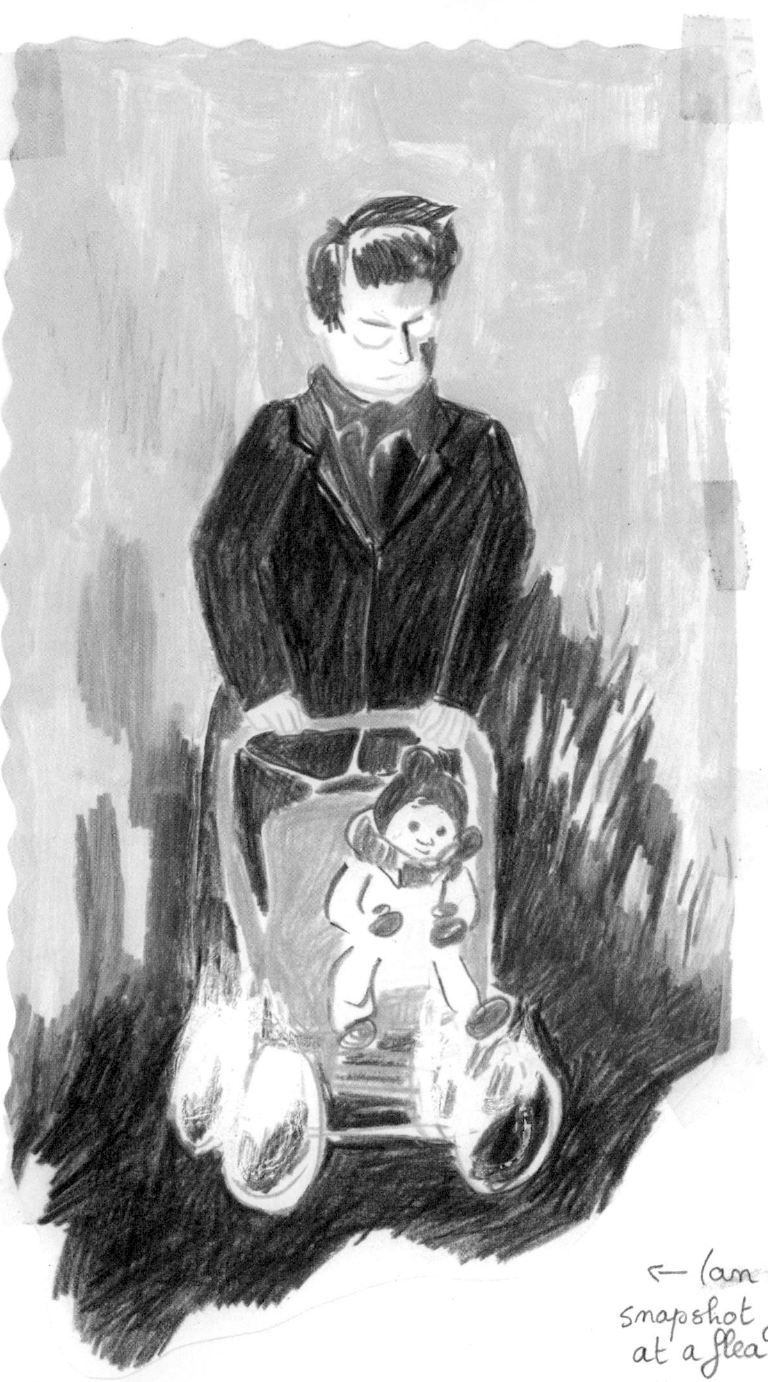

not by him ...

← (an old snapshot found at a flea market)

but by all
men who
leave

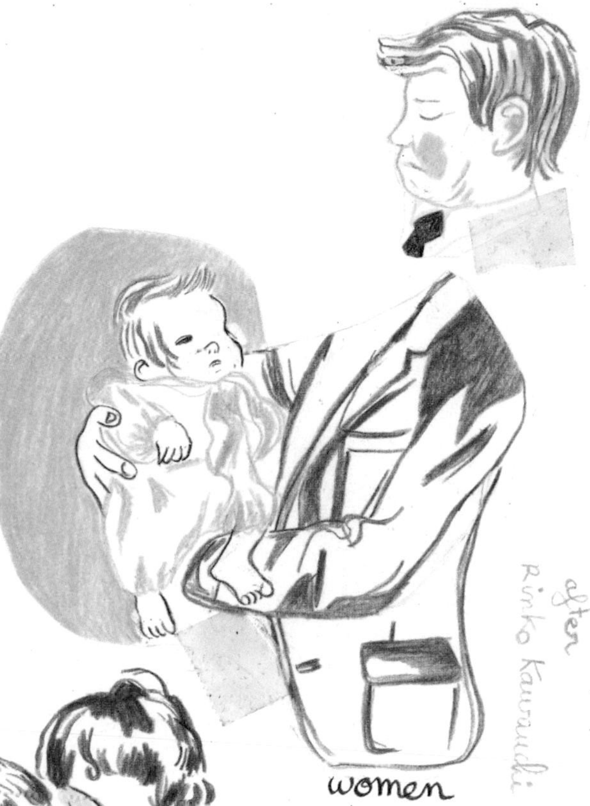
after
Rinko Kawauchi

women
on their
own
to tend
to the
bodies of
their
children.

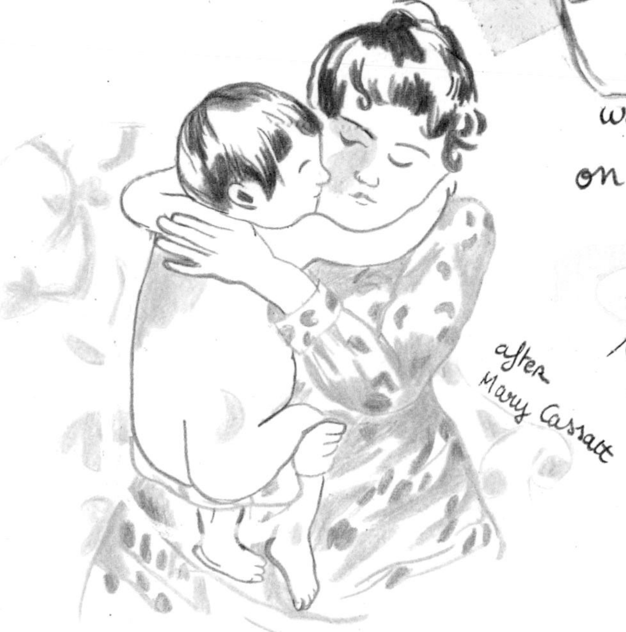
after
Mary Cassatt

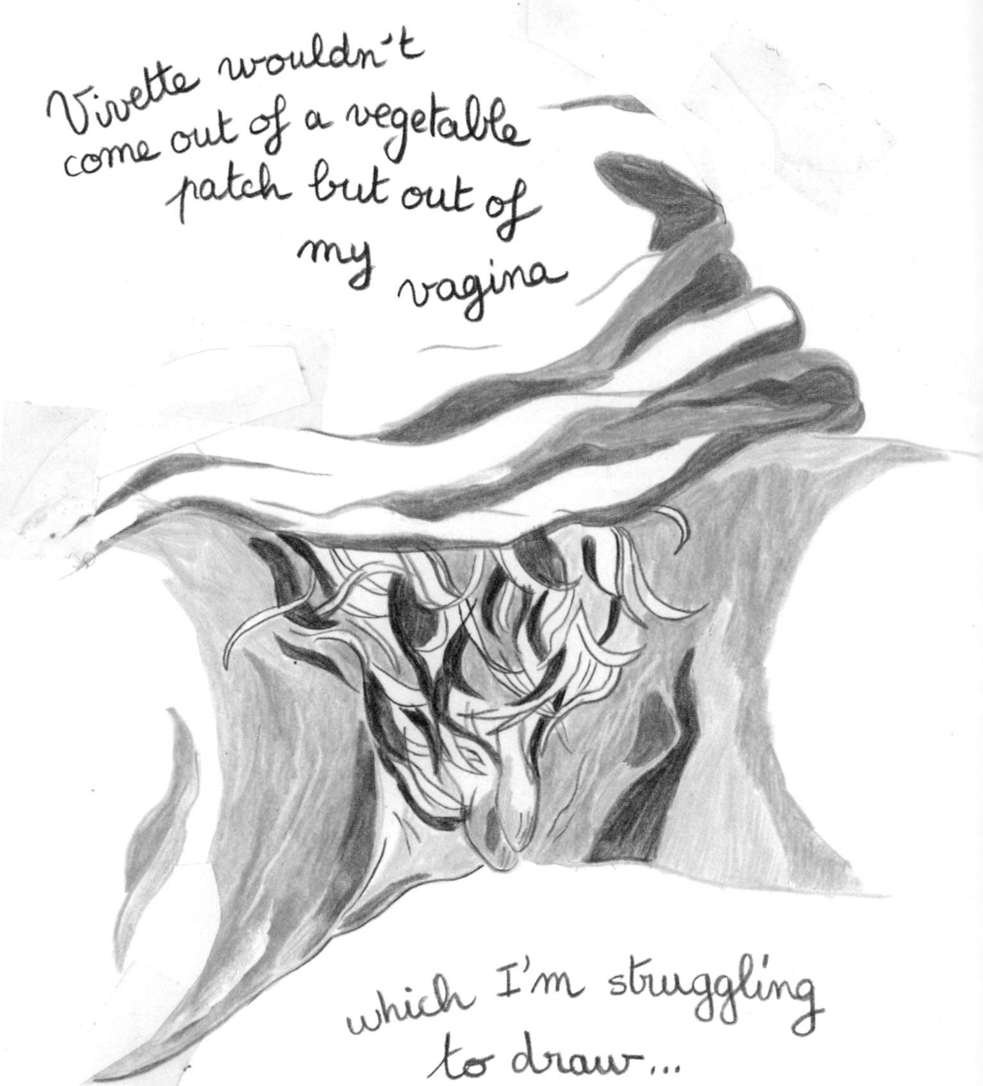
Vivette wouldn't come out of a vegetable patch but out of my vagina
which I'm struggling to draw...

... having lived so long without an image of one.

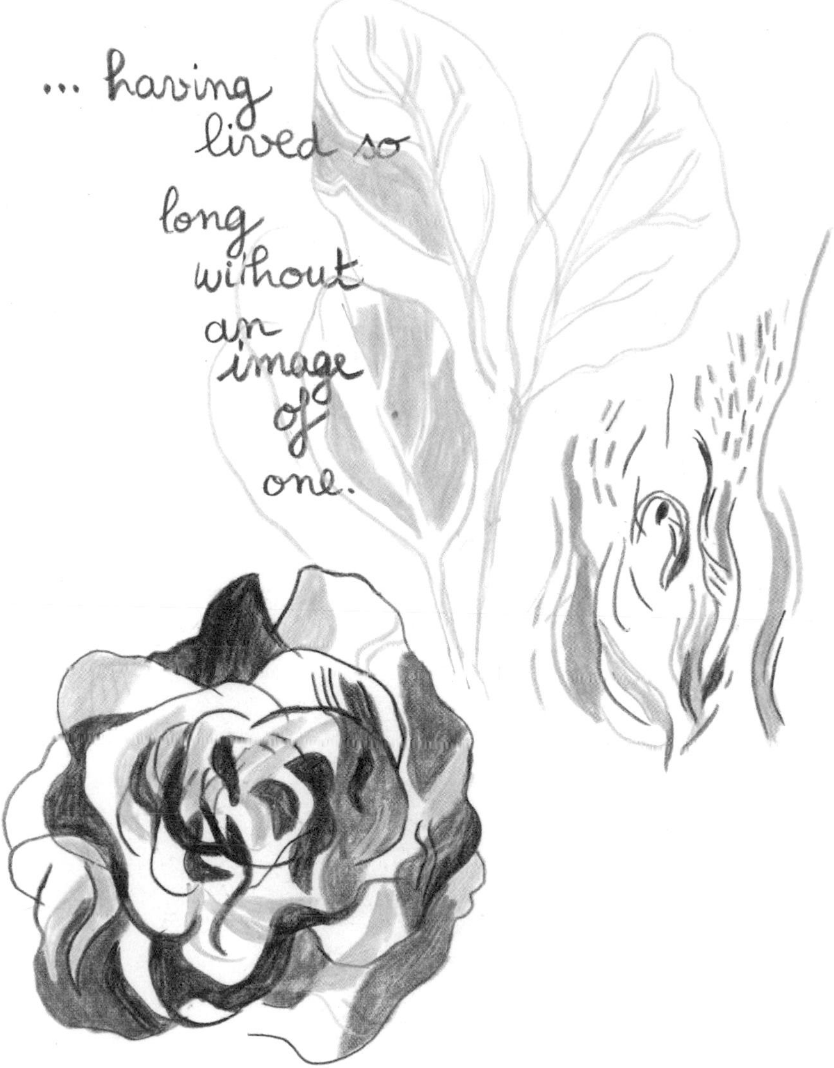

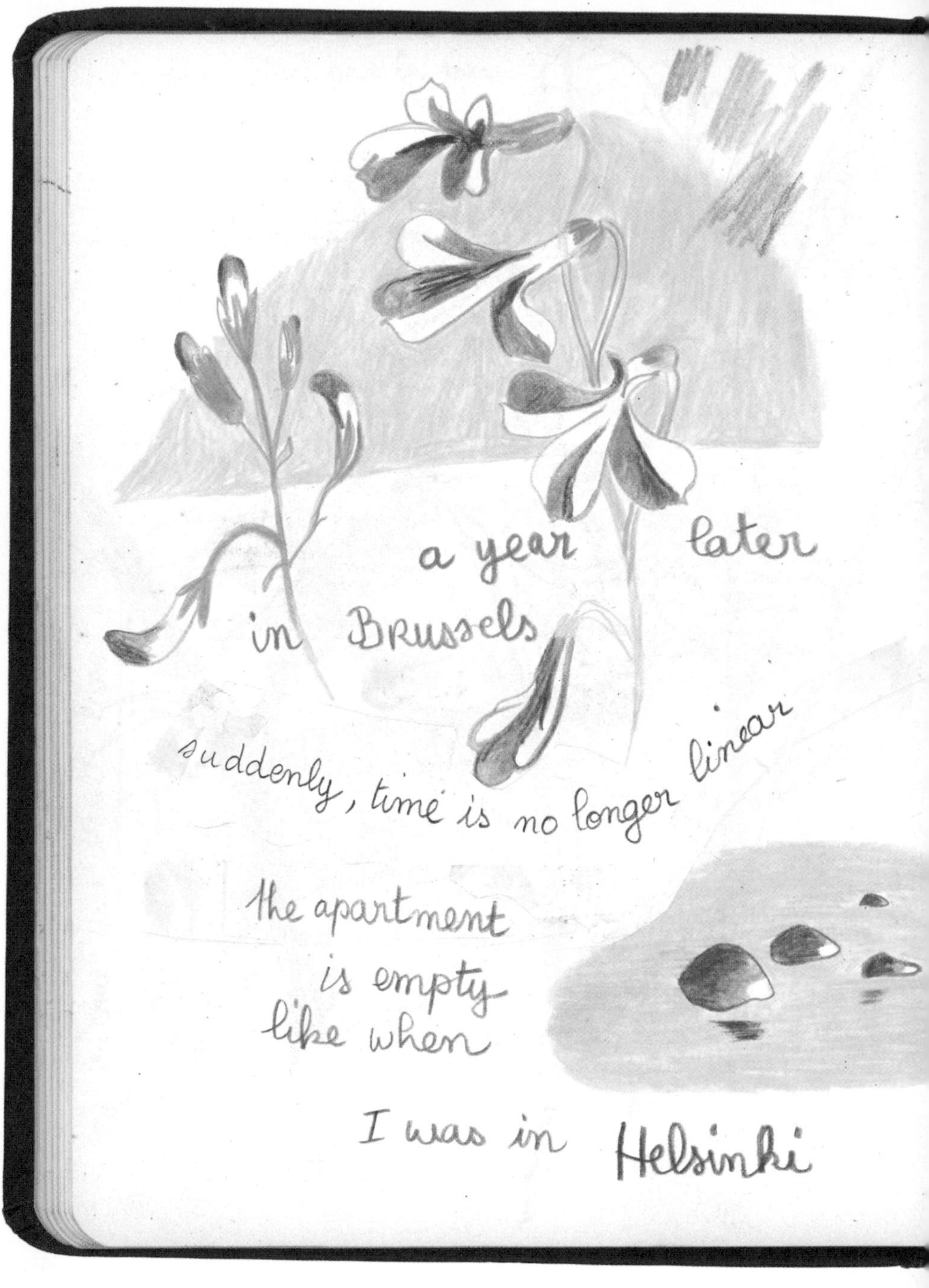
a year later
in Brussels
suddenly, time is no longer linear
the apartment
is empty
like when
I was in Helsinki

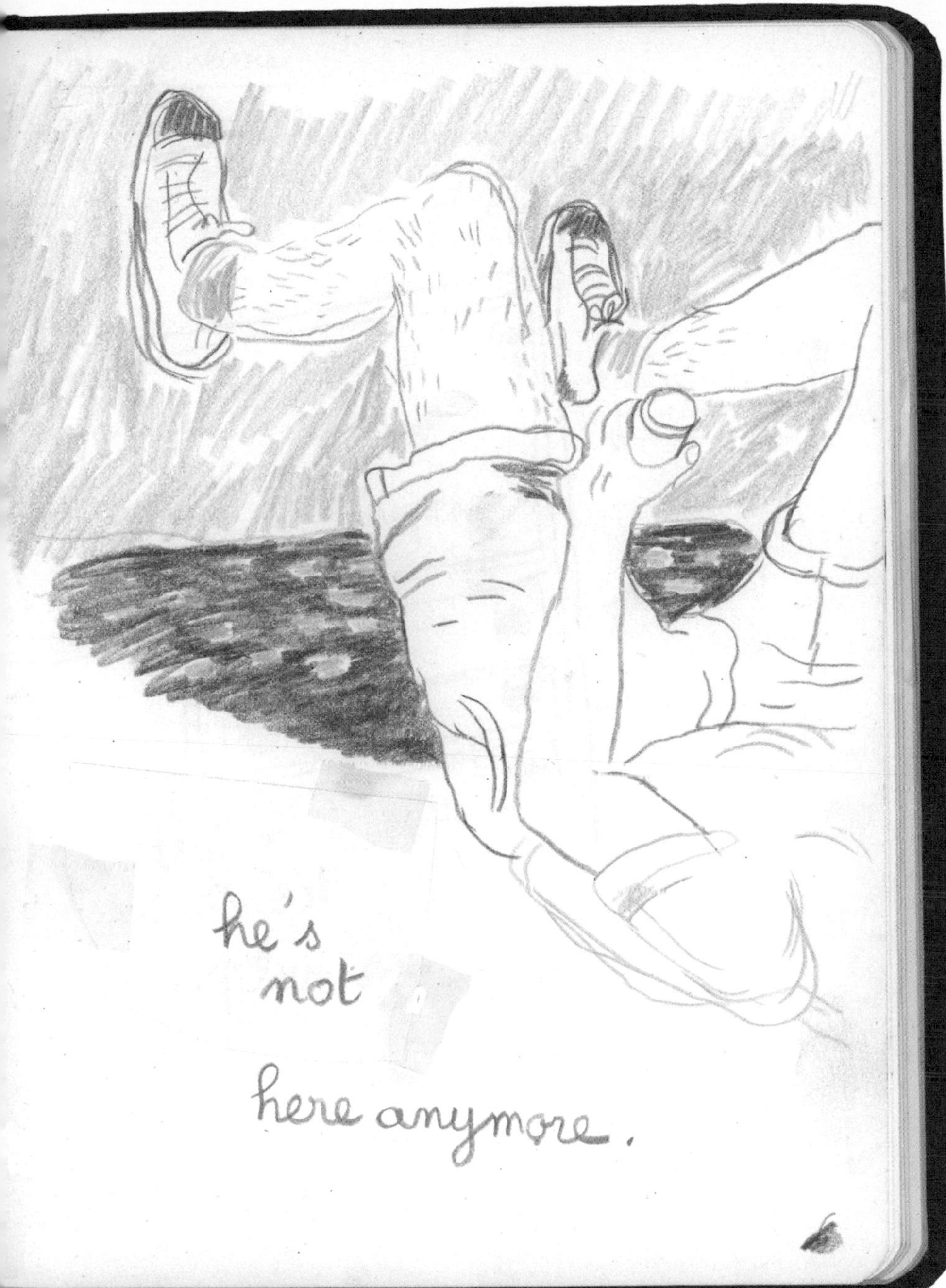
he's
not
here anymore.

I draw
the teapot.

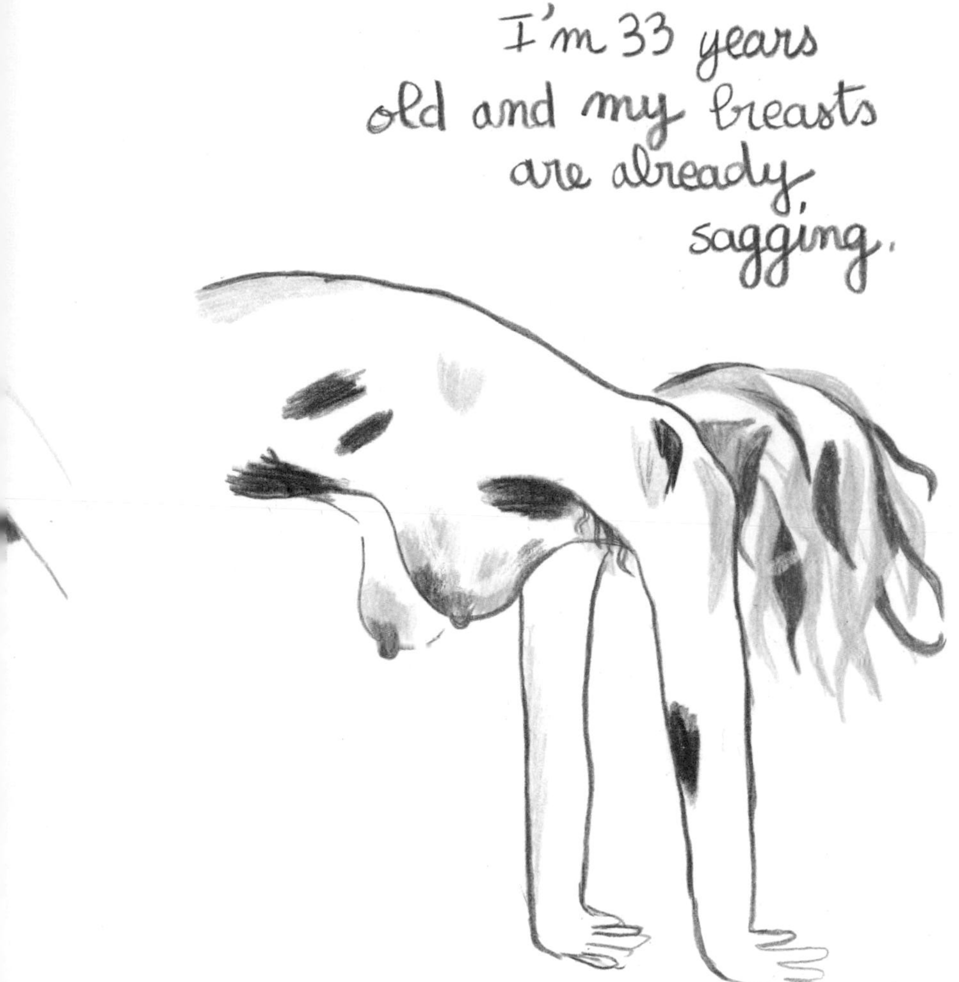
I'm 33 years old and my breasts are already sagging.

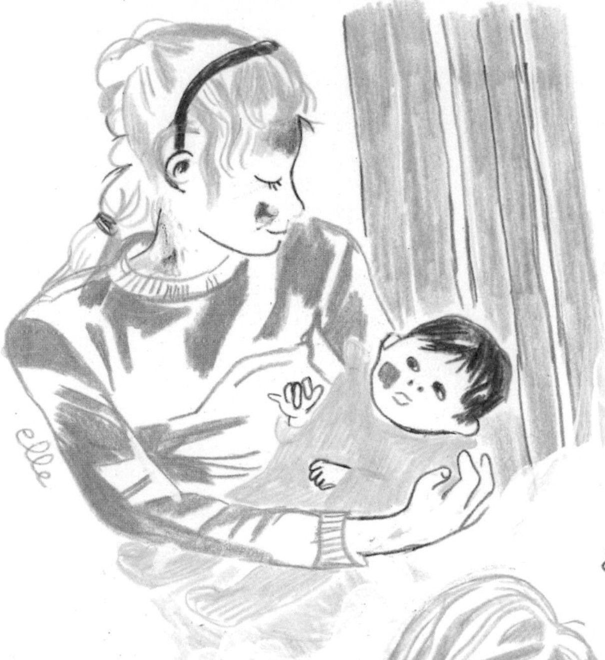
elle

When she was little, my sister used to say she wanted children,

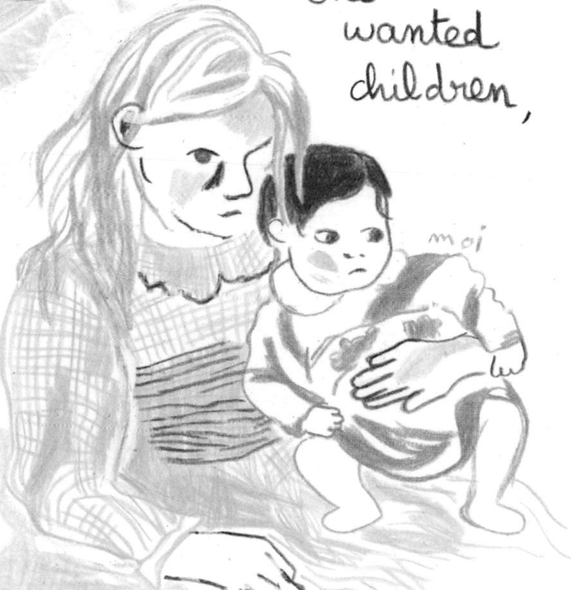
moi

but not a husband.

and I used to say
that if
I had
children,
I'd
want to
be
the father,

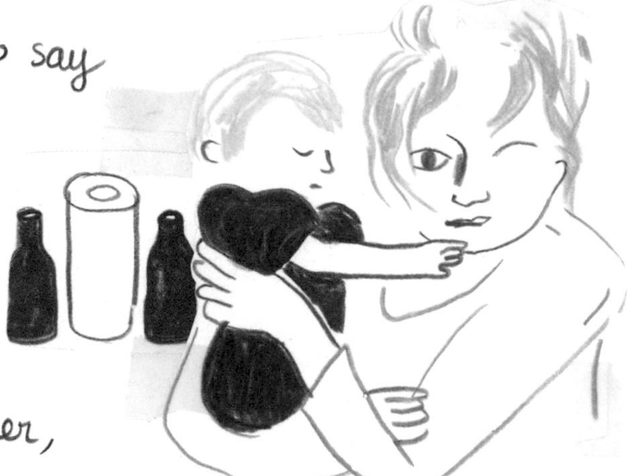

not the mother.

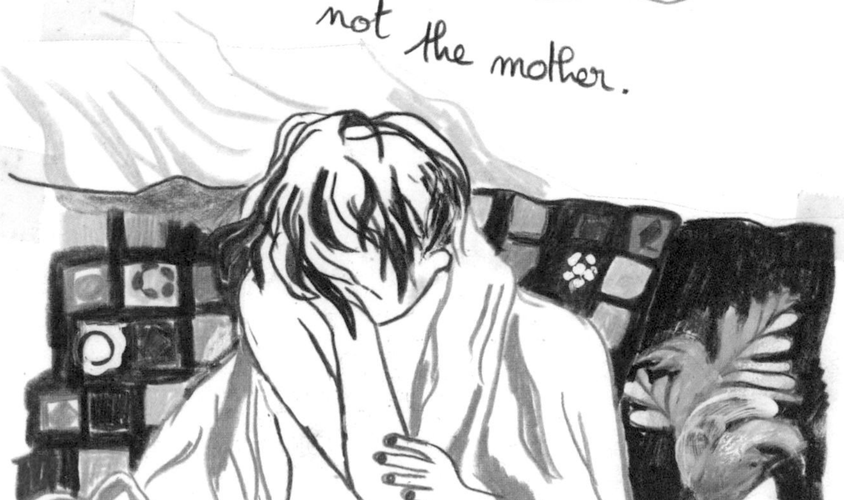

Wanda wakes up on the sofa at her sister's place...
(Barbara Loden, 1970)

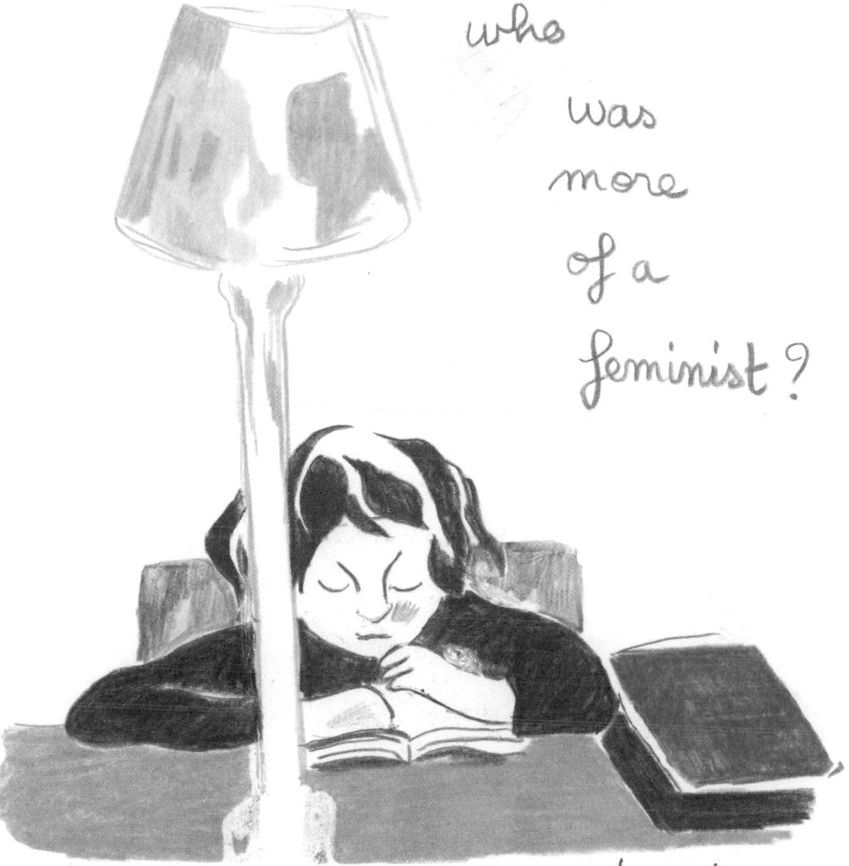
who was more of a feminist?

after Bonnard again.

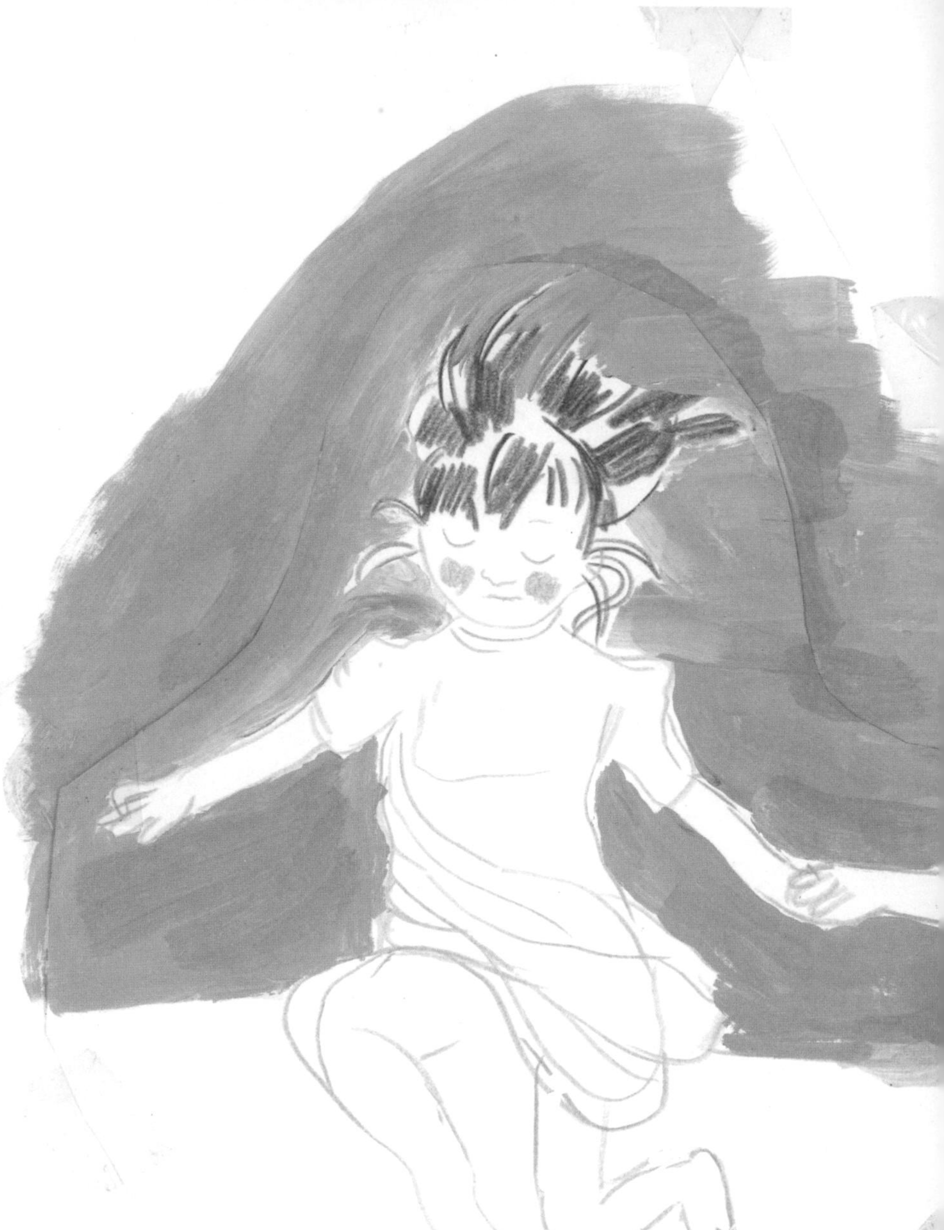

how old was I
   when I started feeling
cheated simply by
      being a girl?

I got my
   first lesson in
sex the year
I learned to
      read.

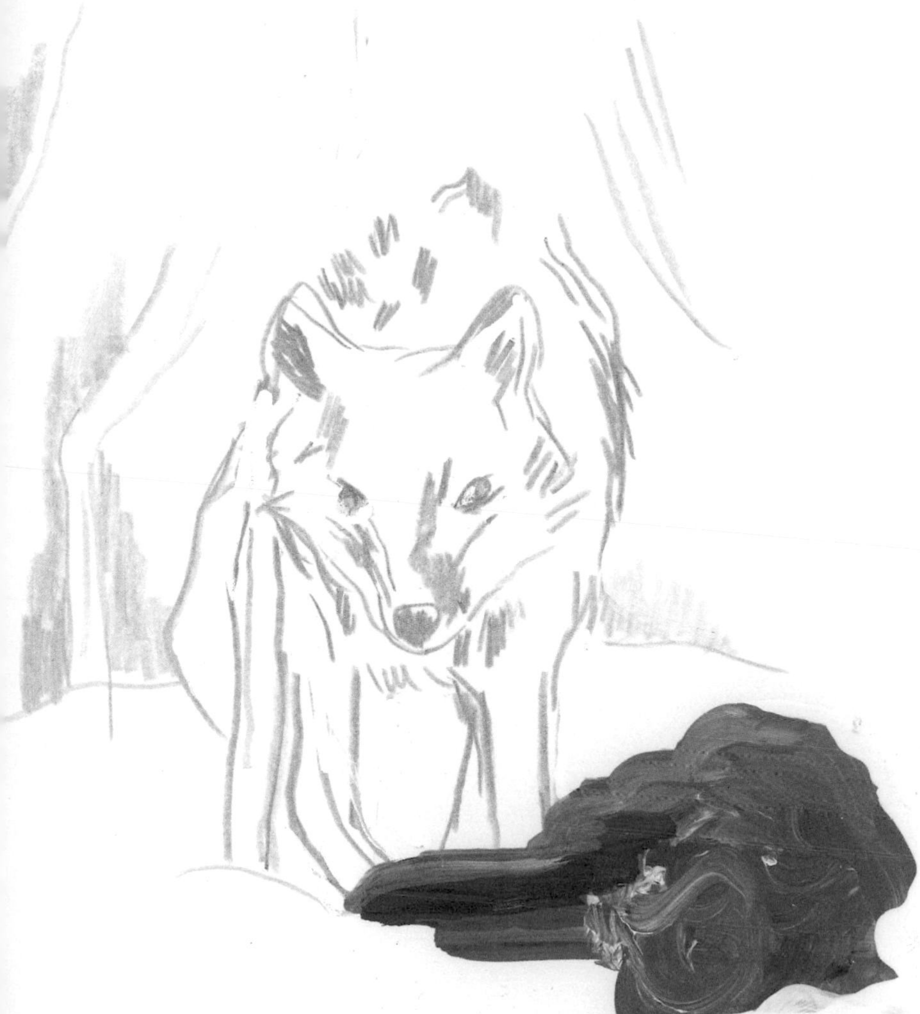

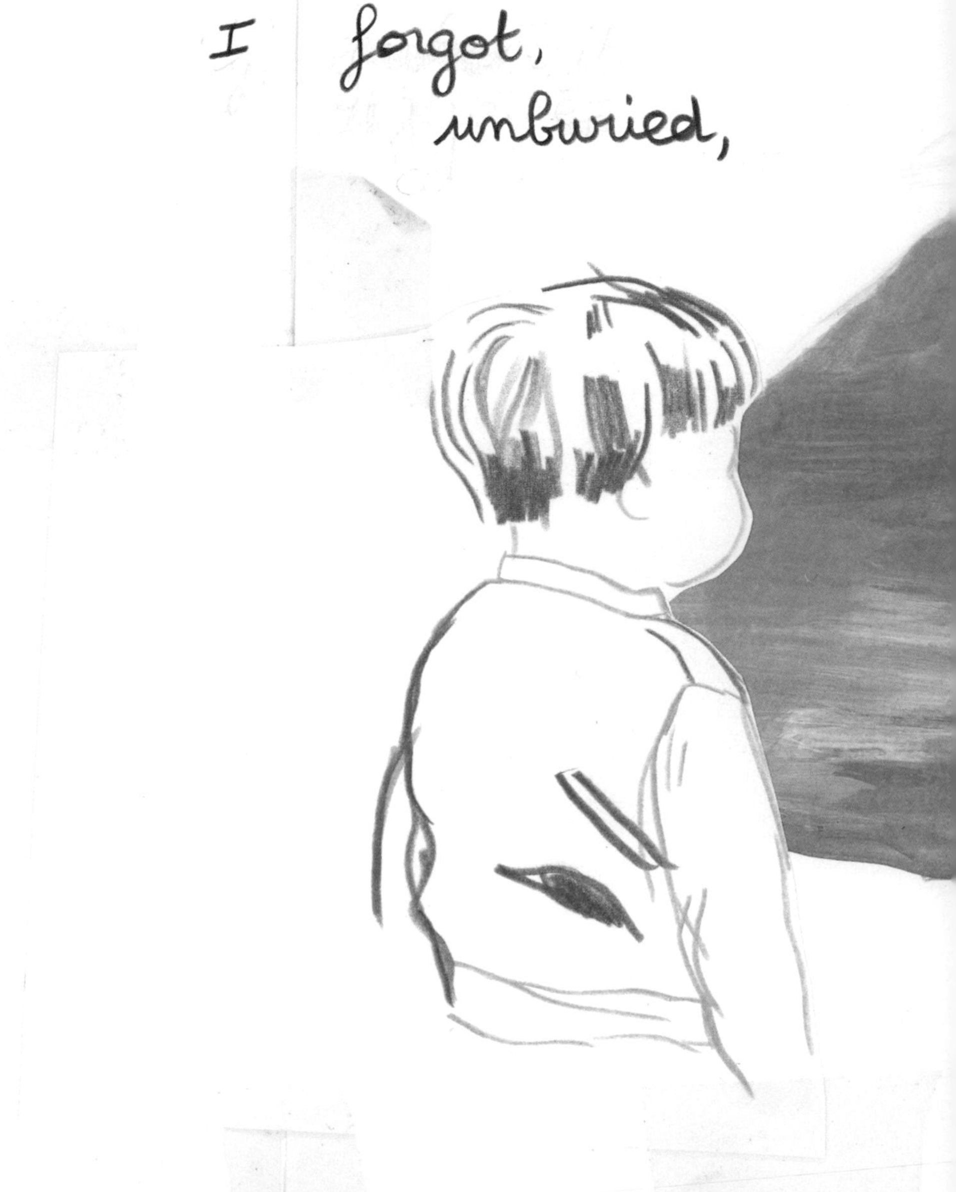
I forgot,
unburied,

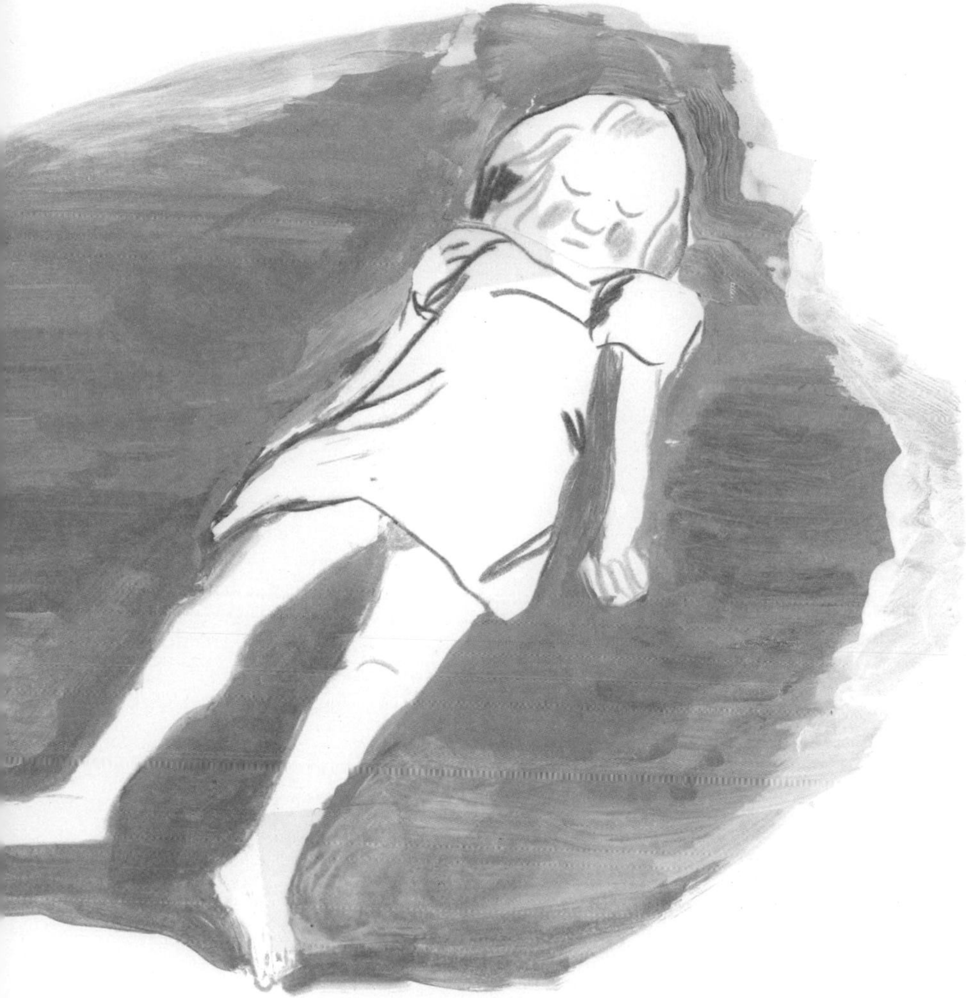

and wrote about
this incident

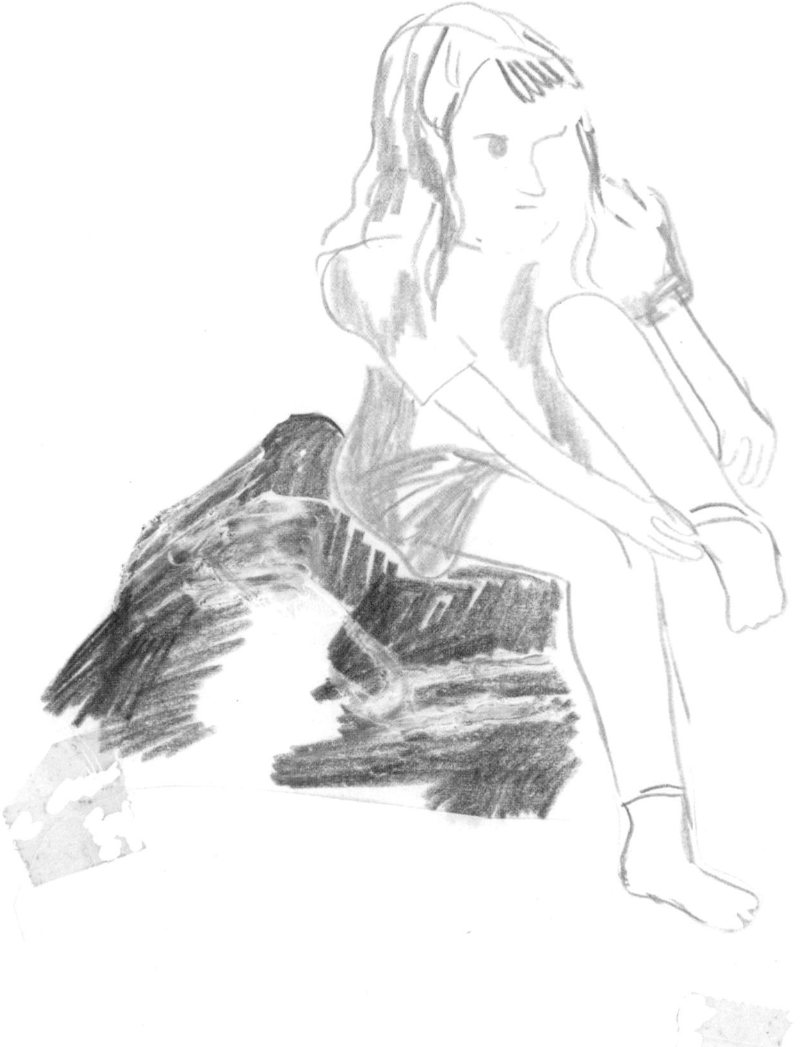

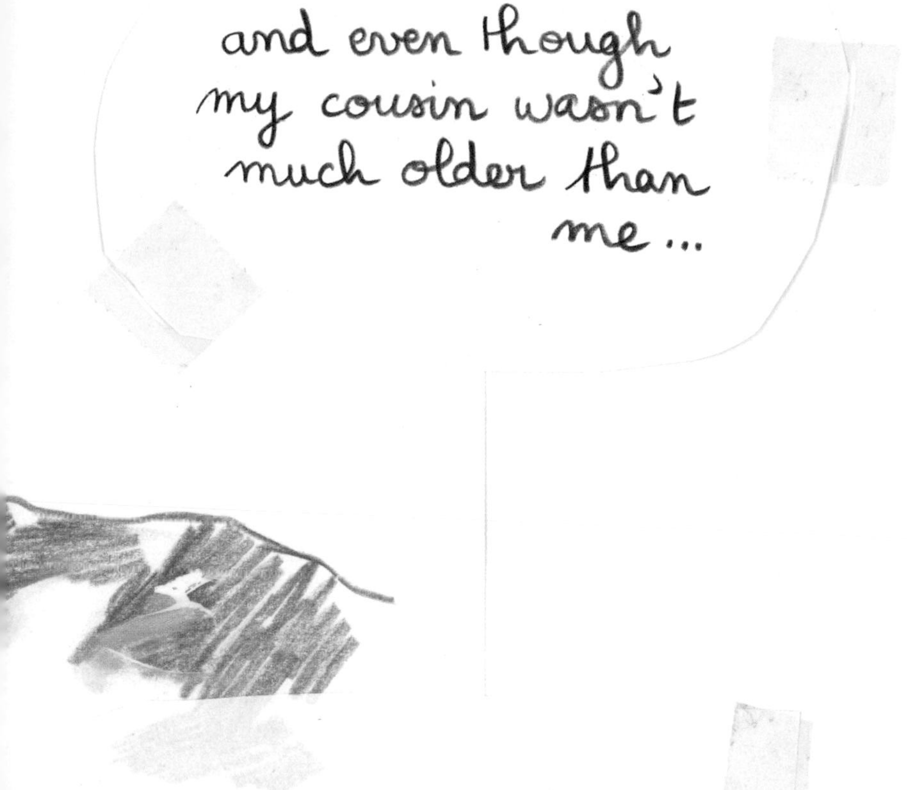
and even though my cousin wasn't much older than me...

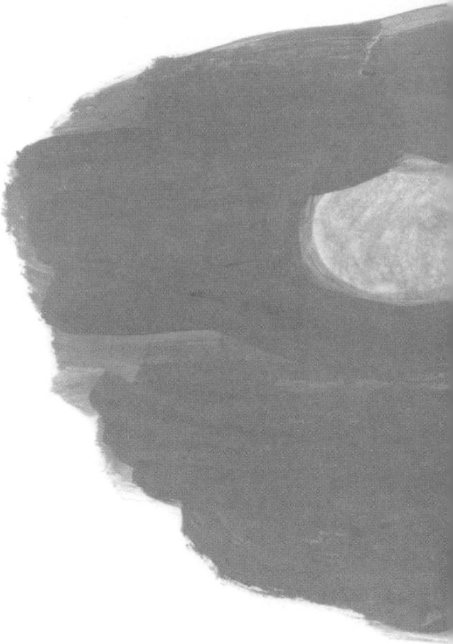

I still can't
dismiss it

as " kids just being kids"

I feel like I'm
carrying the weight
of an old family
story

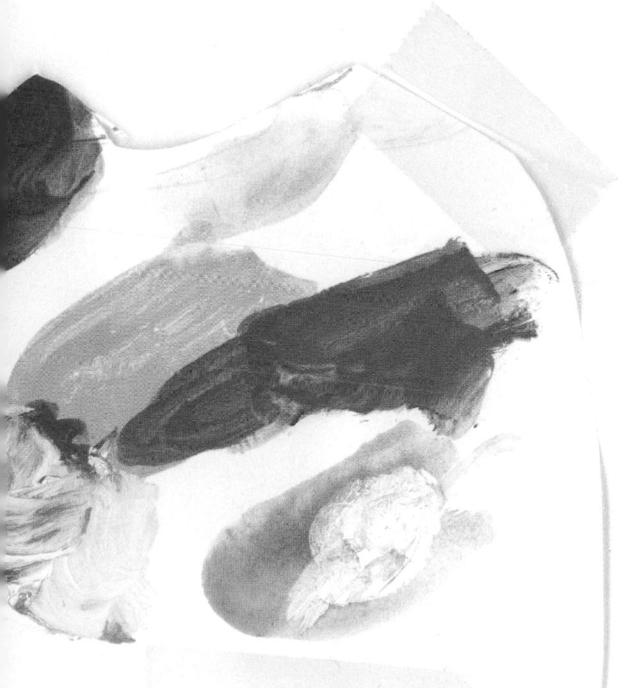

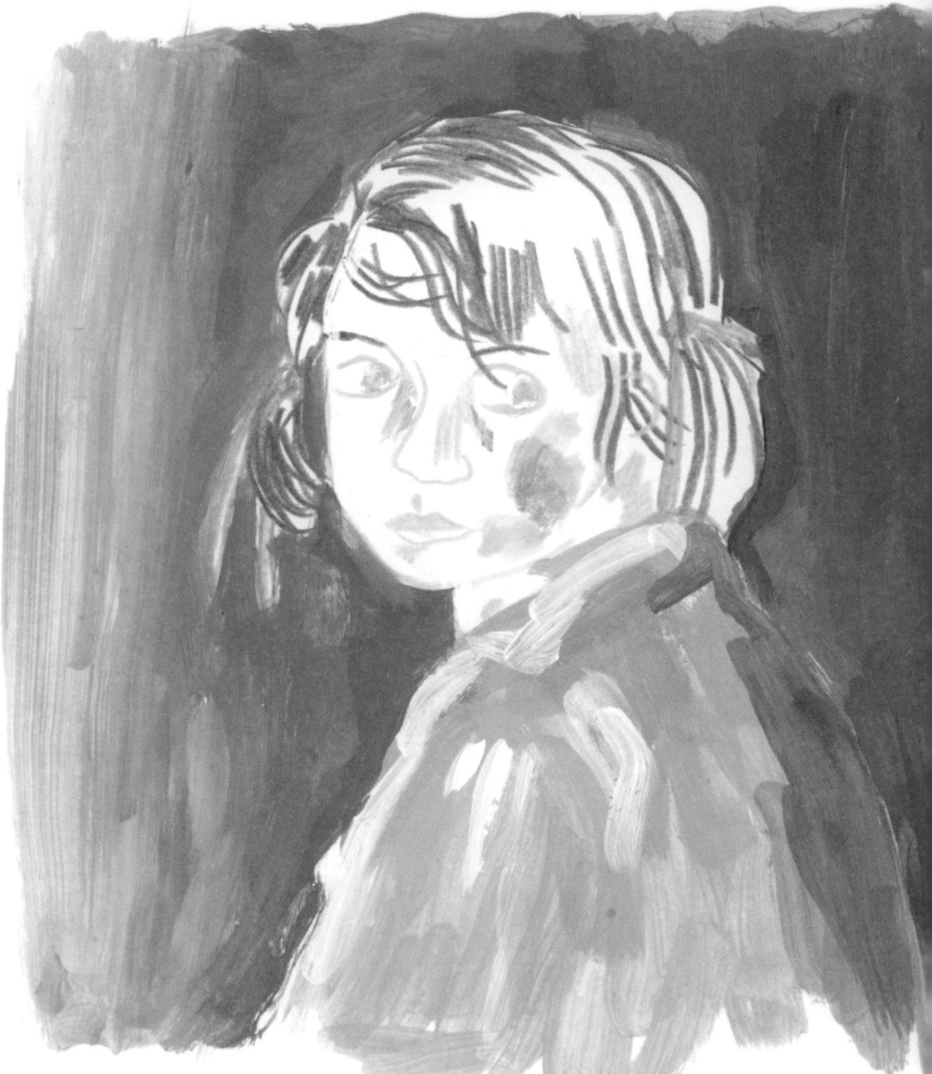

mouchette

but
really
it's
the story
of all
women.

I wanted to
write a book
to say ...

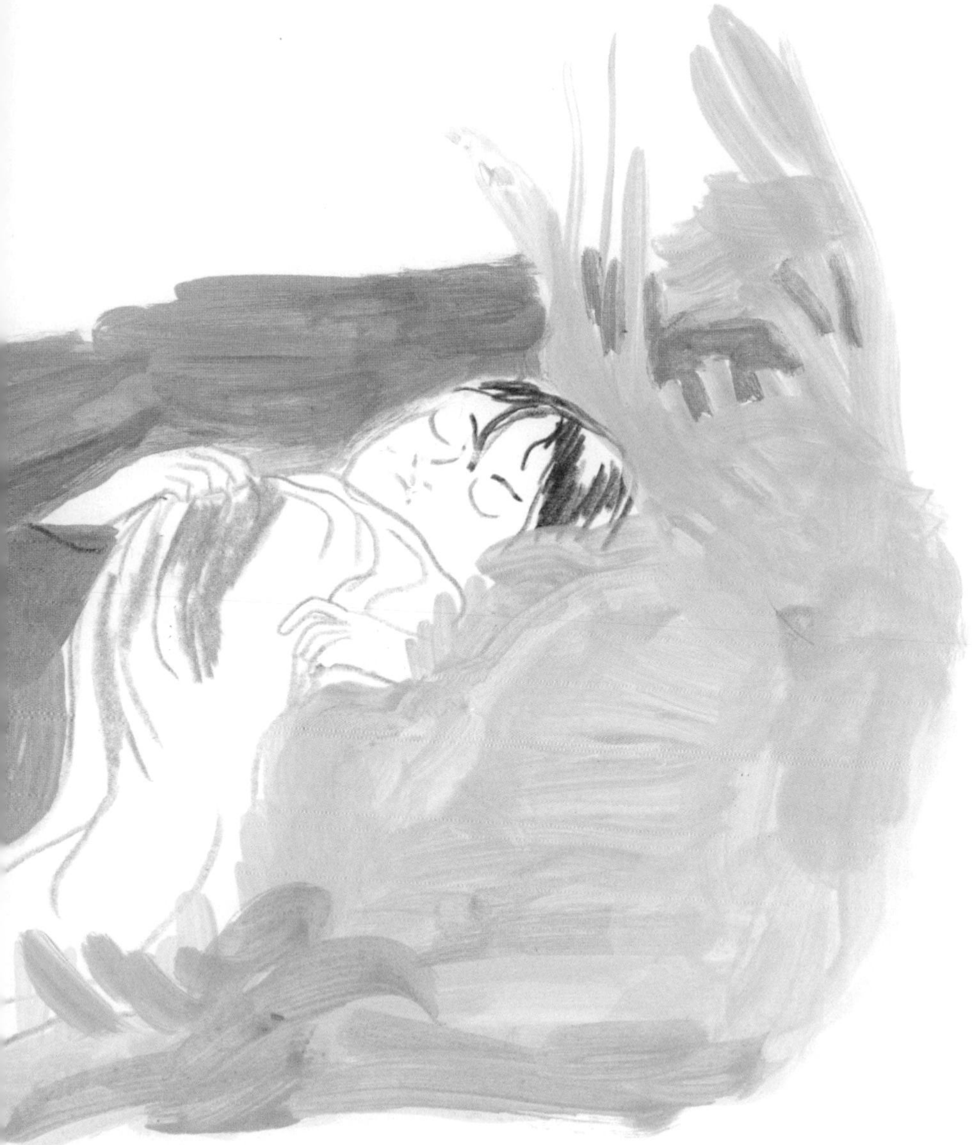

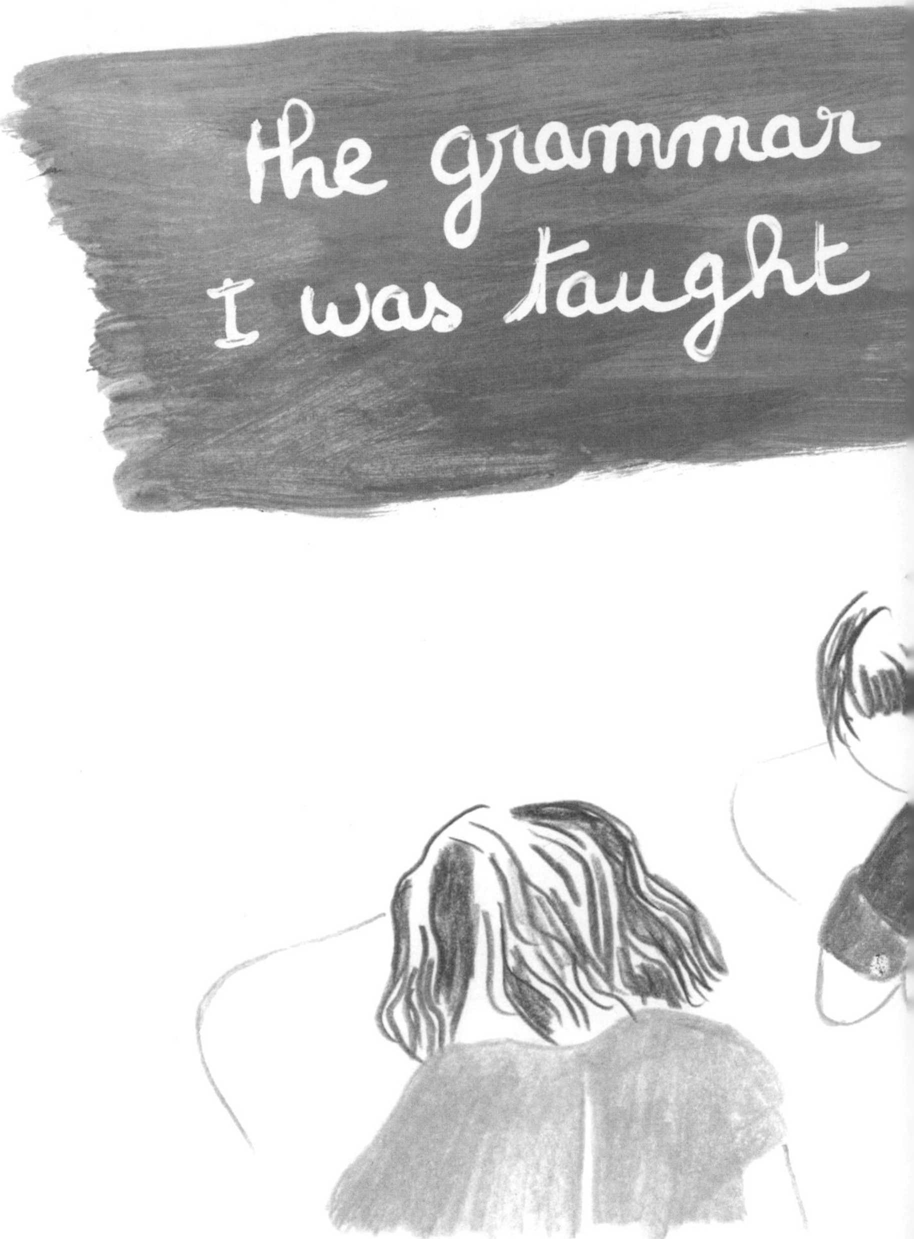
the grammar
I was taught

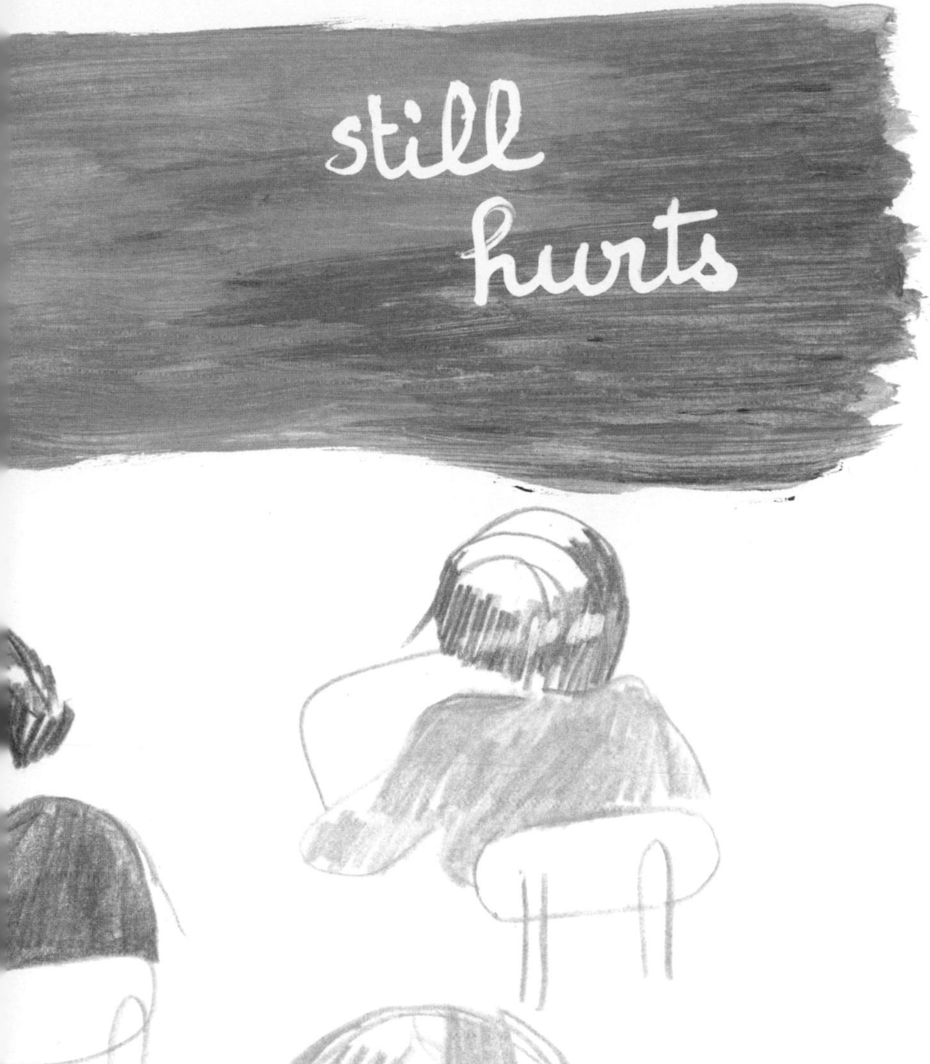
still
hurts

* In French,
the masculine takes precedence.

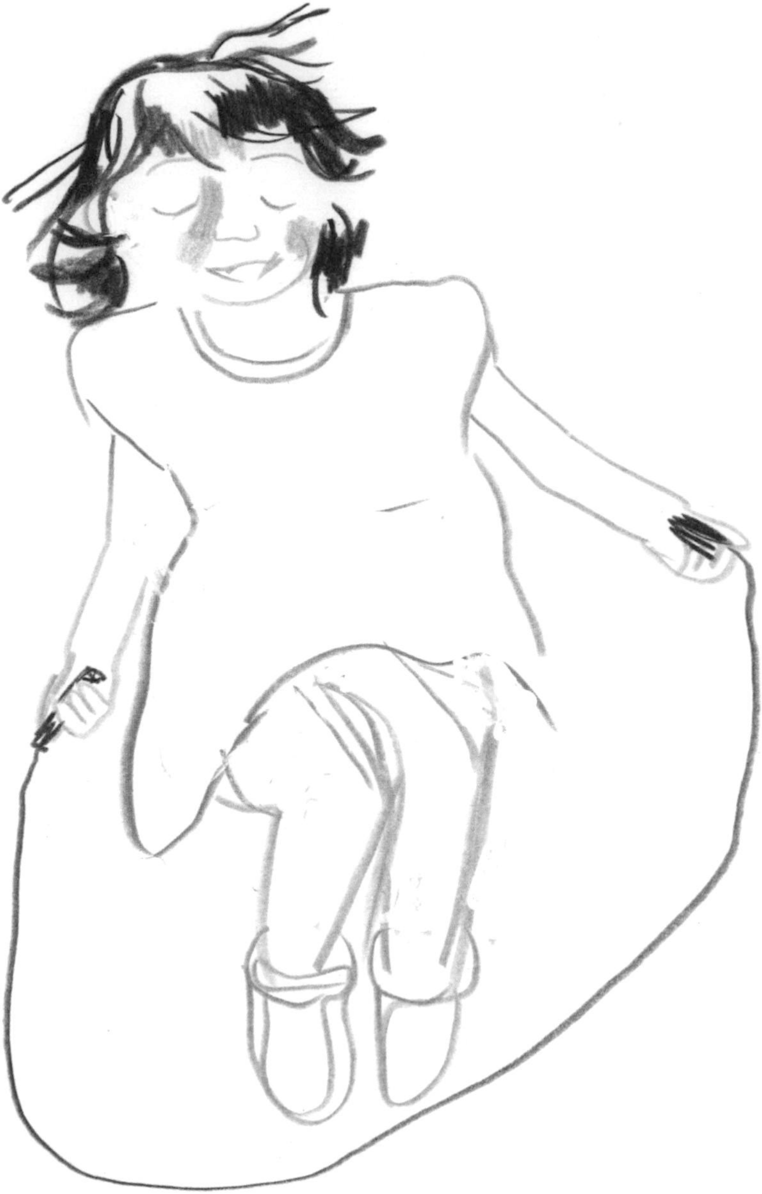

I wanted
that power
too.

why do I
have images
in my head

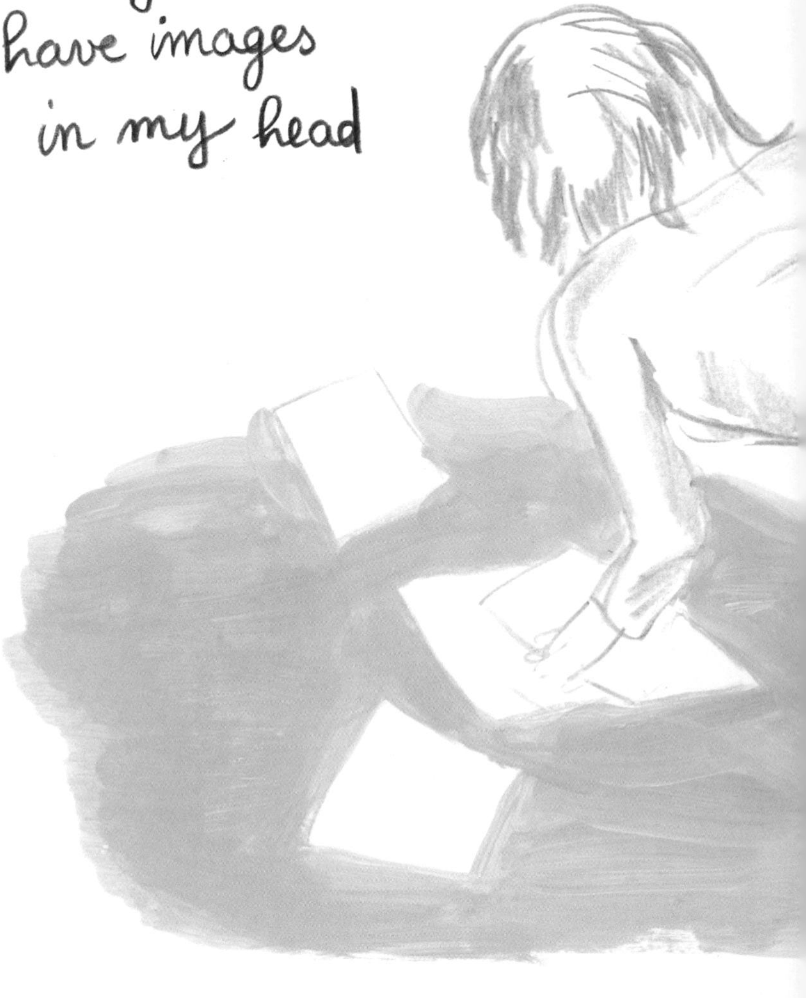

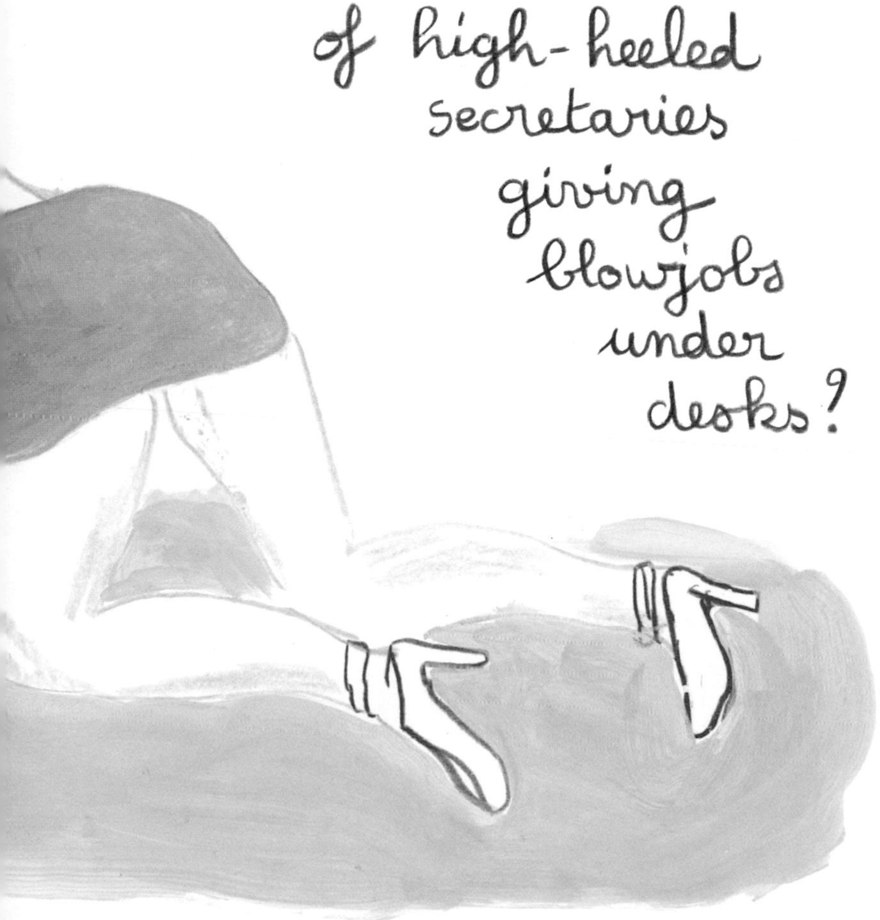
of high-heeled secretaries giving blowjobs under desks?

I wanted
so badly
not to be
a girl

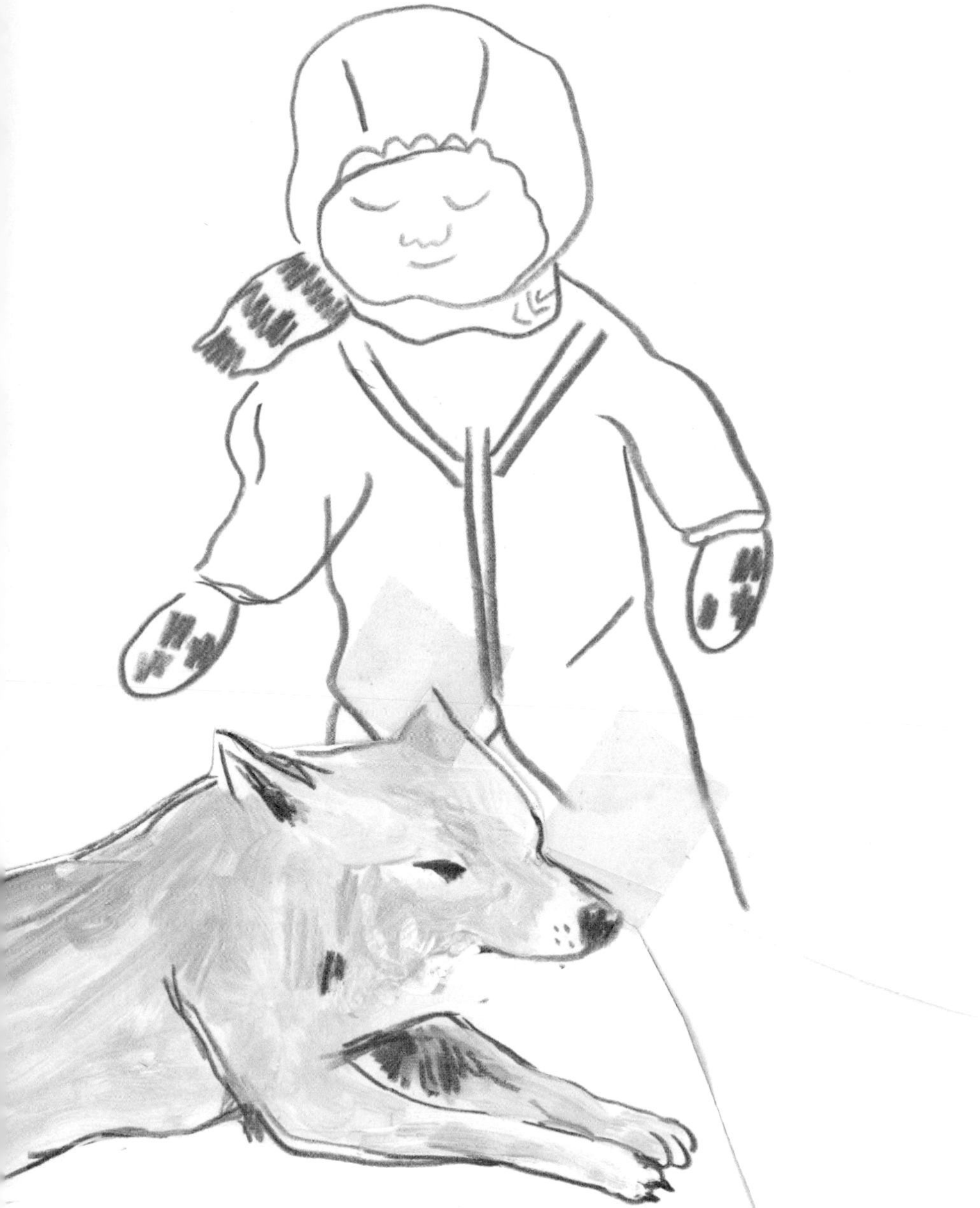

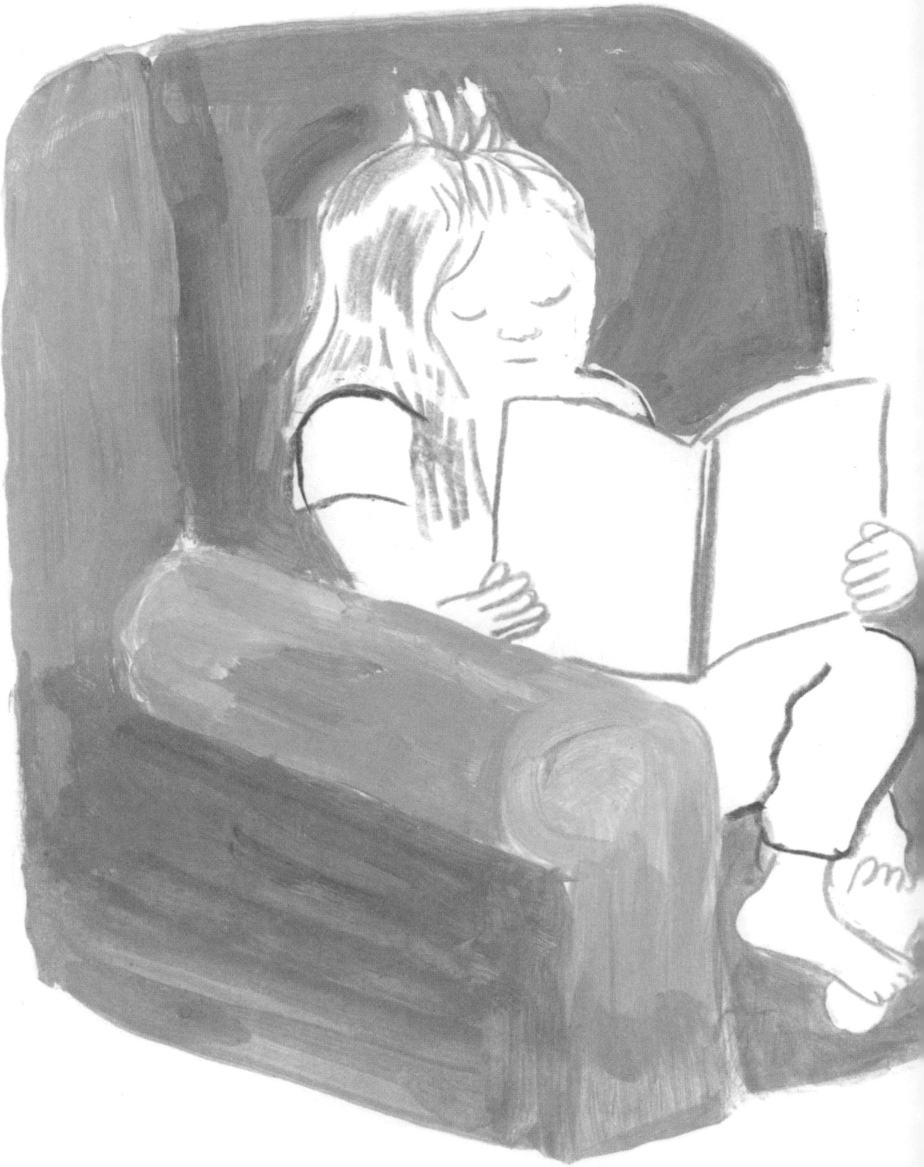

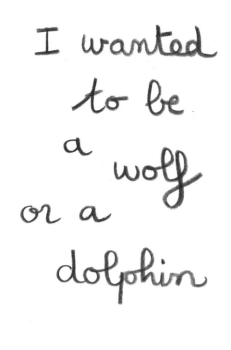

I wanted
to be
a wolf
or a
dolphin

for two months,
I've been
wearing
this
sweater
with a
narwhal
that
says
"gentle
warrior"
on it

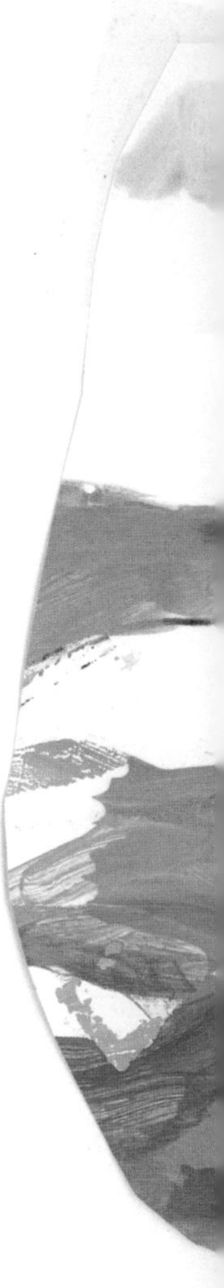

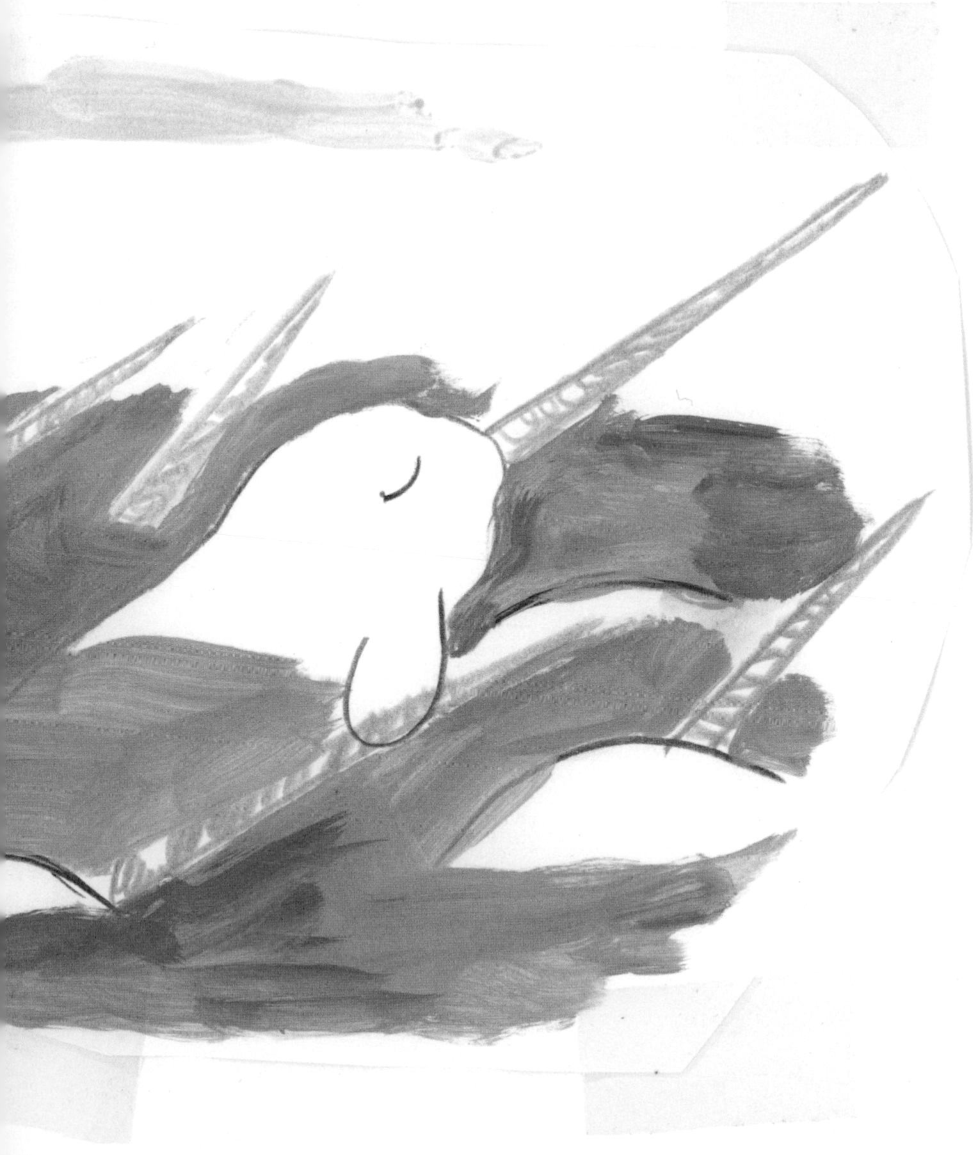

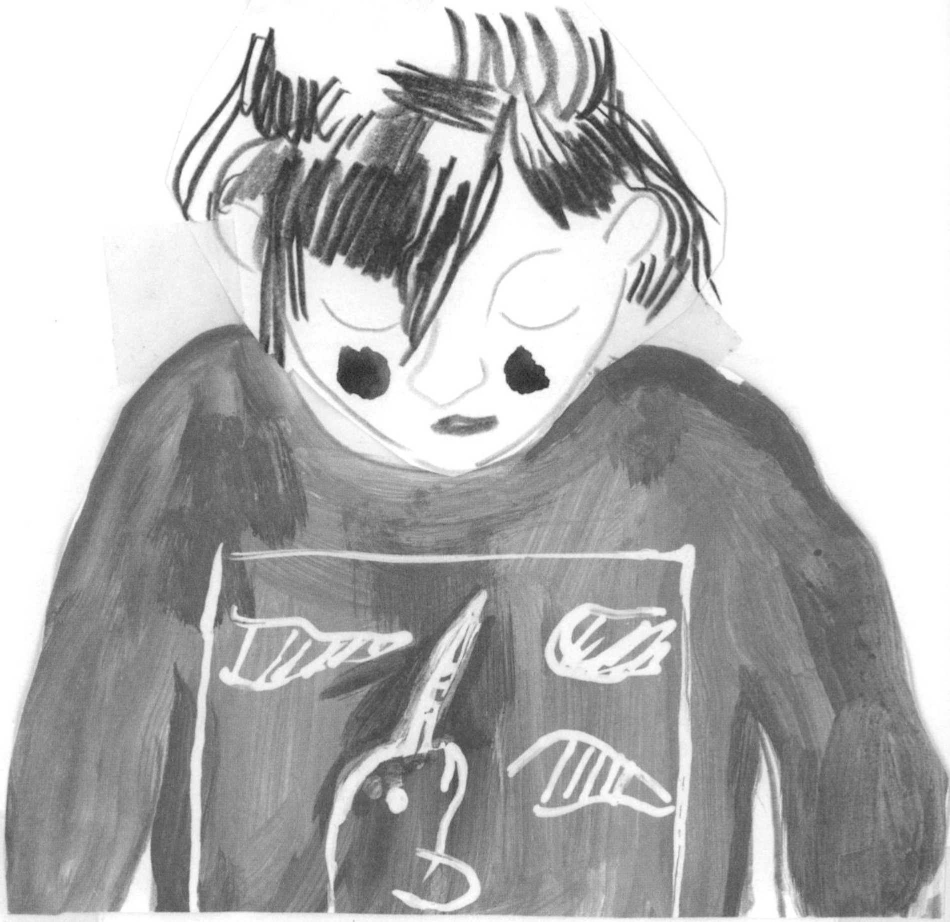

yesterday,
I thought to myself
that's me,

the unicorn -
whale,

the gentle
feminist.

but you know what?

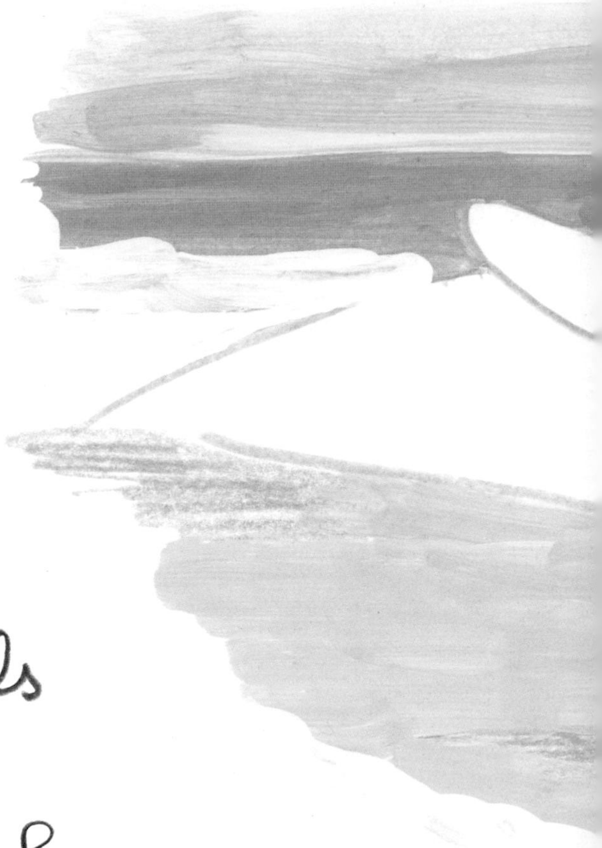

female narwhals

don't have horns.

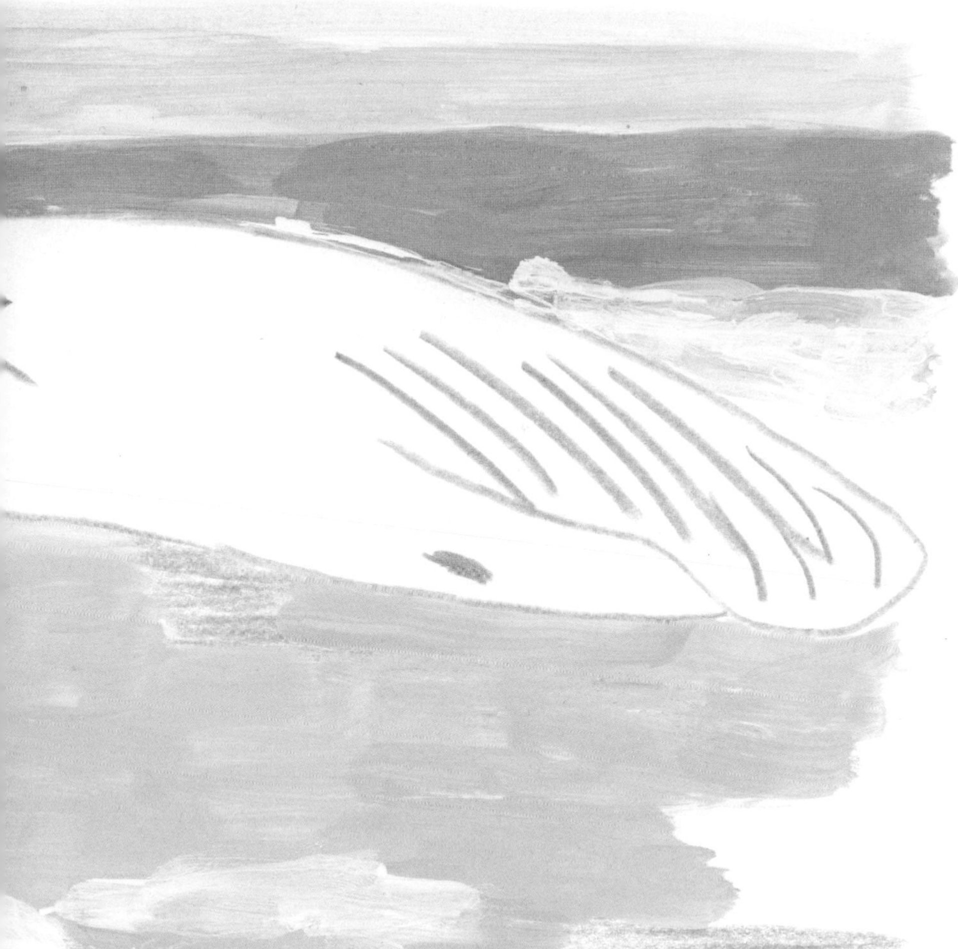

Fall 2014

Helsinki

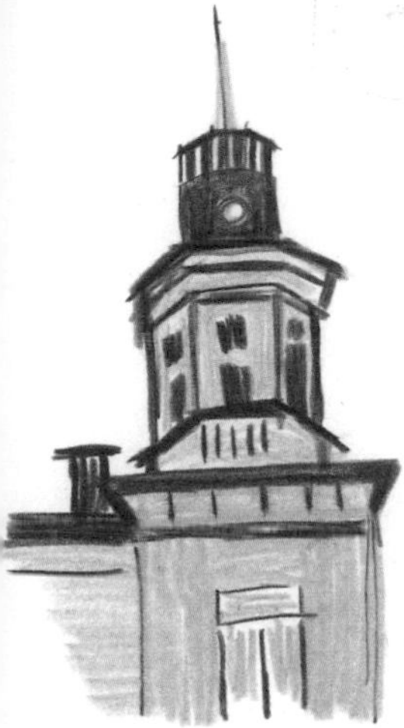

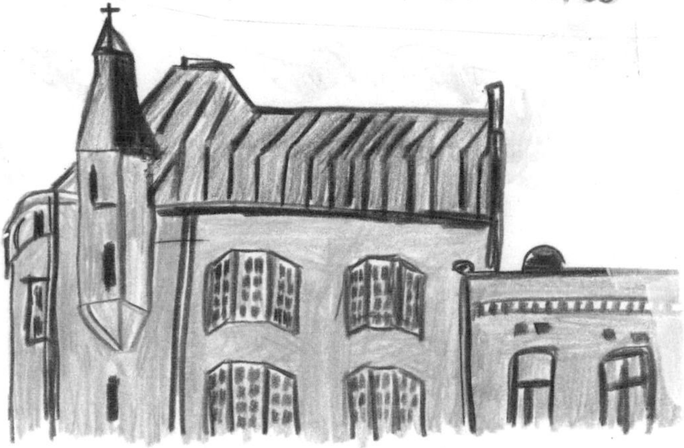

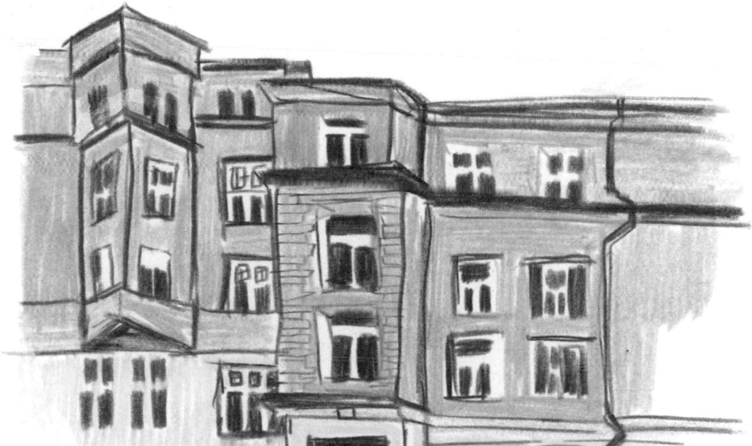

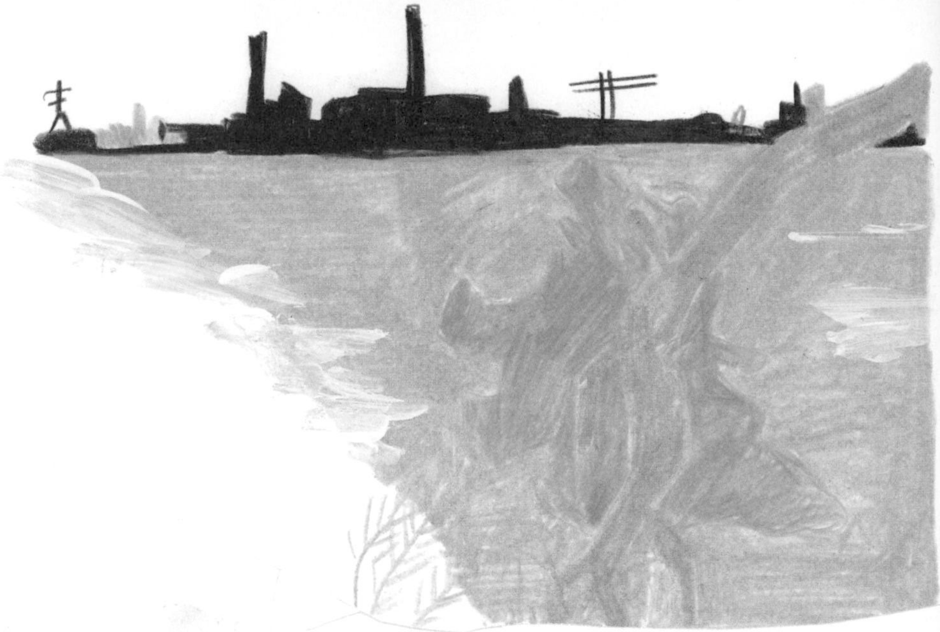
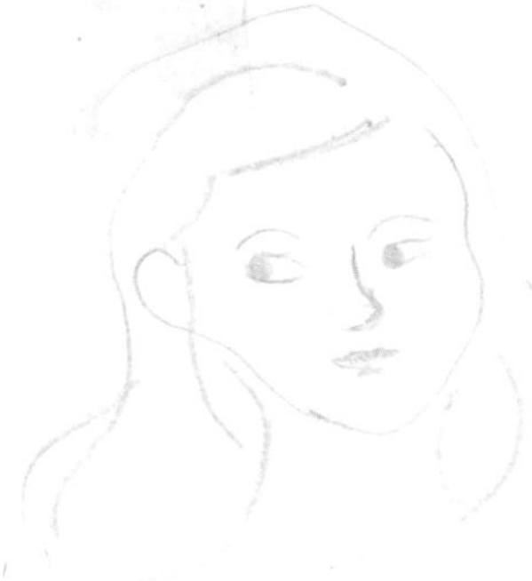

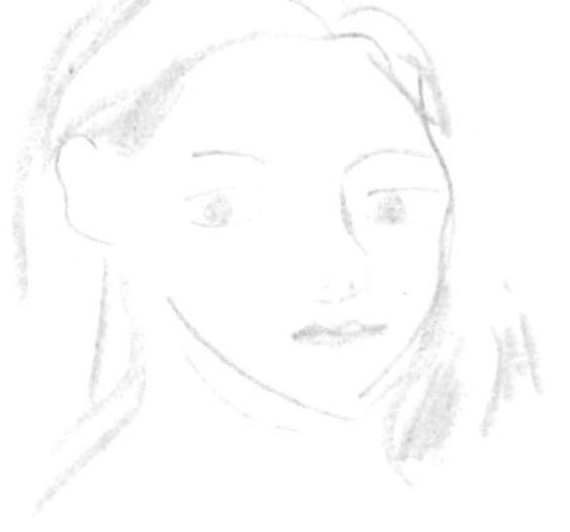
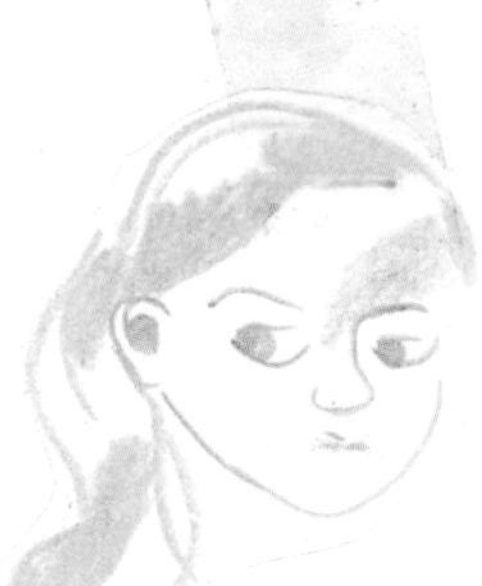

this book, the one in your hands,
was supposed to be about
Tove Jansson*

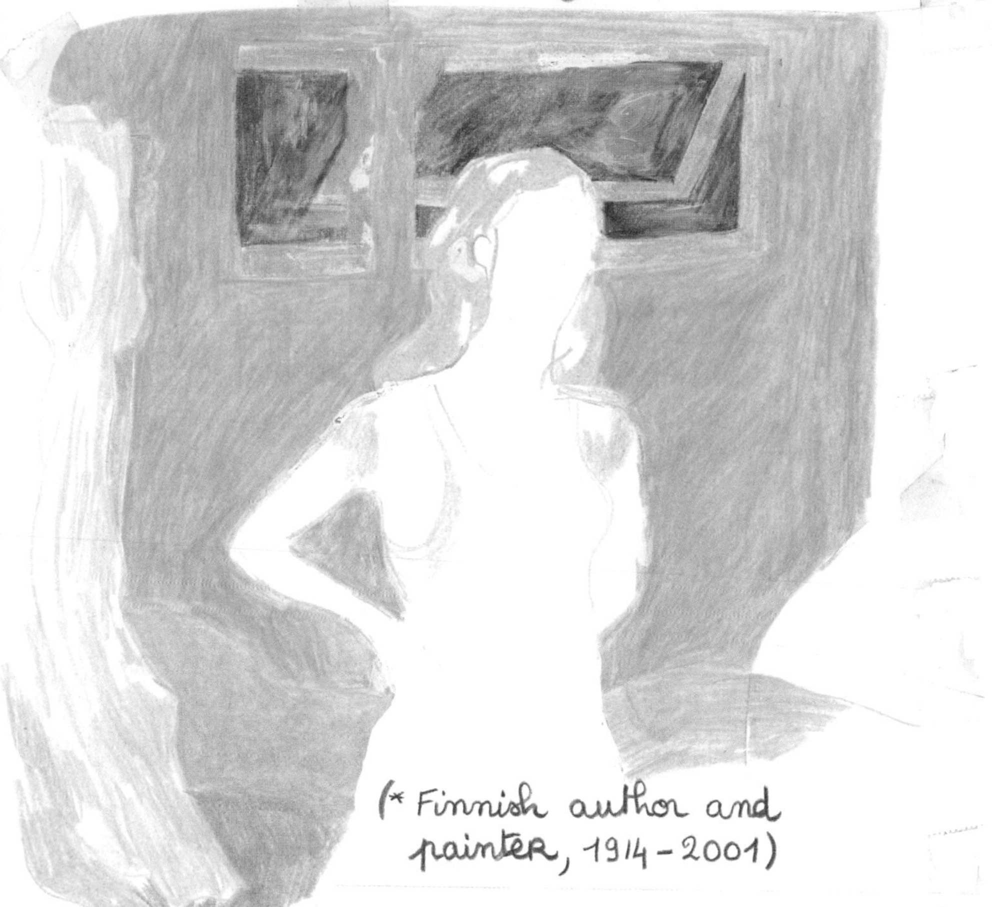

(* Finnish author and
painter, 1914-2001)

October 2014. I go to
Finland to write about her
(fiction or nonfiction, I don't know
yet)

I don't even know why Tove Jansson fascinates me.

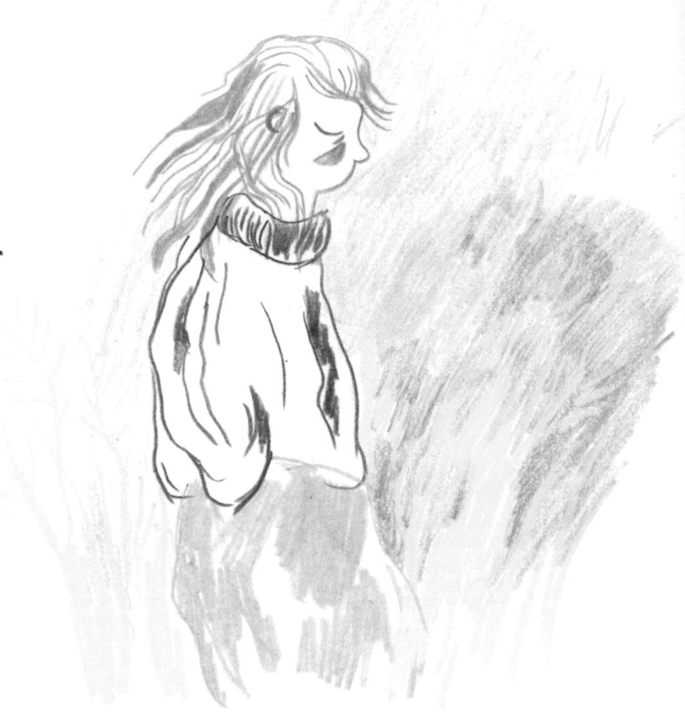

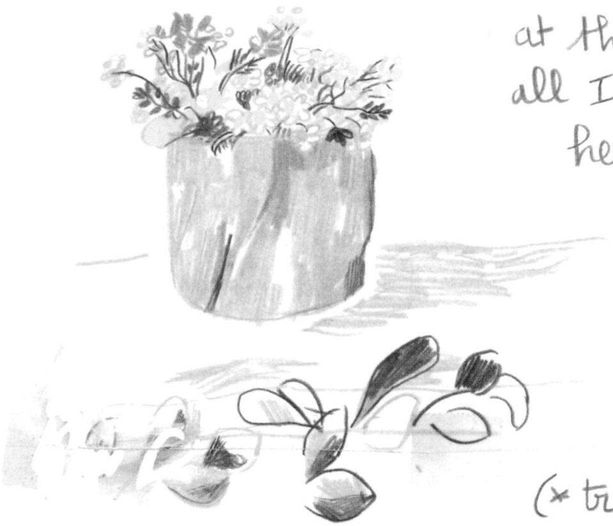

at this point, all I've read of hers are the Moomin books, stories about little white peikkos*

(* trolls in Finnish)

I've fallen in love with the Moomin way of being.

They are "happy idiots who forgive one another and never realize they're being fooled,"

wrote Tove in 1961.

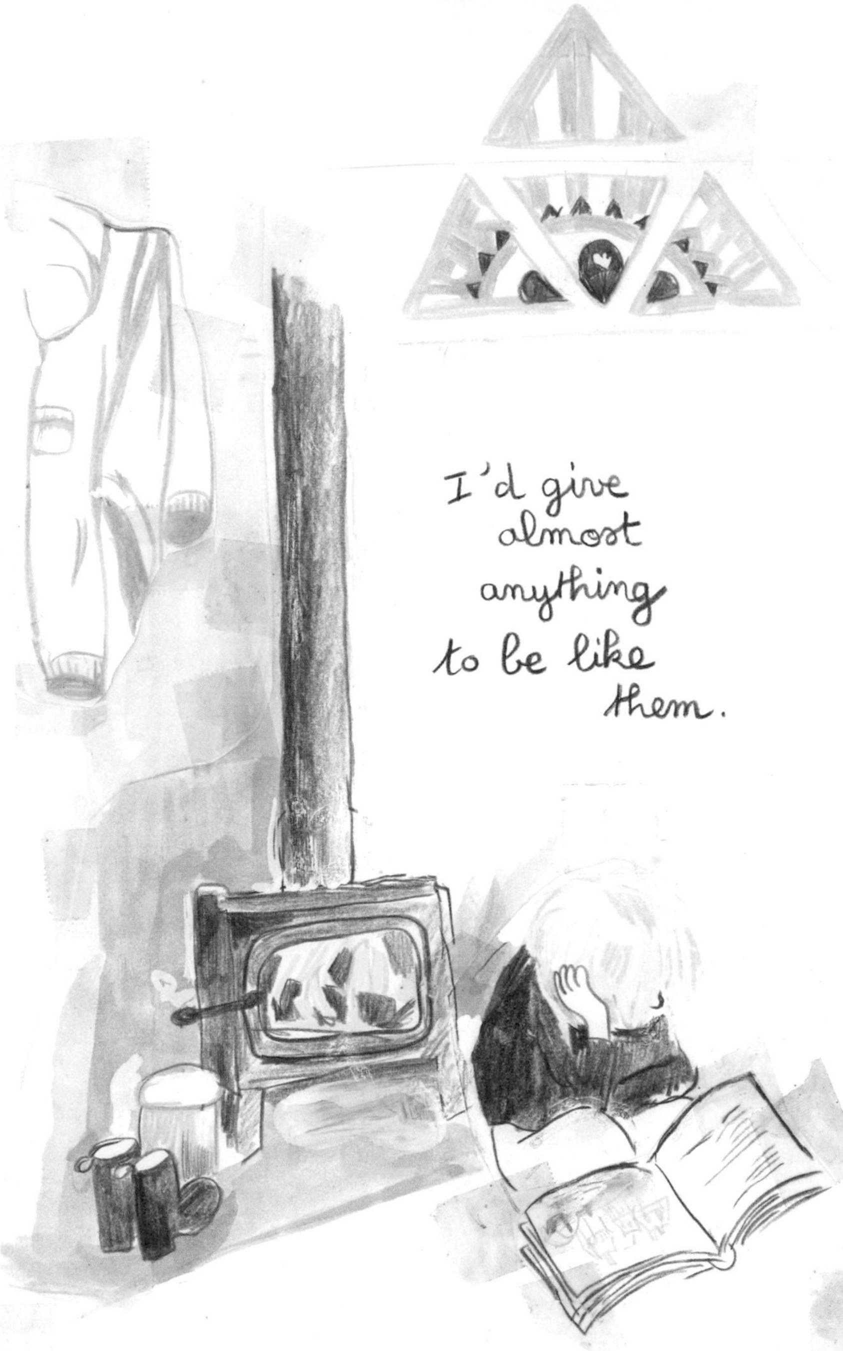
I'd give almost anything to be like them.

It's night when I arrive in Helsinki.

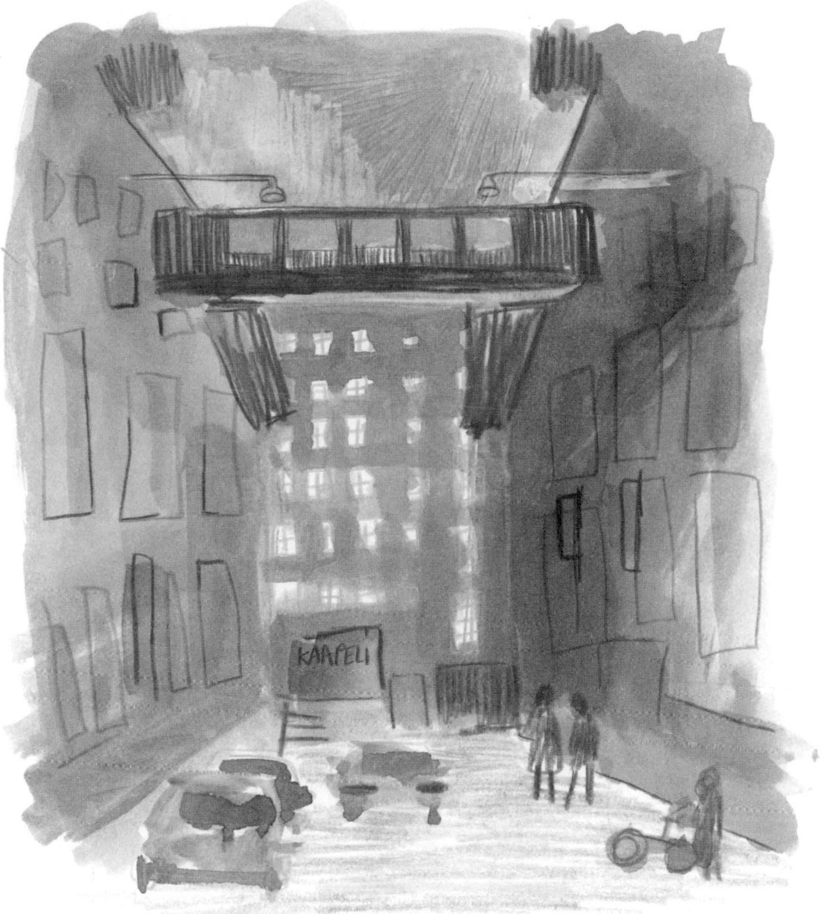
KAAPELI

For the first few weeks, I live in a space that's much too big for me, in an old cable factory: the Kaapelitehdas.

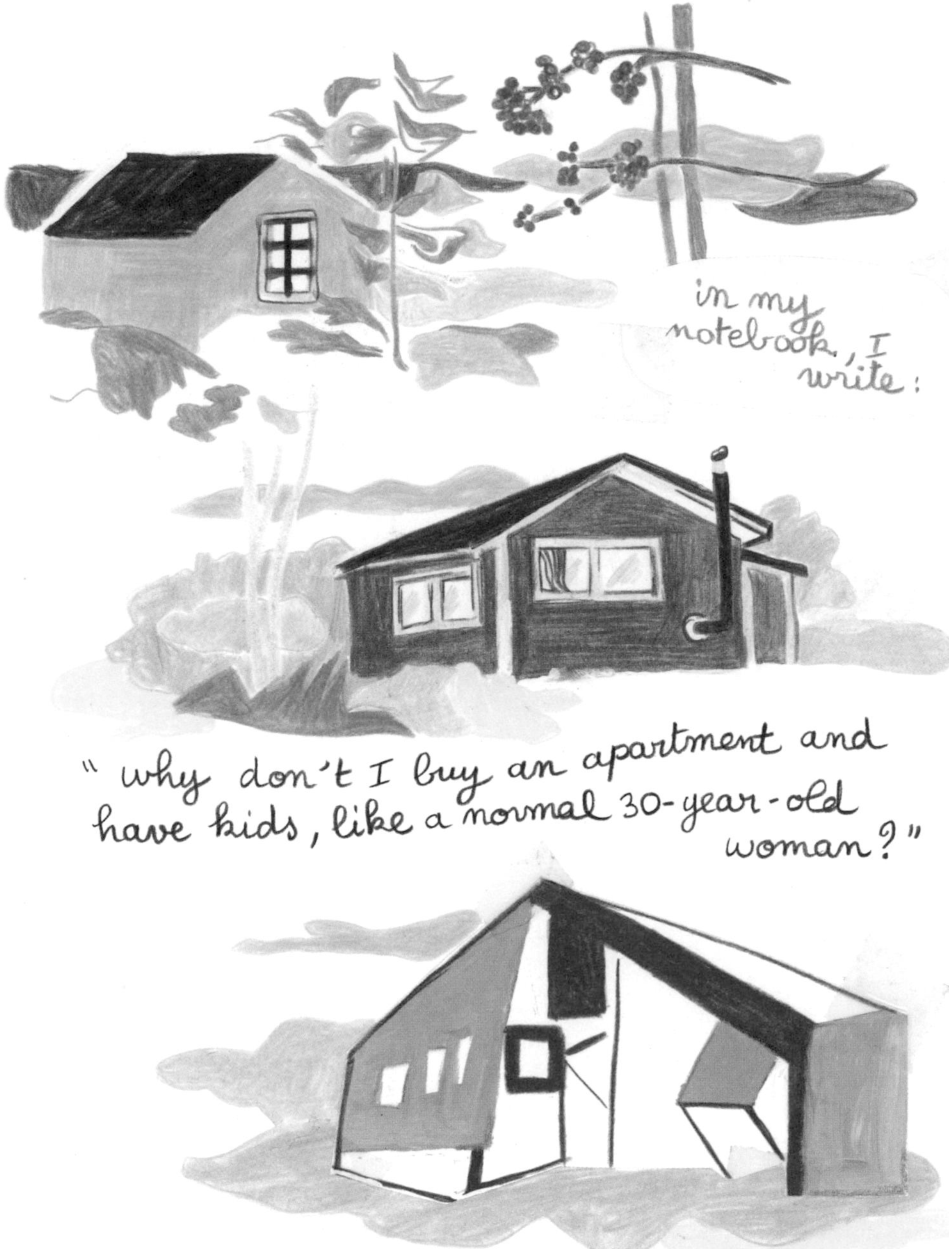
in my notebook, I write:
"why don't I buy an apartment and have kids, like a normal 30-year-old woman?"

I discover the charming mökkis, little wooden cabins where Finns spend their summers and weekends.

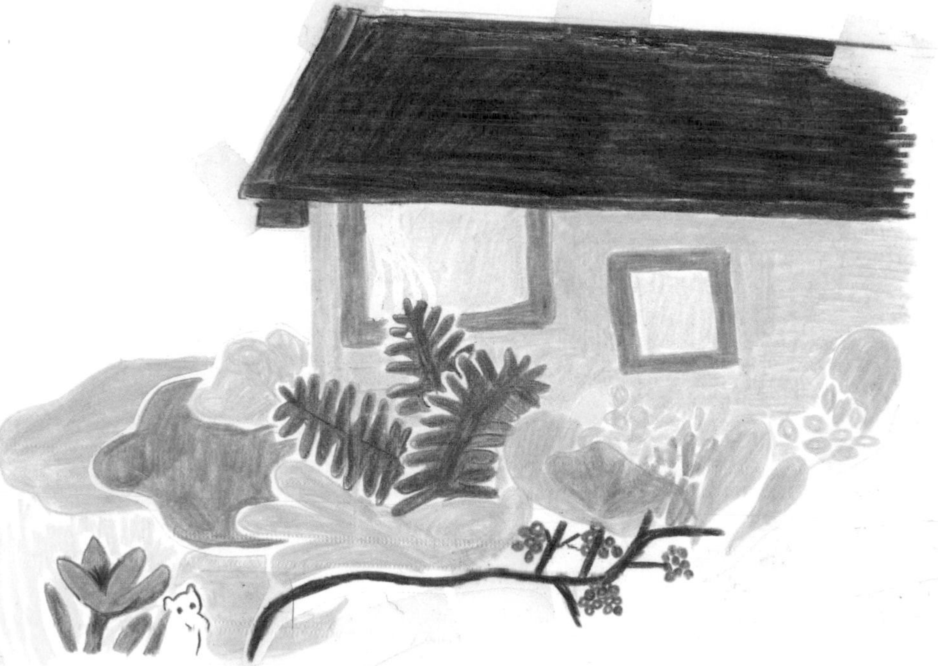

Jérôme is far away
- I feel alone

he tells me there should be
fold-and-pack cabins,
take-away houses that shelter you
wherever you go.

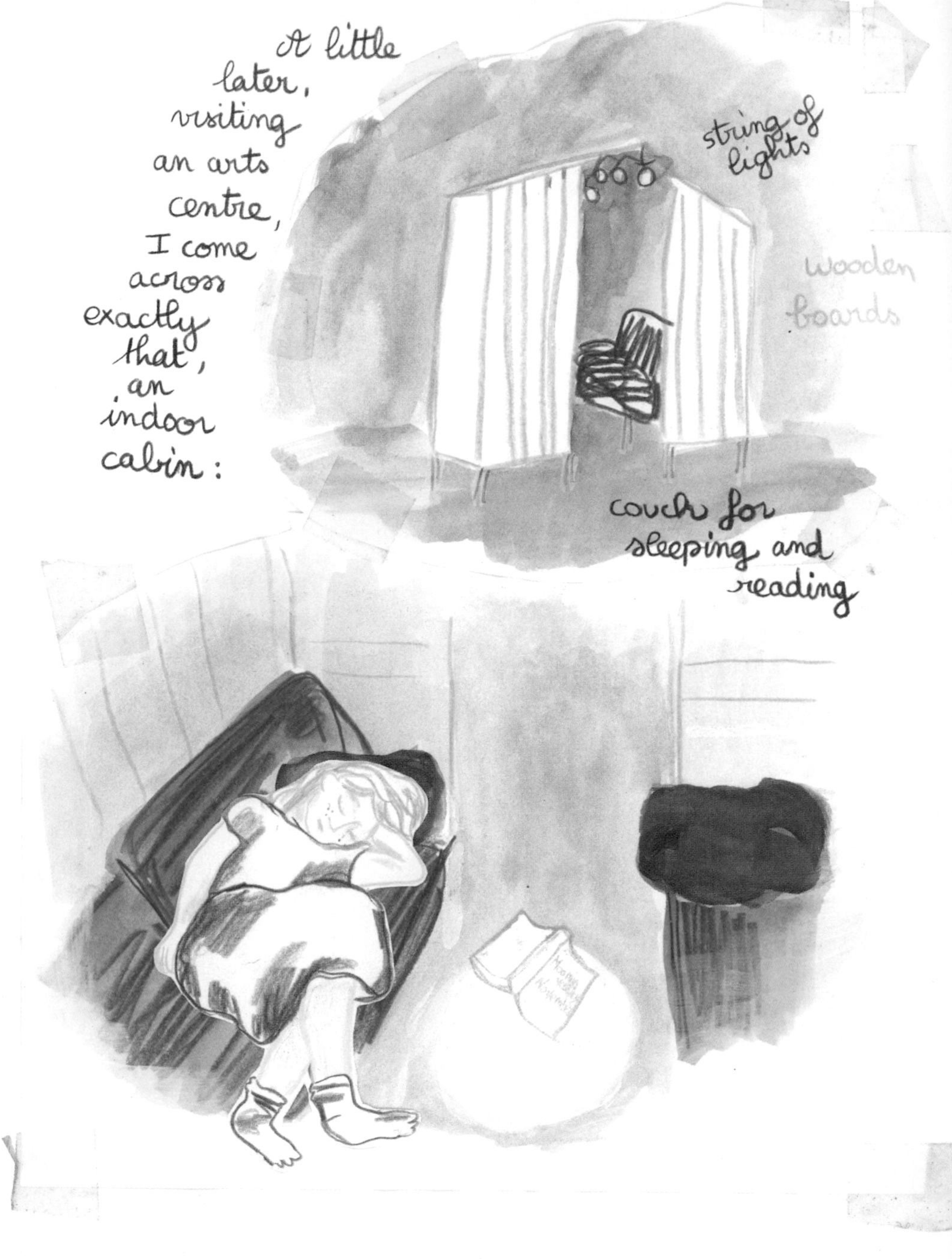
A little later, visiting an arts centre, I come across exactly that, an indoor cabin:
string of lights
wooden boards
couch for sleeping and reading

in Lauttasaari, an island-neighbourhood in Helsinki, my friend Julie's place has an enclosed balcony.

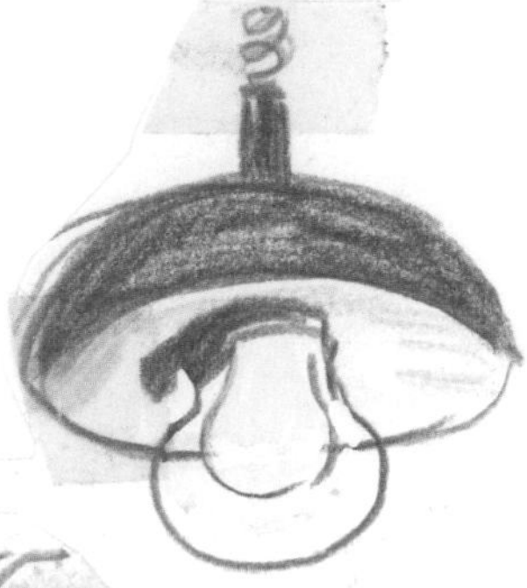

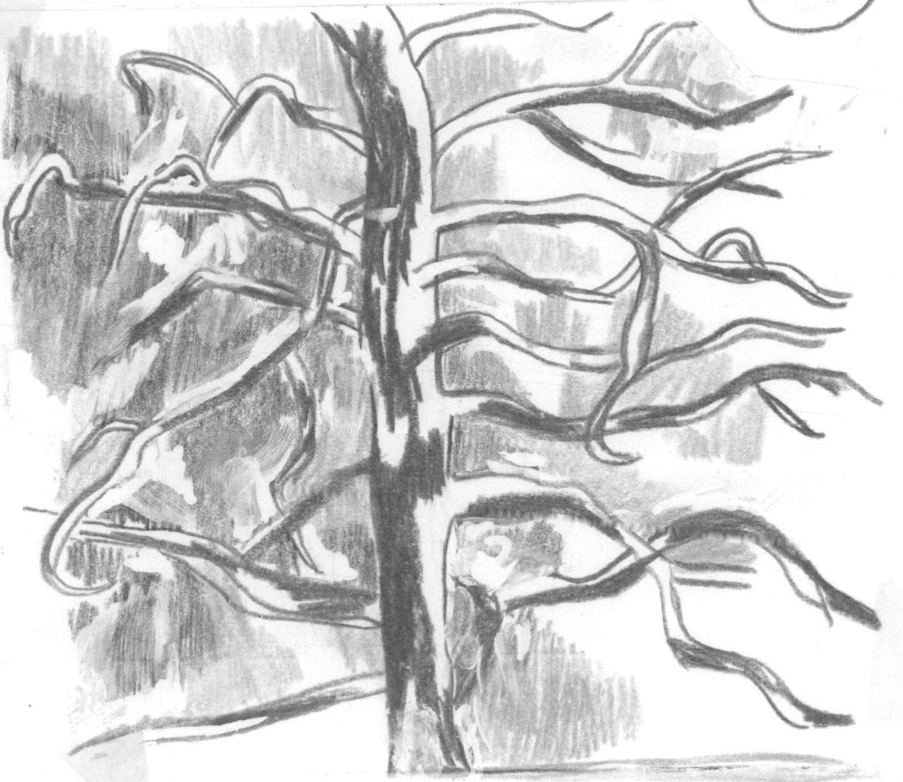

It looks out onto this tree.

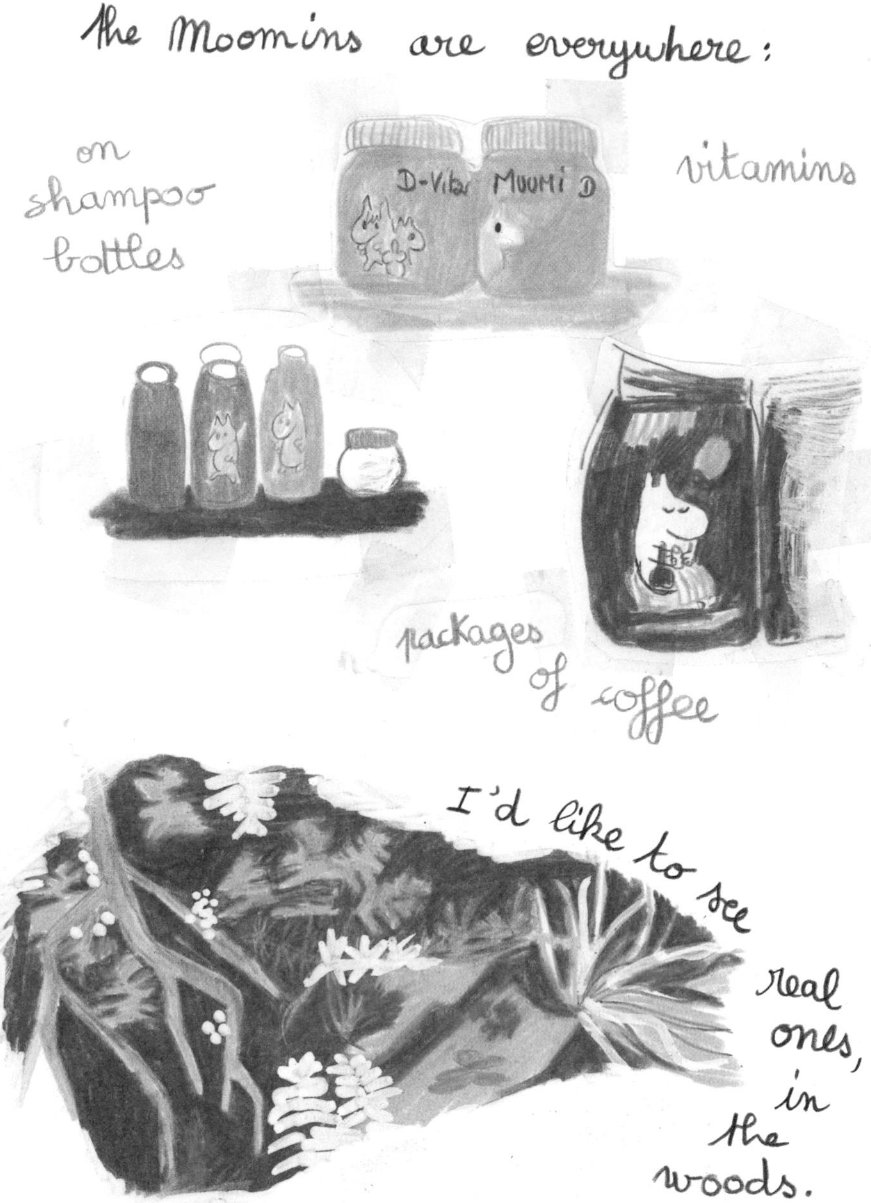
the Moomins are everywhere:
on shampoo bottles
D-Vita MUUMI D
vitamins
packages of coffee
I'd like to see real ones, in the woods.

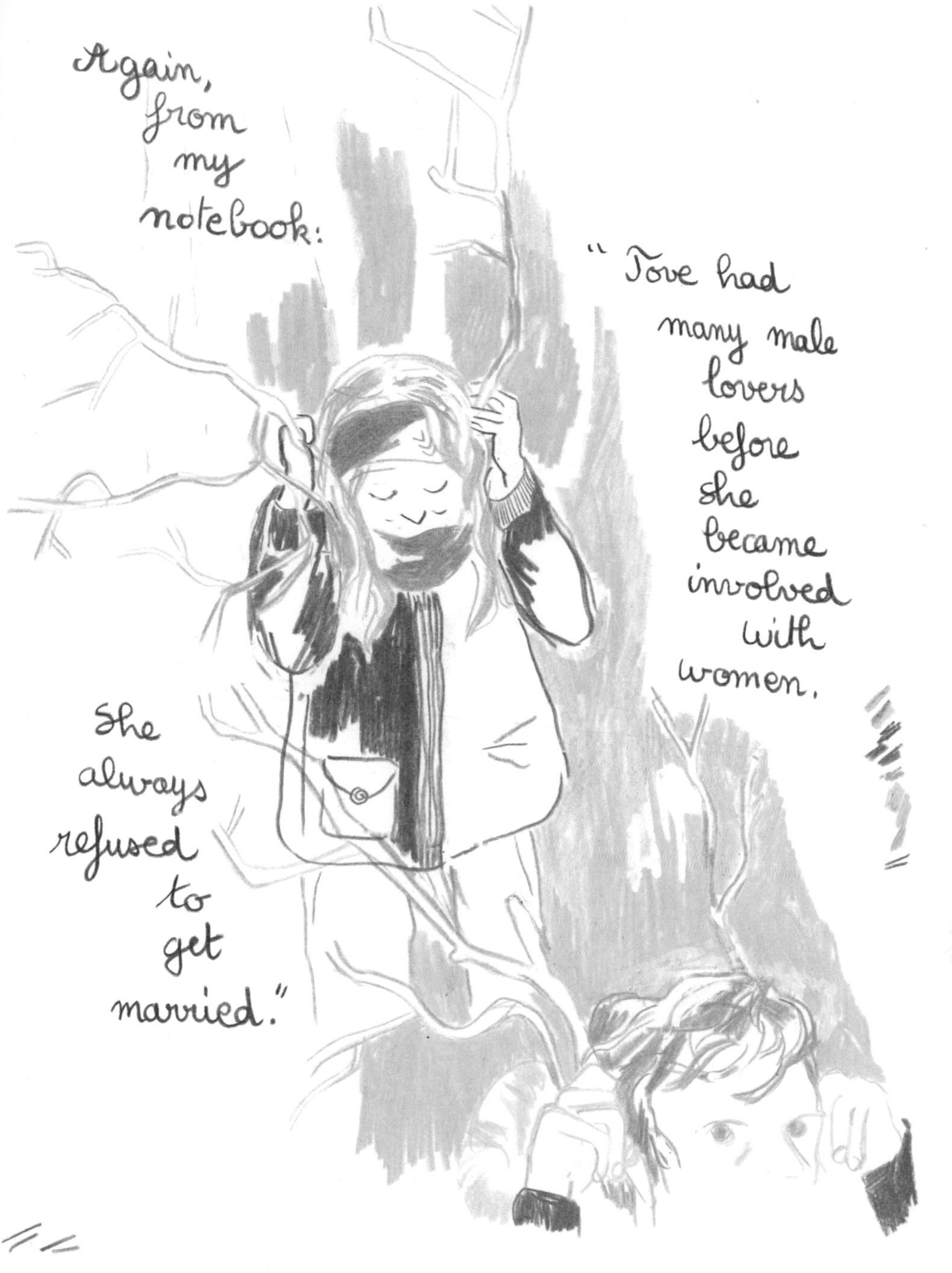
Again, from my notebook:
"Tove had many male lovers before she became involved with women.
She always refused to get married."

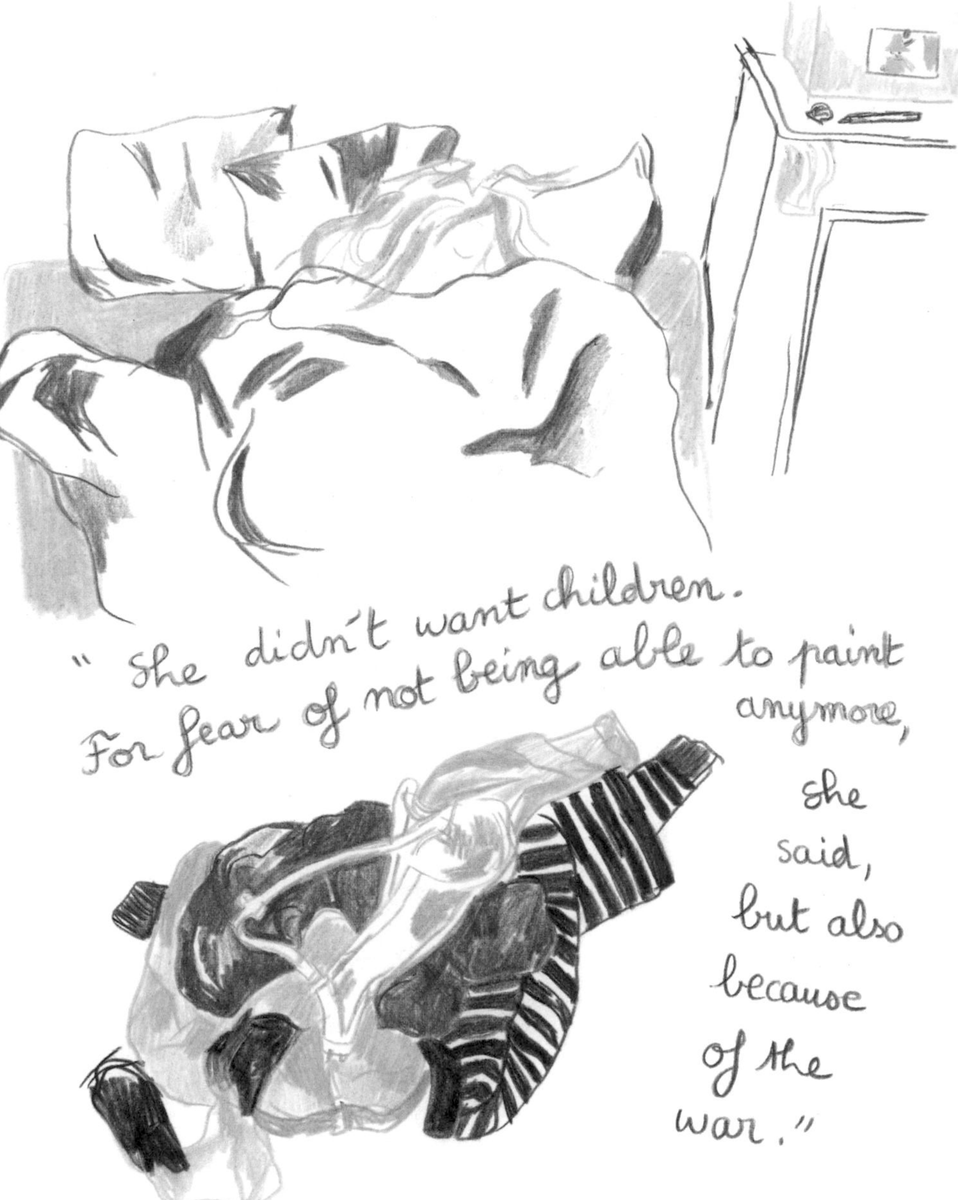
"She didn't want children.
For fear of not being able to paint anymore,
she said,
but also because of the war."

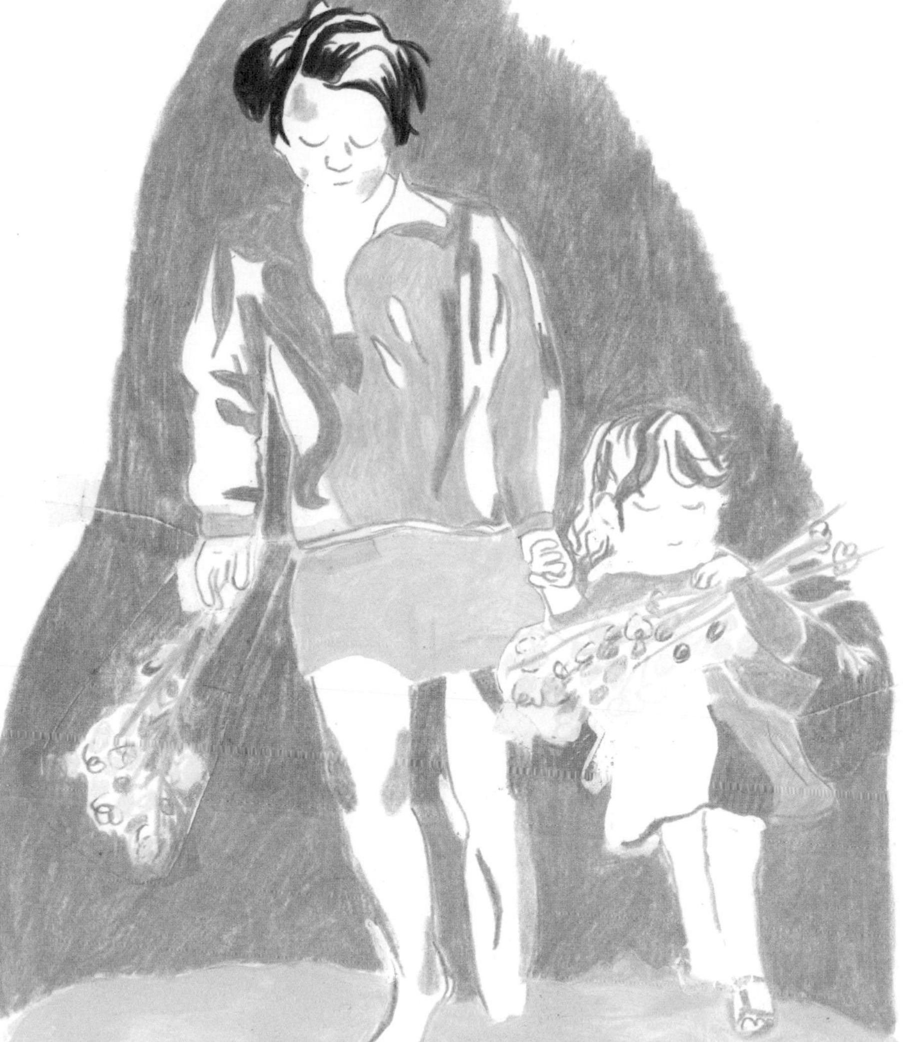

(Later, the terrorist attacks in France and Belgium would give me the same excuse.)

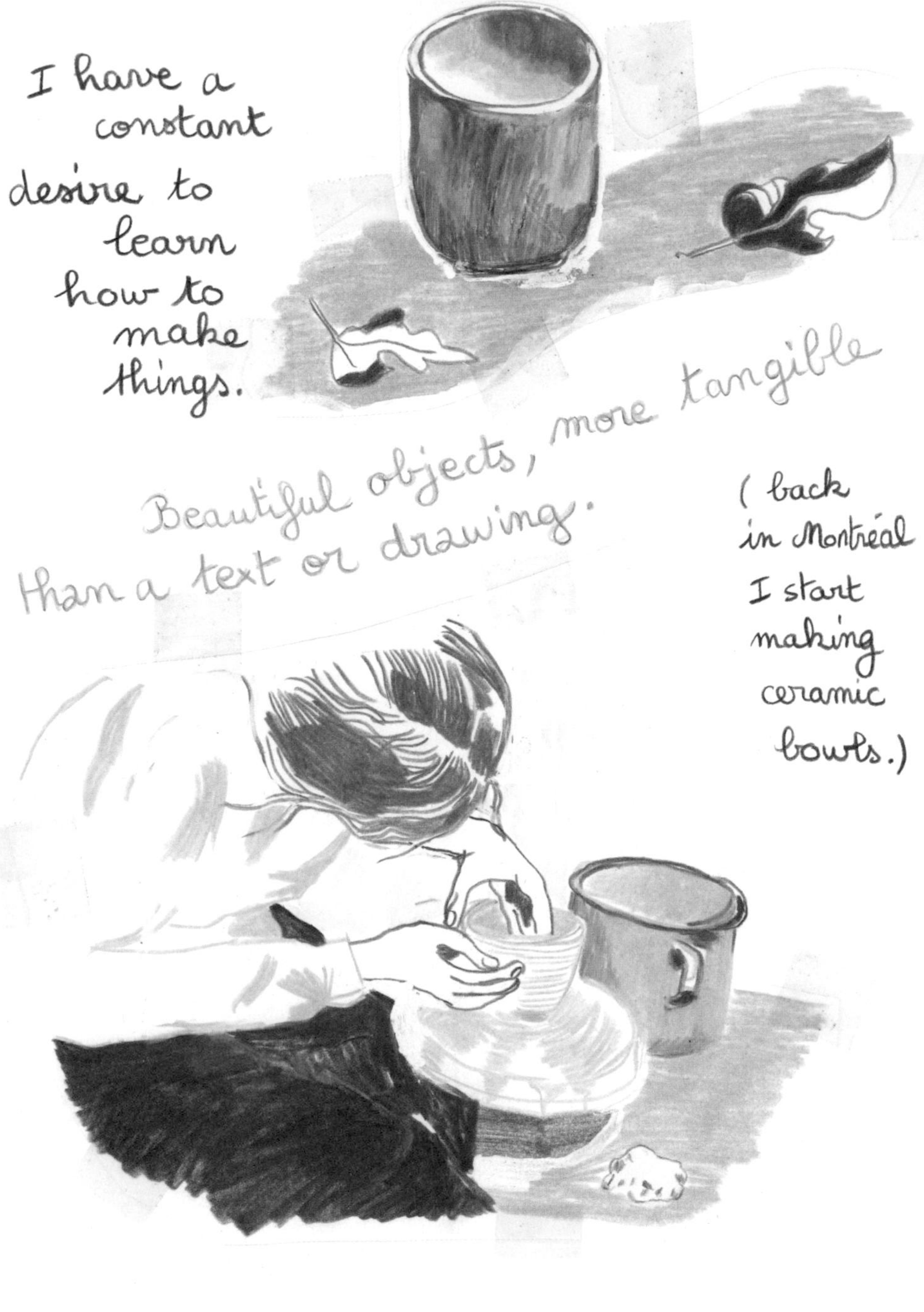
I have a constant desire to learn how to make things.
Beautiful objects, more tangible than a text or drawing.
(back in Montréal I start making ceramic bowls.)

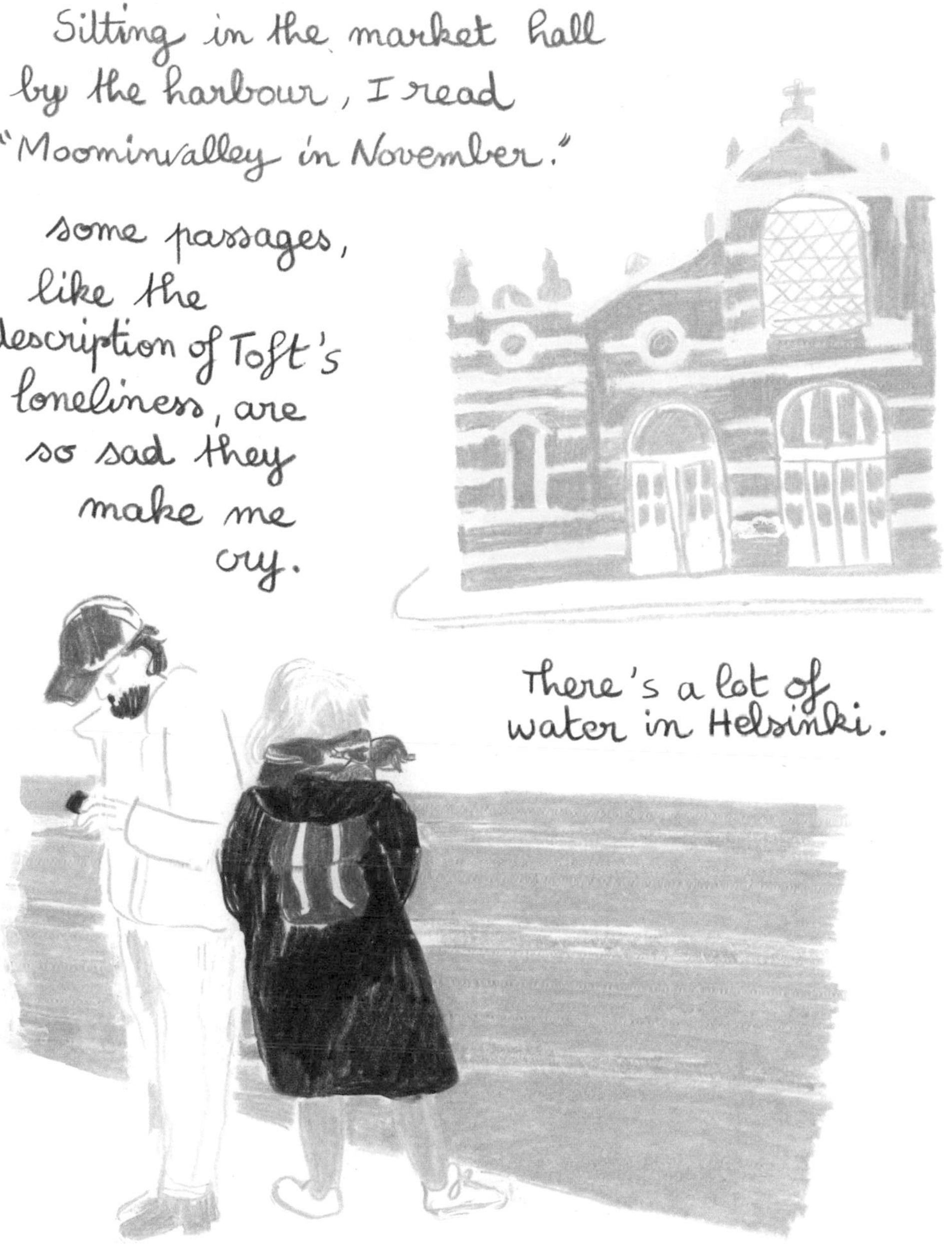
Sitting in the market hall by the harbour, I read "Moominvalley in November."
some passages, like the description of Toft's loneliness, are so sad they make me cry.
There's a lot of water in Helsinki.

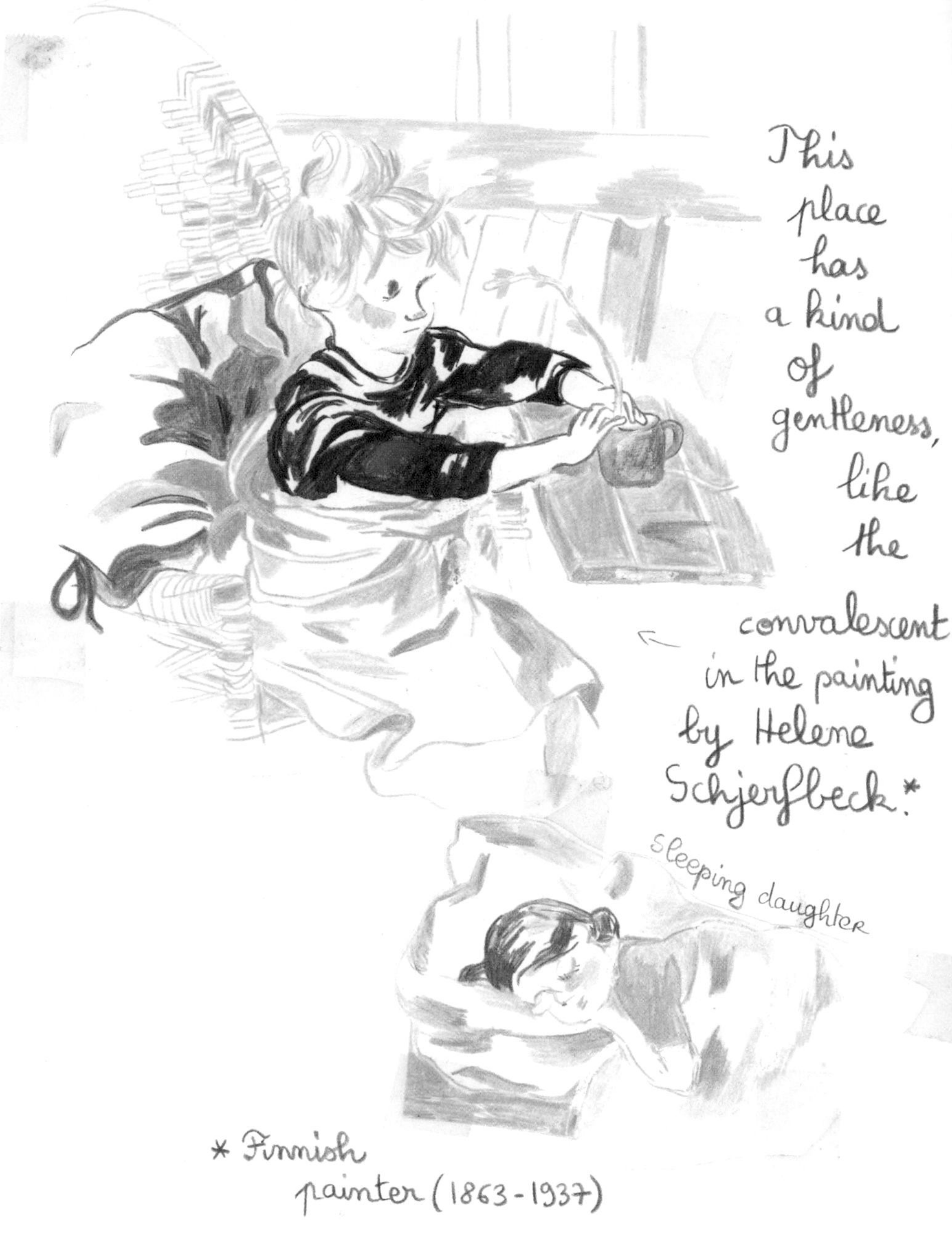
This place has a kind of gentleness, like the convalescent in the painting by Helene Schjerfbeck.*
Sleeping daughter
* Finnish painter (1863-1937)

but it chills me, too,

   like the look in the eyes of the
     little peasant
girl in the
  painting by
Eero Järnefelt*

* Finnish painter (1863-1937)

I've been going to the Yrjönkatu pool.

There are separate days for women and men.

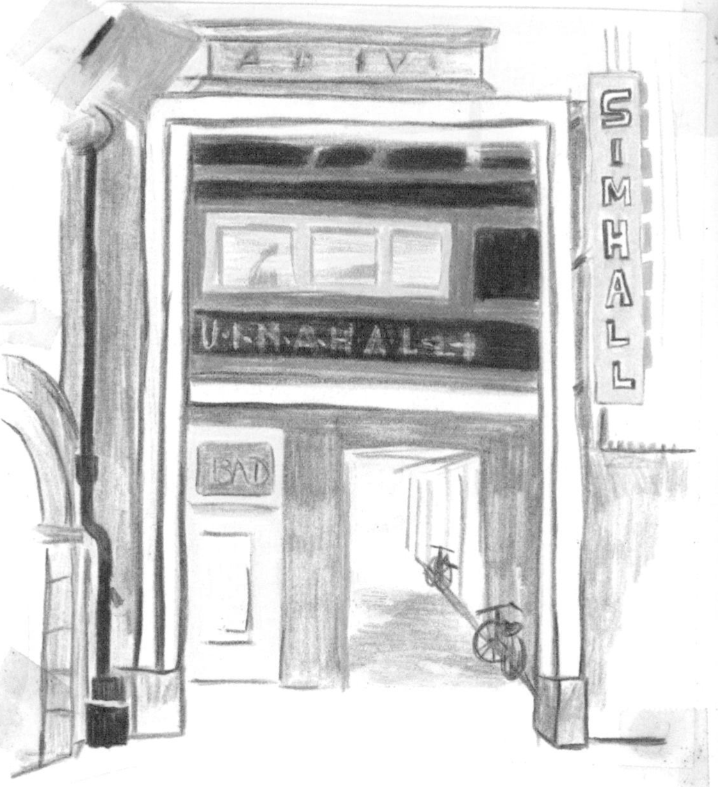
SIMHALL
UINAHALLI
BAD

You can swim naked.

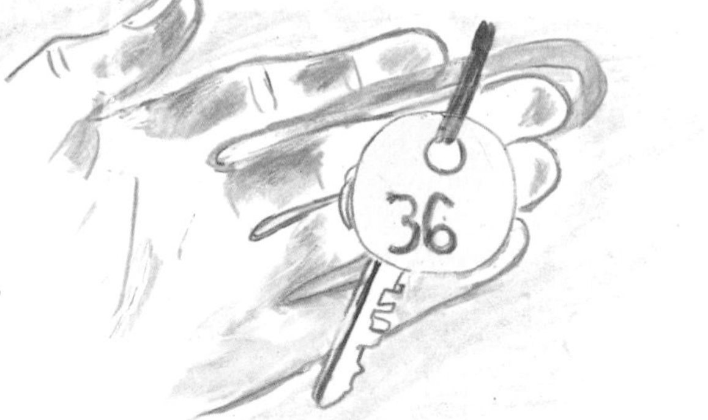
36

I wonder whether
Tove Jansson
ever swam here.

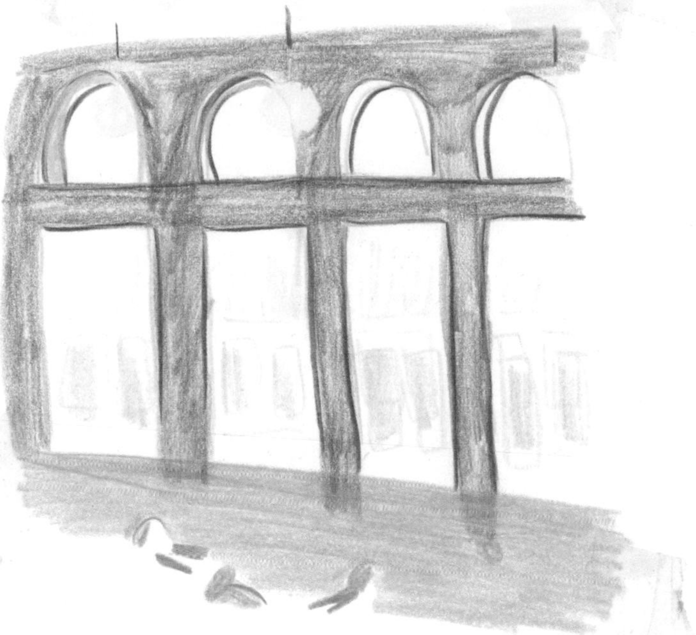

There's a small woman who swims very slowly. She has only one breast.

Who decided that one body
is more beautiful than that?

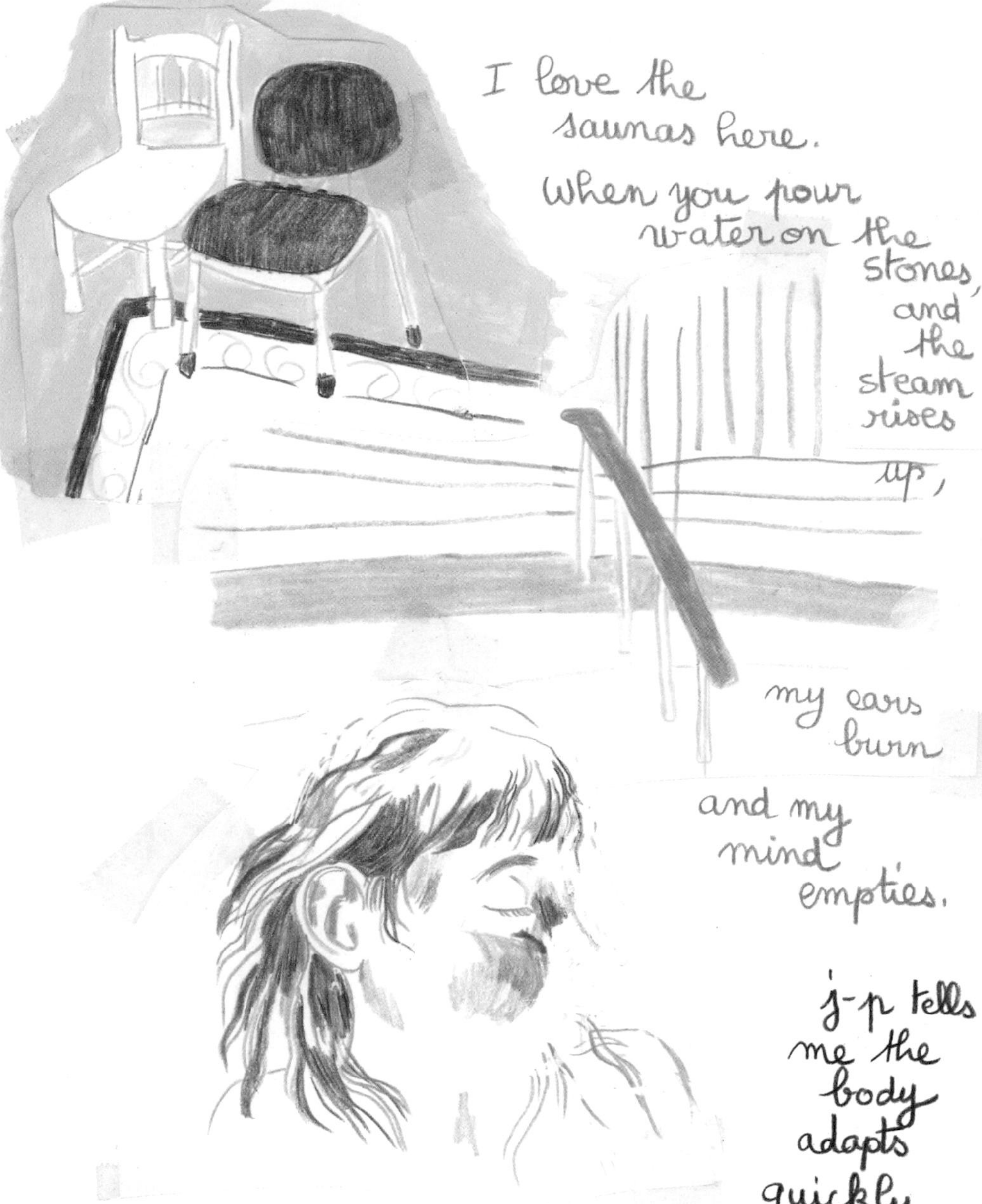
I love the saunas here.
When you pour water on the stones, and the steam rises up,
my ears burn
and my mind empties.
j-p tells me the body adapts quickly,

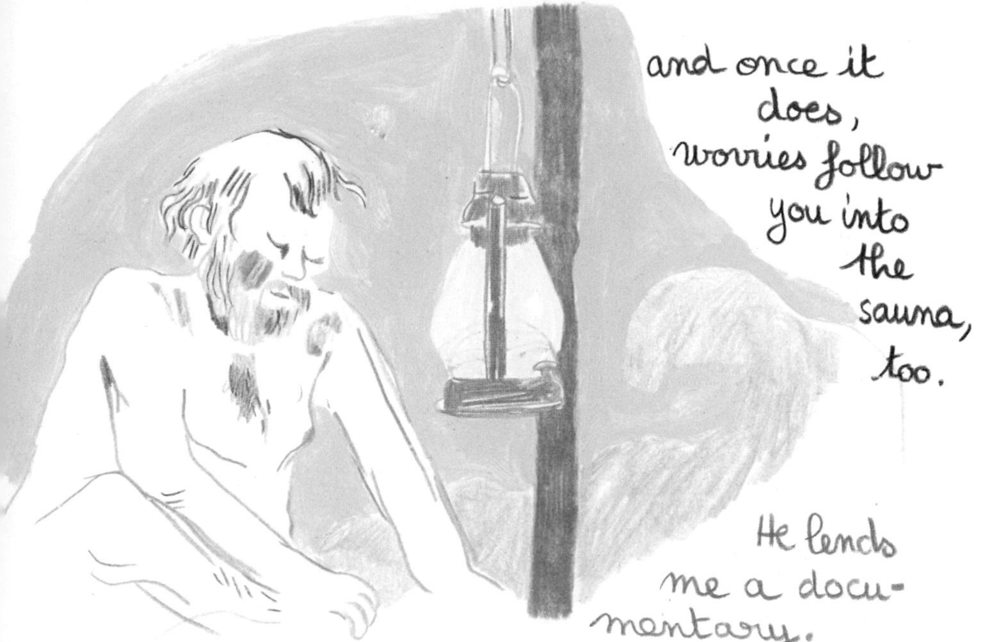
and once it does, worries follow you into the sauna, too.

He lends me a documentary. In it, a man takes a sauna with a bear.

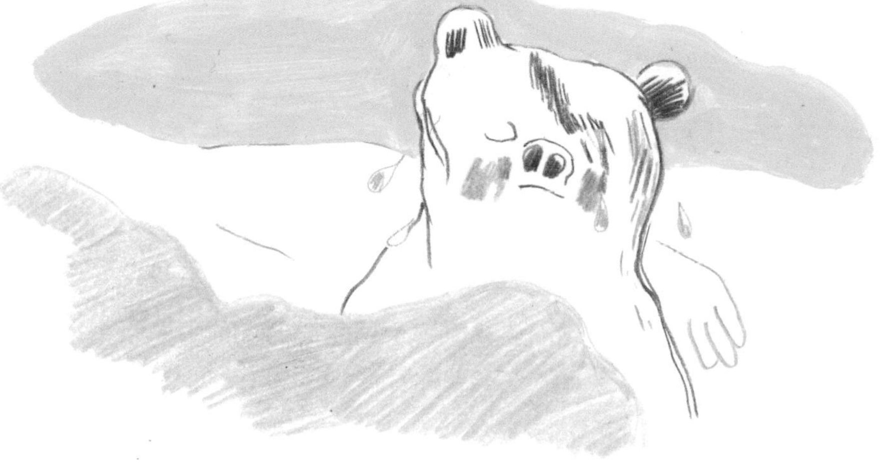

I move to the island of Suomenlinna

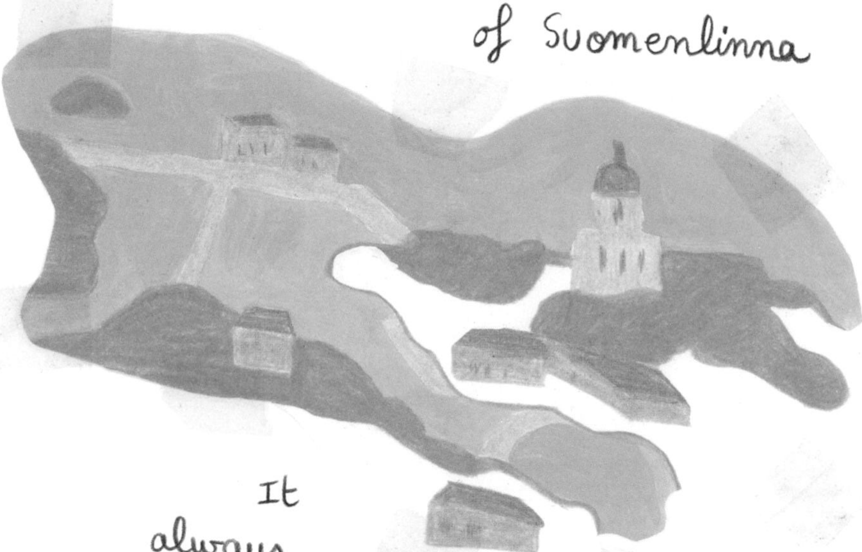

It always seems that to feel comfortable in a place, I need to get my bearings first.

(when I'm sure of what's around me, I can start my work.)

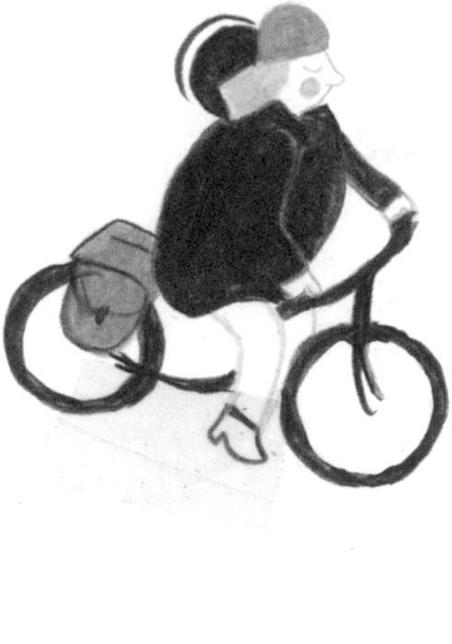

Tove Jansson wrote an essay about the island "Oar," in 1971.

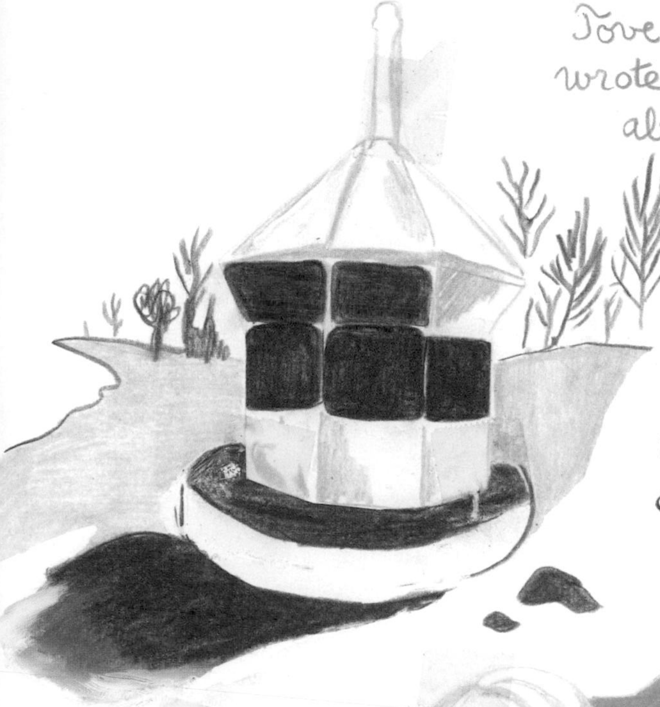

She sees them as a symbol of constructive solitude.

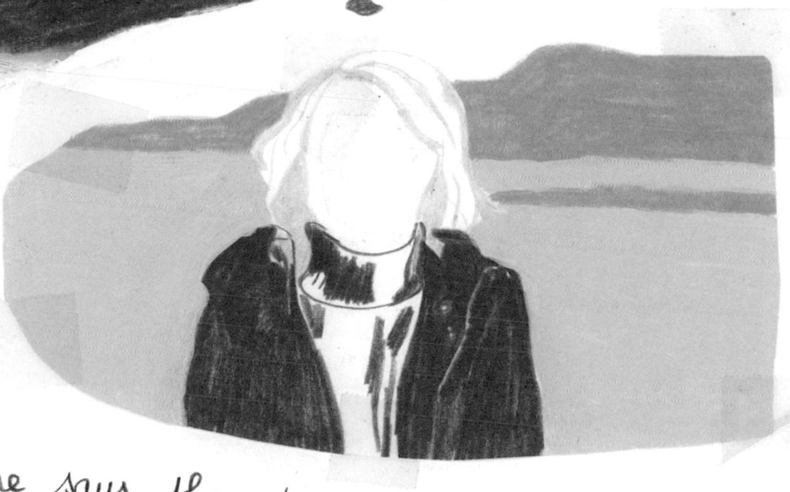

She says there's no true freedom if we can't be alone with ourselves.

She'd already bought her
own island, Klovharun, several
                    years earlier.
A patch of rock with a
cabin, a sanctuary. The photos are
enough to make anyone dream.

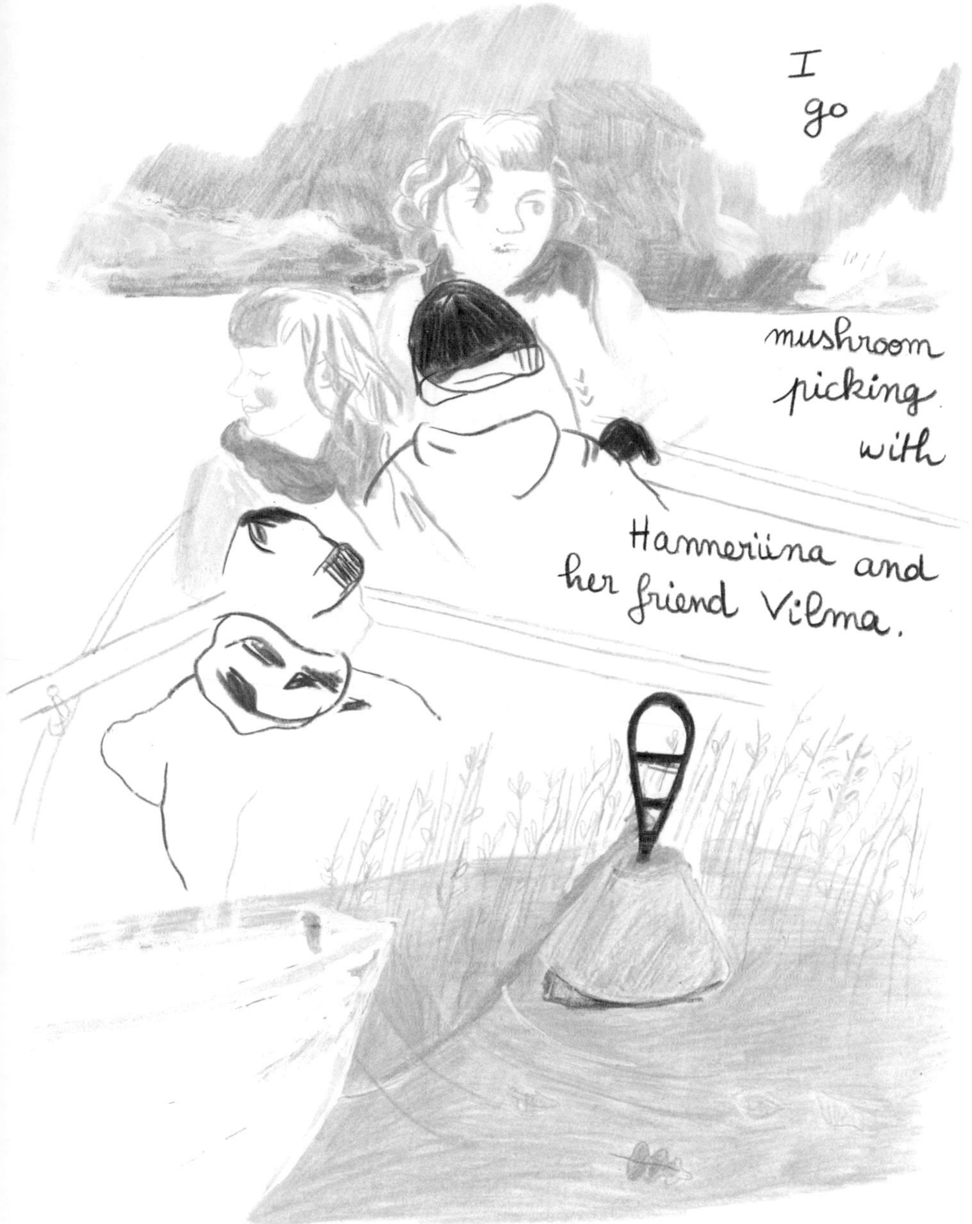
I go mushroom picking with Hanneriina and her friend Vilma.

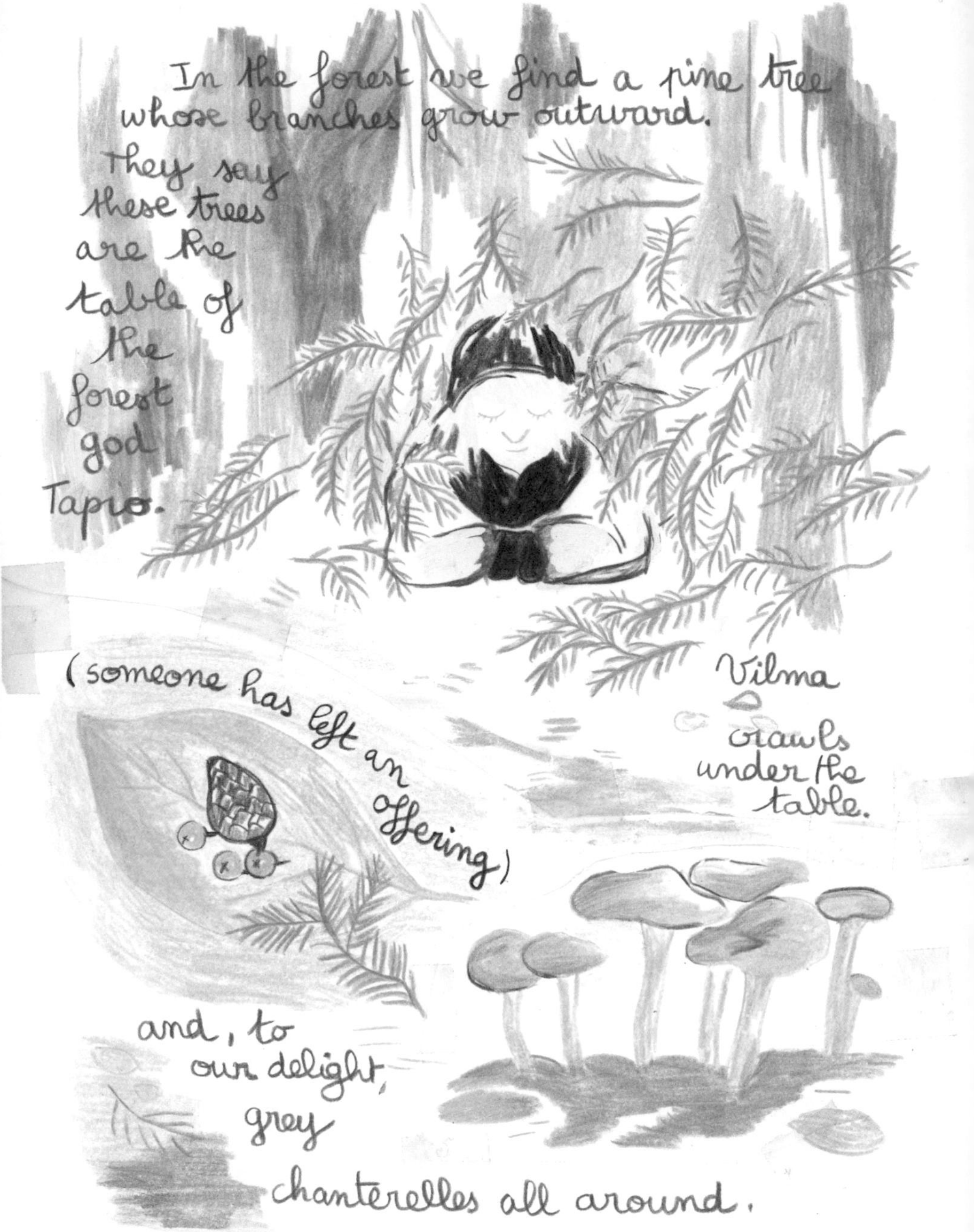
In the forest we find a pine tree whose branches grow outward.
They say these trees are the table of the forest god Tapio.
(someone has left an offering)
Vilma crawls under the table.
and, to our delight, grey chanterelles all around.

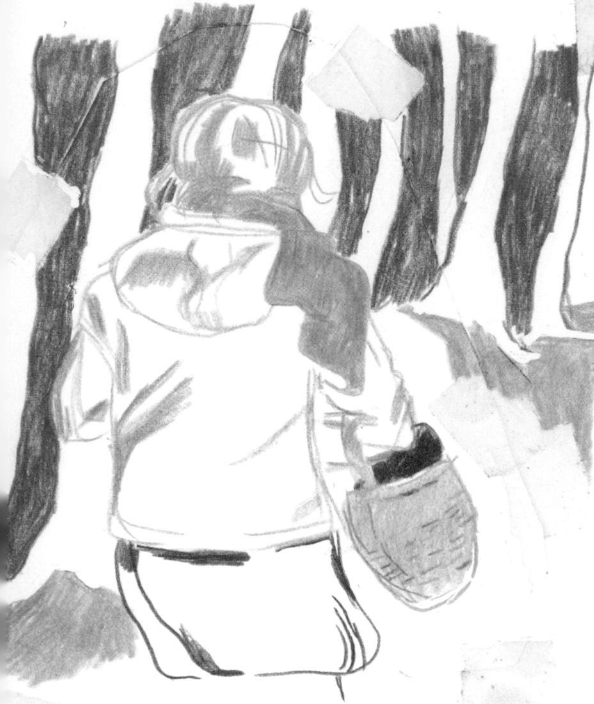

H. tells me women's shirts don't fit her. the sleeves are too tight, from all the summer days spent rowing her boat.

I think of my huge calves, maybe because of all the walking?

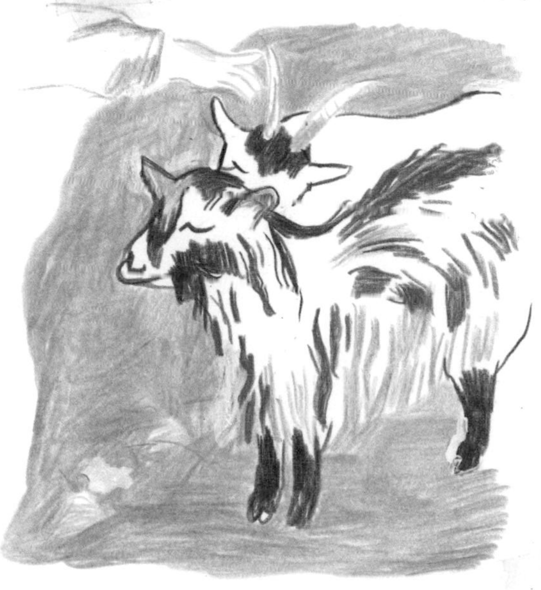

I admire these Finns,
who sail and row, and know
the names of the trees
    and mushrooms,

   who plant potatoes
   like H.,

      and like
      Tove Jansson.

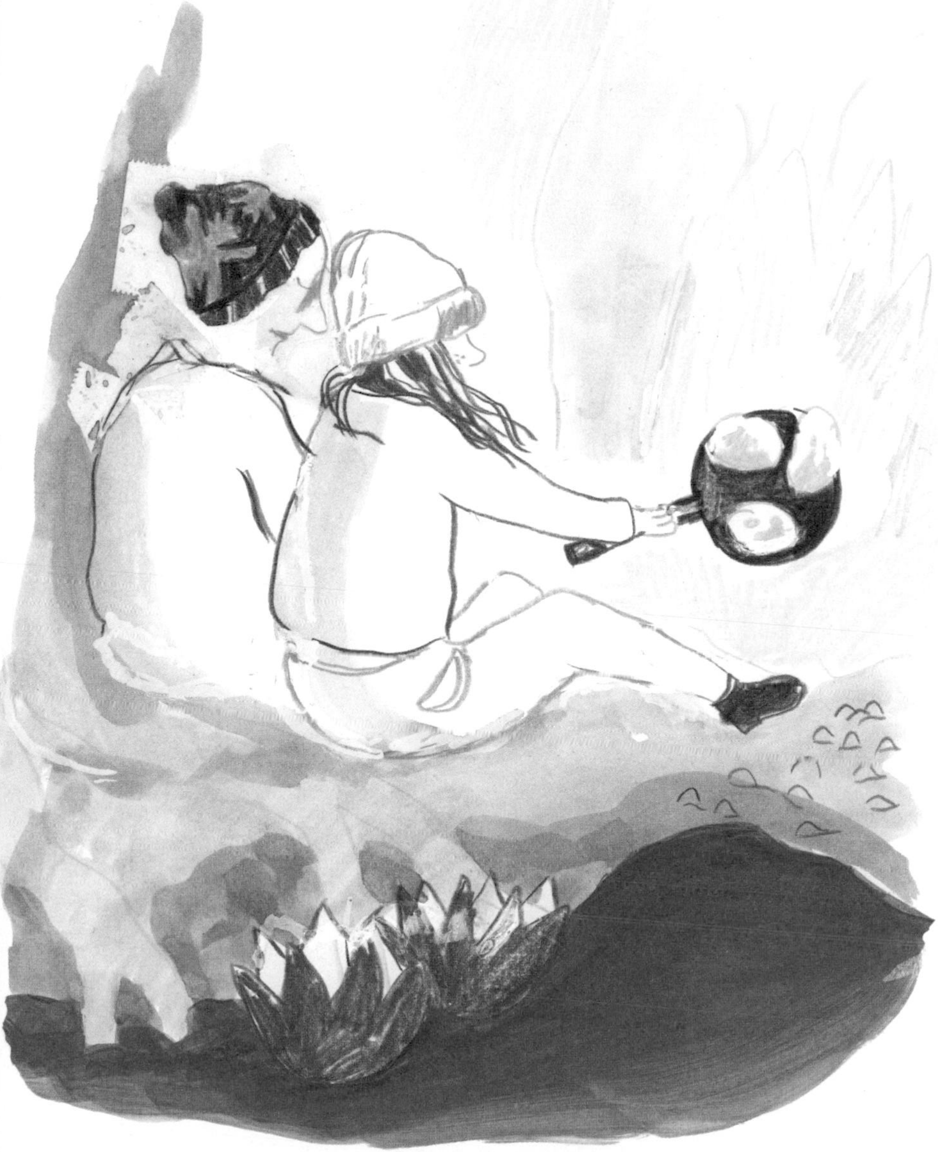

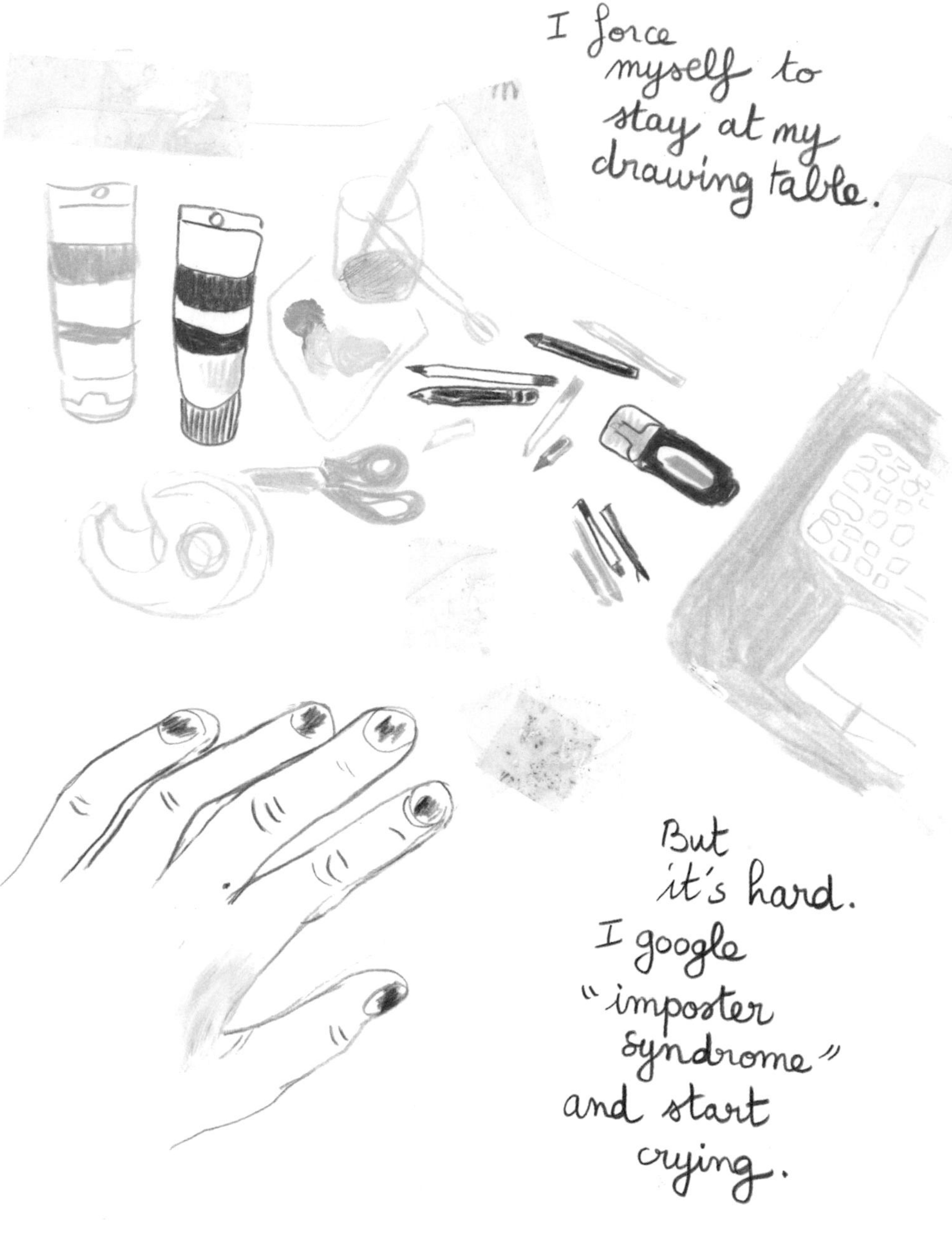
I force myself to stay at my drawing table.
But it's hard. I google "imposter syndrome" and start crying.

I wanted to visit the island with the lighthouse where the moomins supposedly lived...

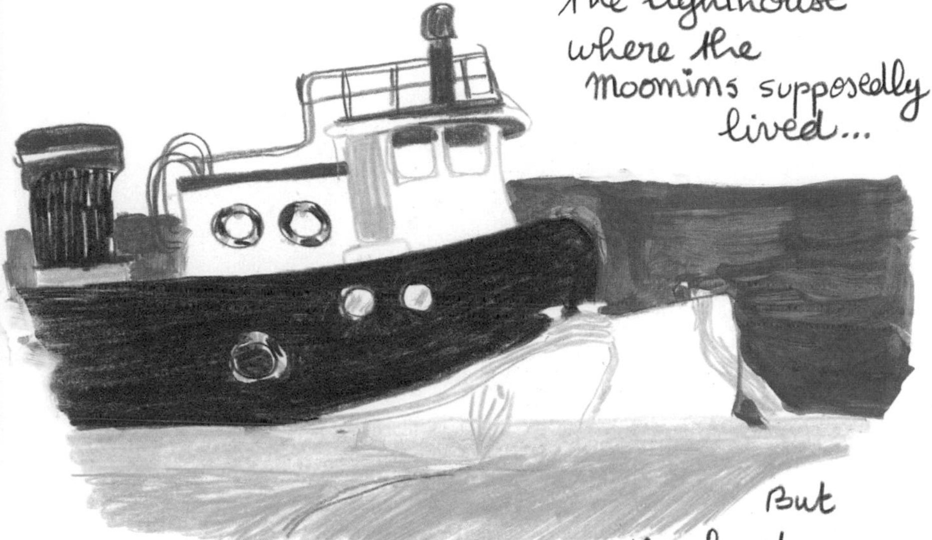

But the boats have stopped for the winter.

I pace, feeling restless.

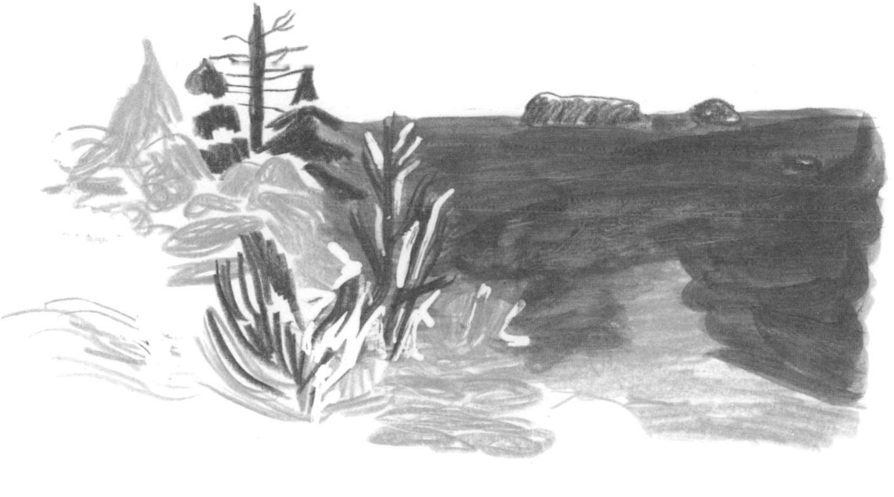

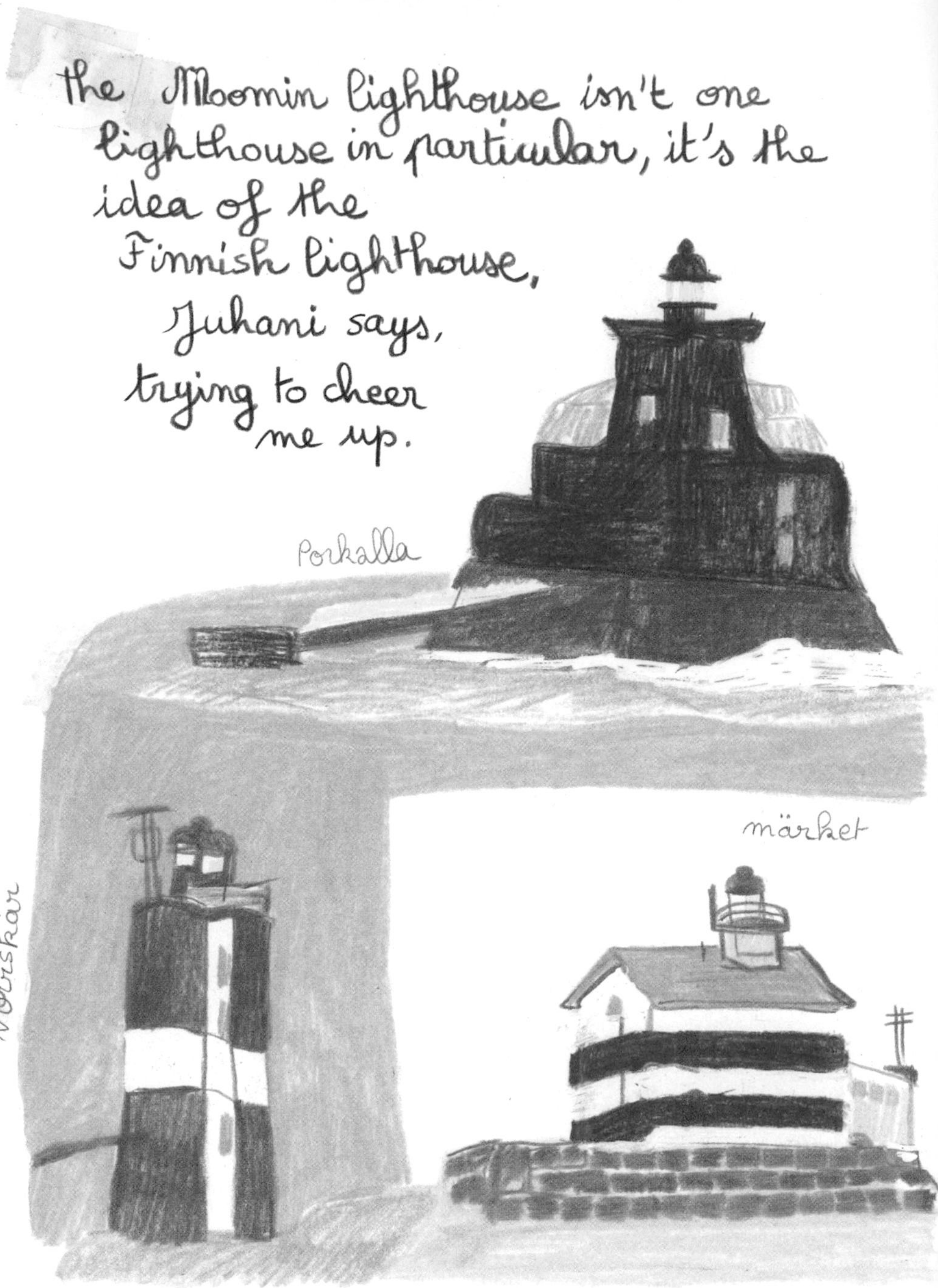
the Moomin lighthouse isn't one lighthouse in particular, it's the idea of the Finnish lighthouse,
Juhani says, trying to cheer me up.
Porkalla
märket
Norrskär

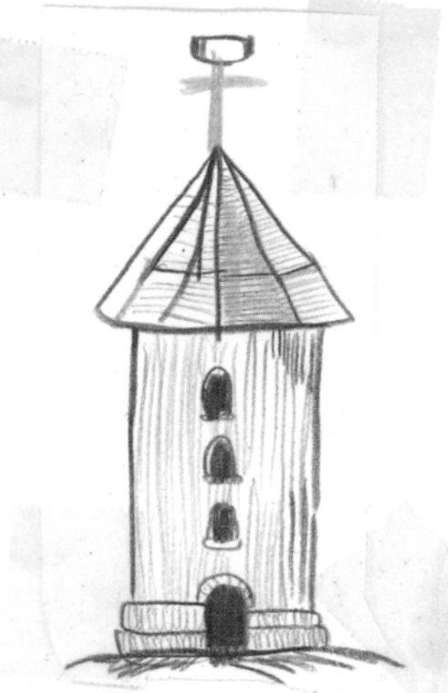

the Glosholm lighthouse,
an old tower whose
location was no longer
deemed judicious,
inspired the
Moomin house
(it was destroyed in 1940)

drawing
from 1863

not far from
there is Söderskär,
now in
disuse.

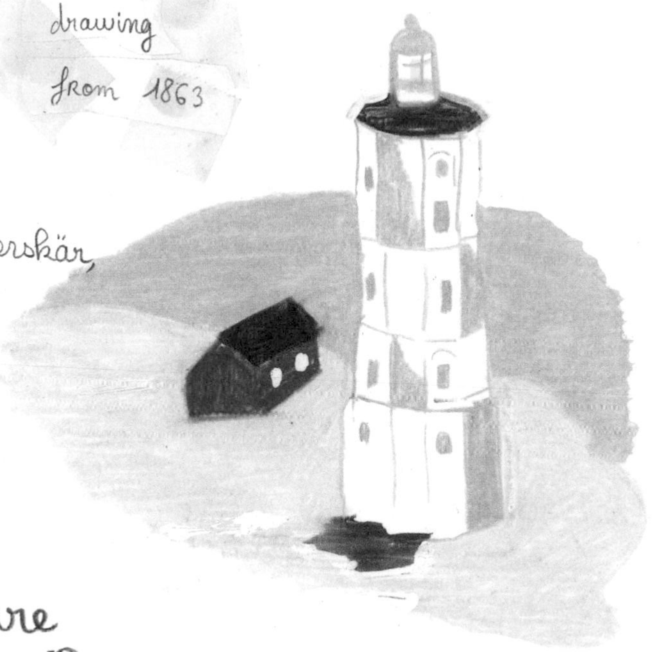

there are
tours in the
summer, and you
can even sleep there, but
it's expensive.

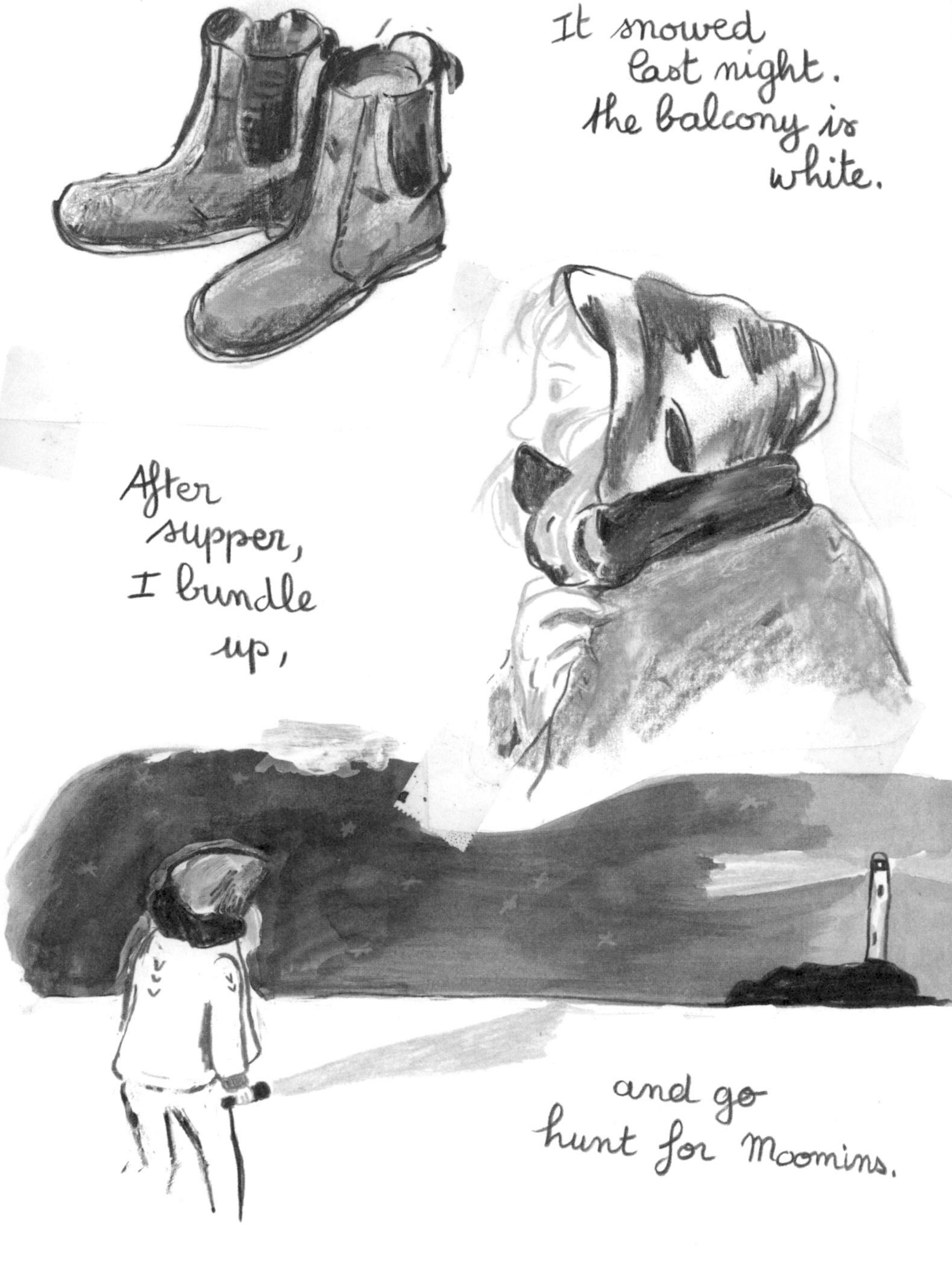
It snowed last night. the balcony is white.
After supper, I bundle up,
and go hunt for Moomins.

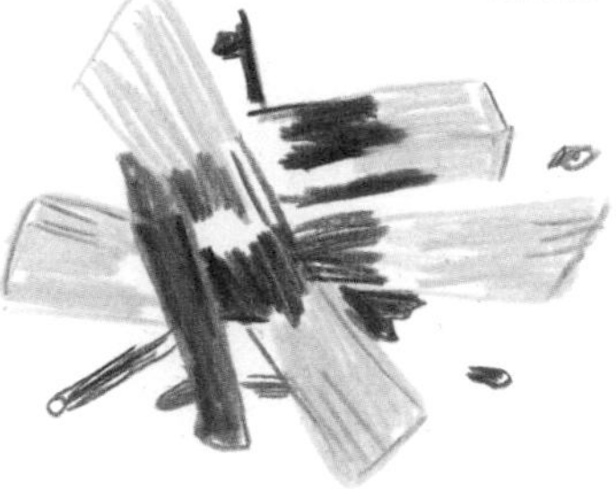

There's a fire smouldering on the beach. I collect wood to keep it going.

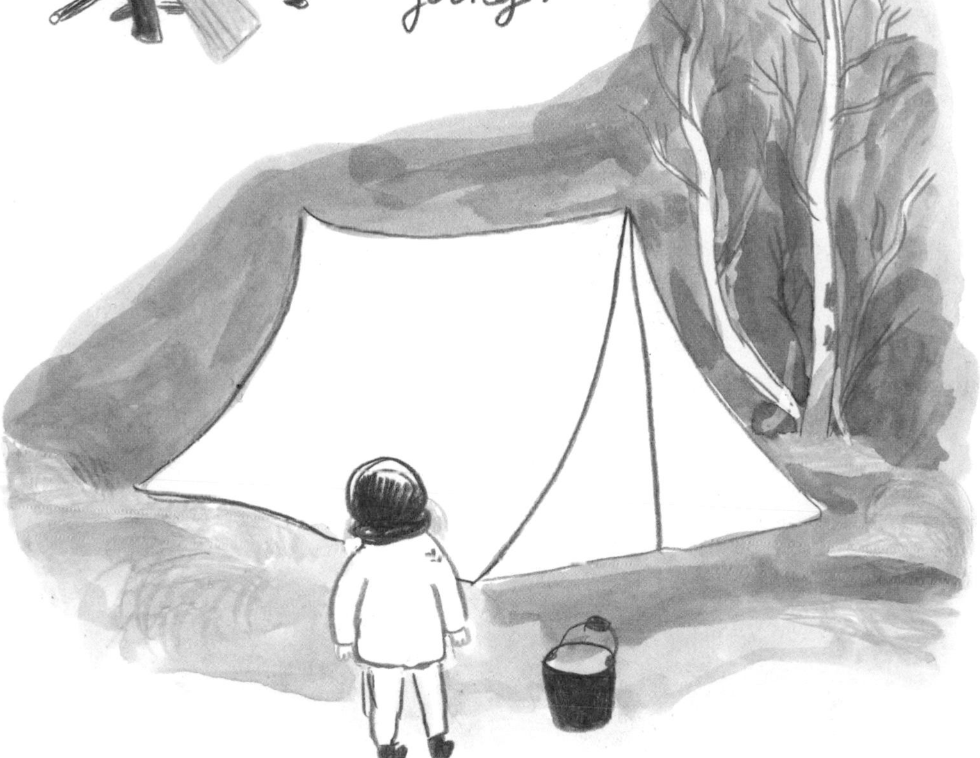

I imagine Snufkin (a solitary and adventurous character in the Moomin books) built the fire.

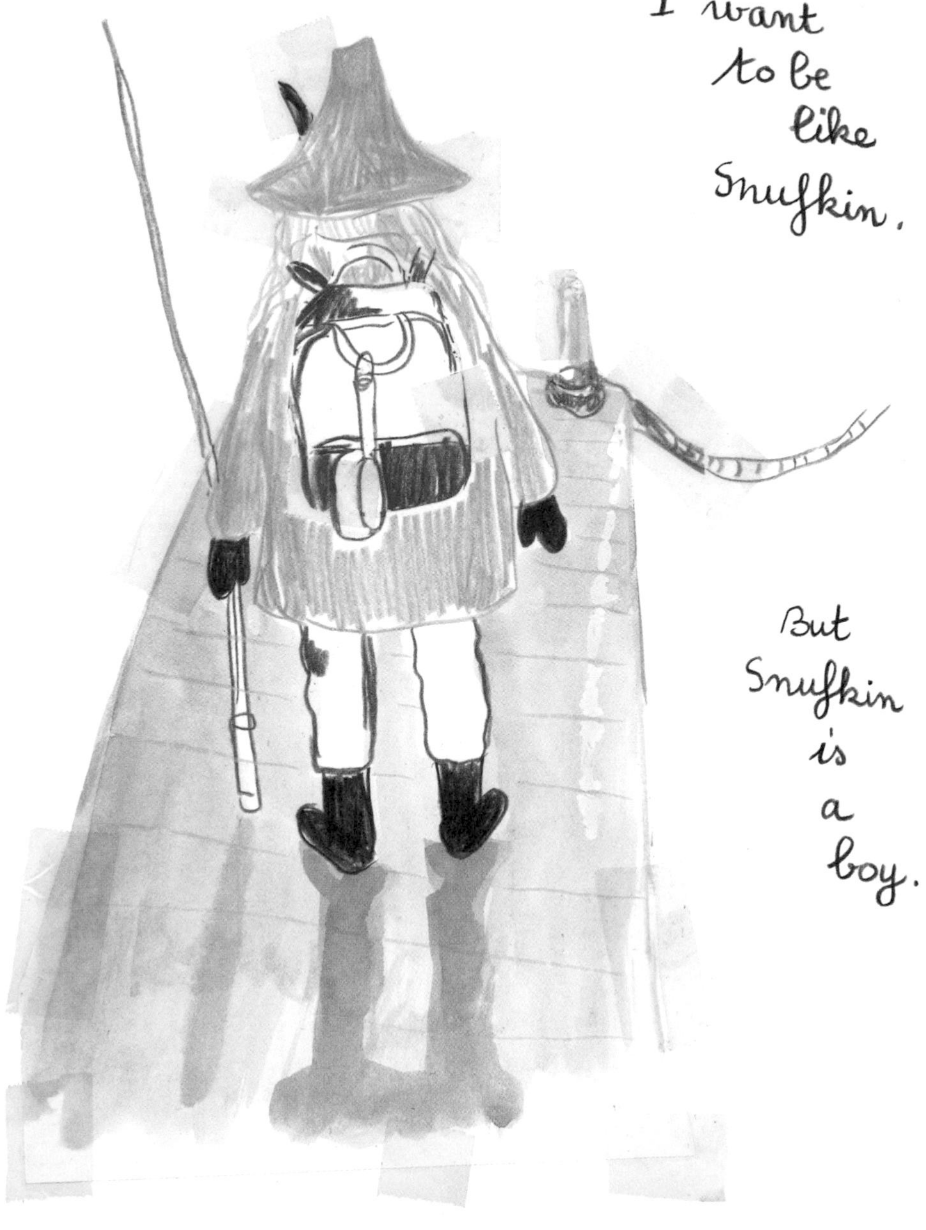
I want to be like Snufkin.
But Snufkin is a boy.

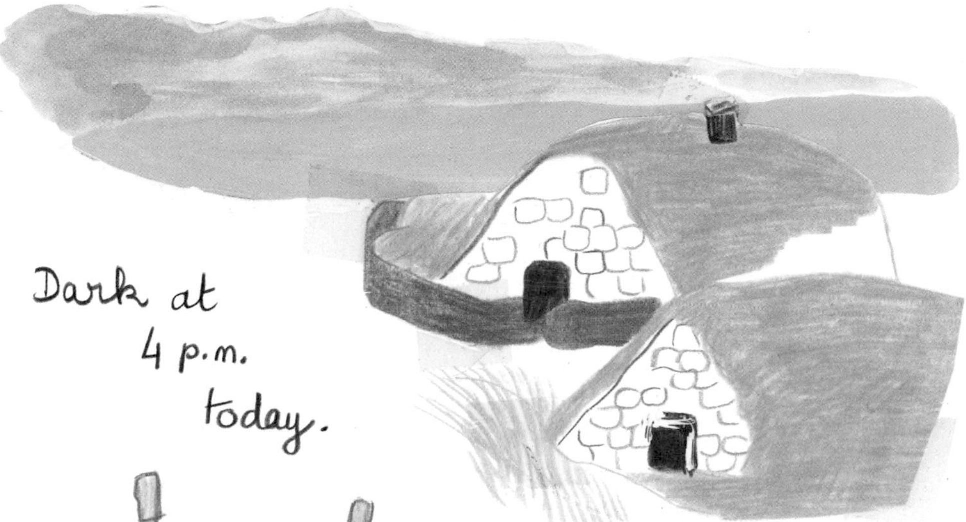

Dark at 4 p.m. today.

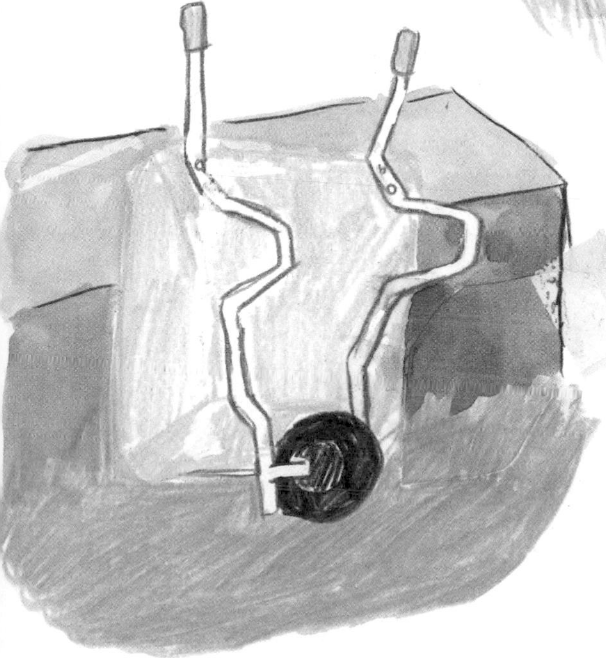

I wander the island in the fog, trying to etch it into my memory.

my period is so painful I have to stop and crouch down on the path.

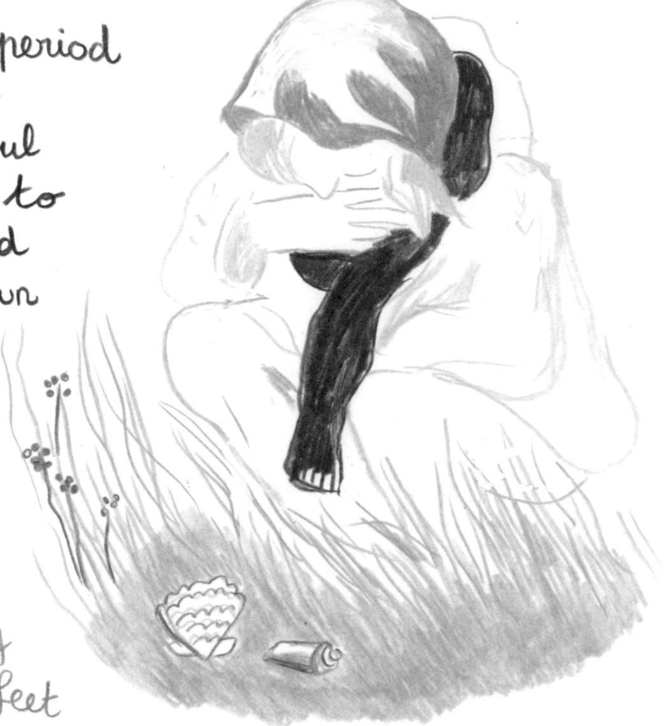

At my feet, I find little shells bordering the flower beds, just like in Moominmamma's garden.

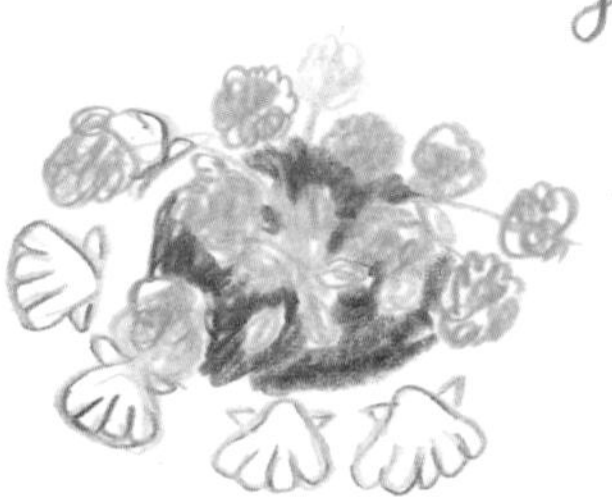

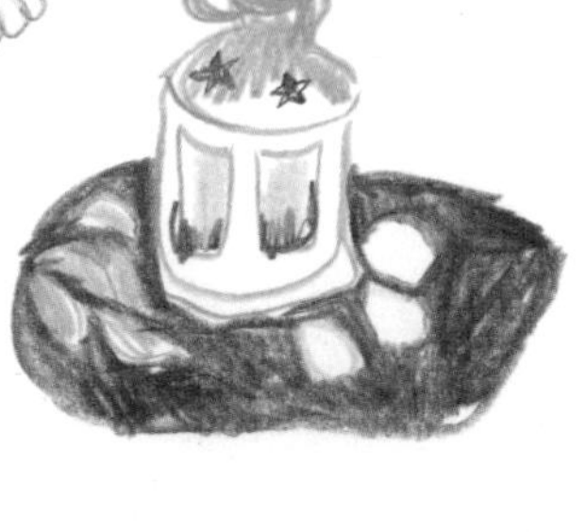

I leave Helsinki in two days.

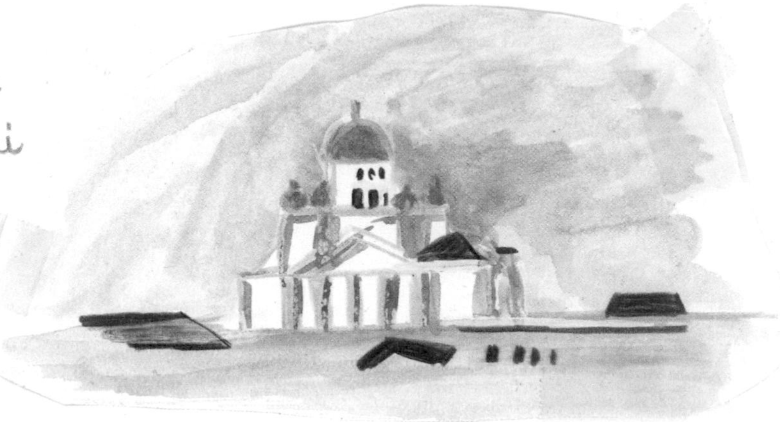

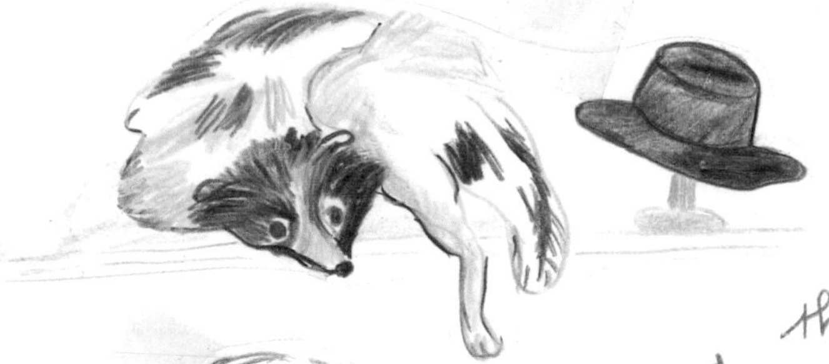

Julie and I find a fox boa in a thrift store, and we take pictures of each other, posing like Tove in her self-portraits.

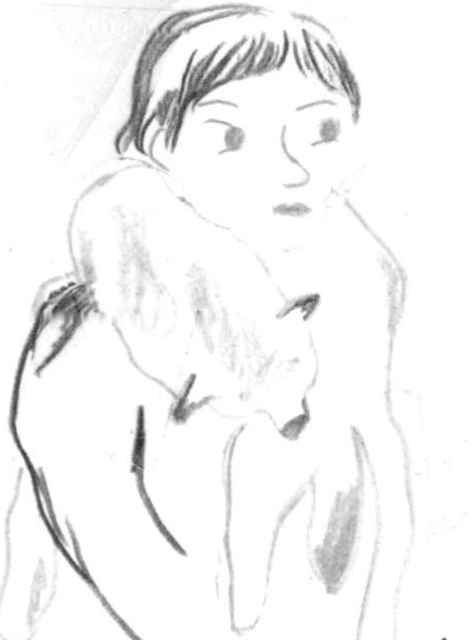

← (lynx boa, 1942)

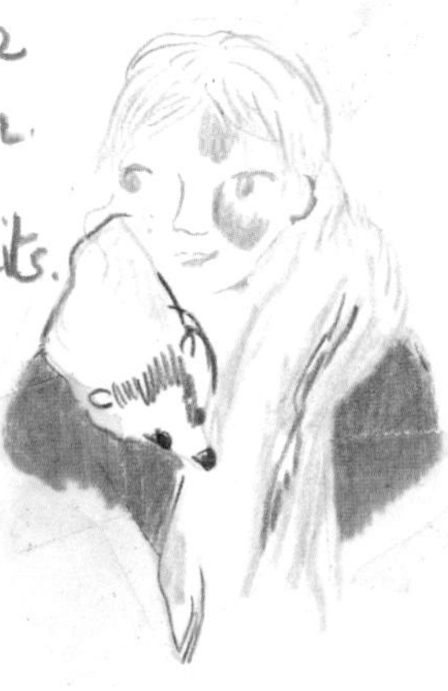

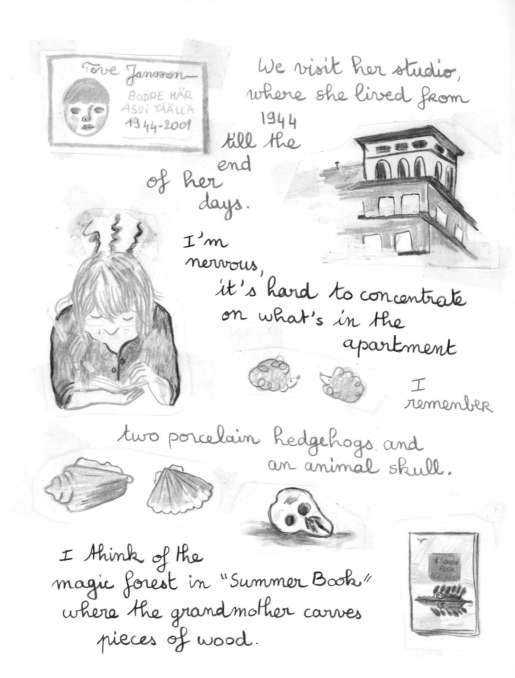

Tove Jansson
BODDE HÄR
ASUI TÄÄLLÄ
1944-2001

We visit her studio, where she lived from 1944 till the end of her days.

I'm nervous, it's hard to concentrate on what's in the apartment

I remember two porcelain hedgehogs and an animal skull.

I think of the magic forest in "Summer Book" where the grandmother carves pieces of wood.

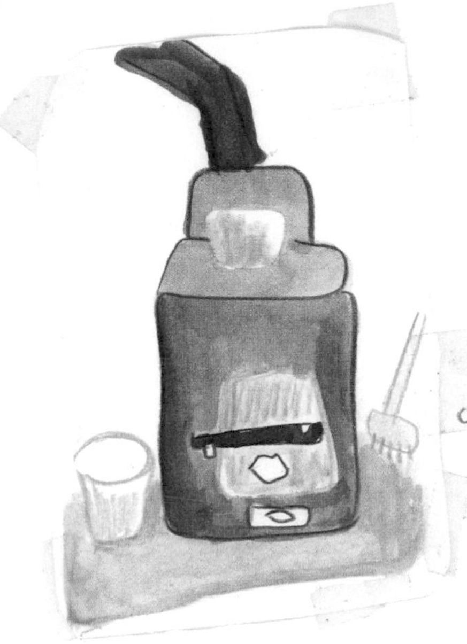

there's a traditional stove (probably with a family of Moomins behind it, since that's where they lived when they were city-dwellers)

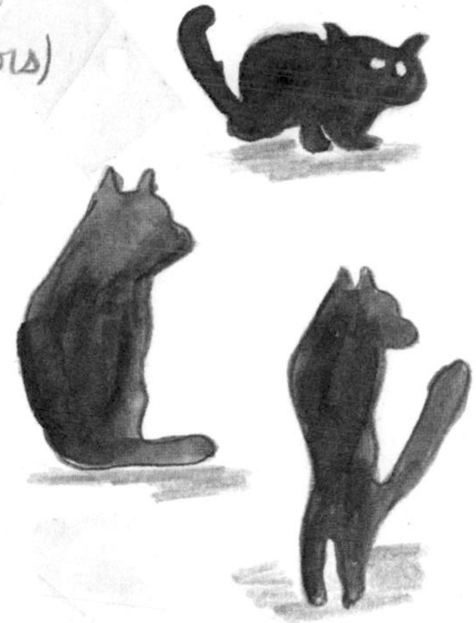

and magnificent prints of cats by Tuuliki Pietilä, Tove's life partner

And tall statues, sculpted by her father, Viktor.

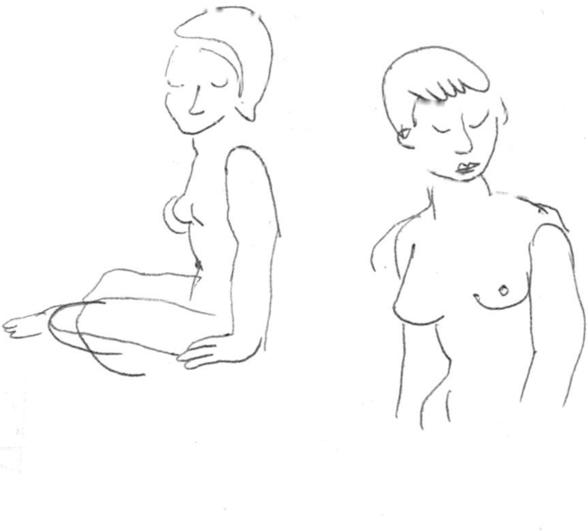

When the studio was renovated in the sixties, Tove said she didn't need a kitchen because she didn't like to cook.

But she had a second storey added so she could see the sea from her window.

From there,
you can see Helsinki's
observation towers
and, I imagine,
sometimes
a comet
too.

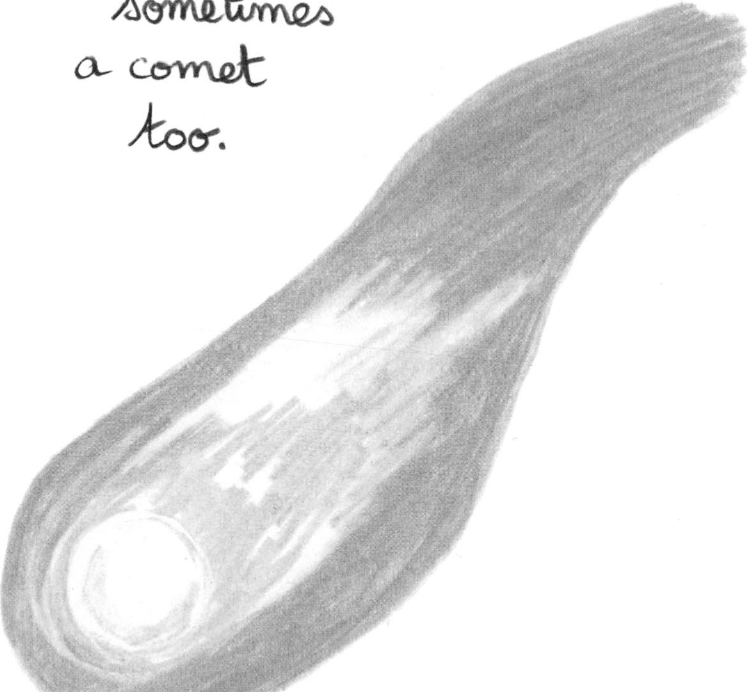

The child's dream

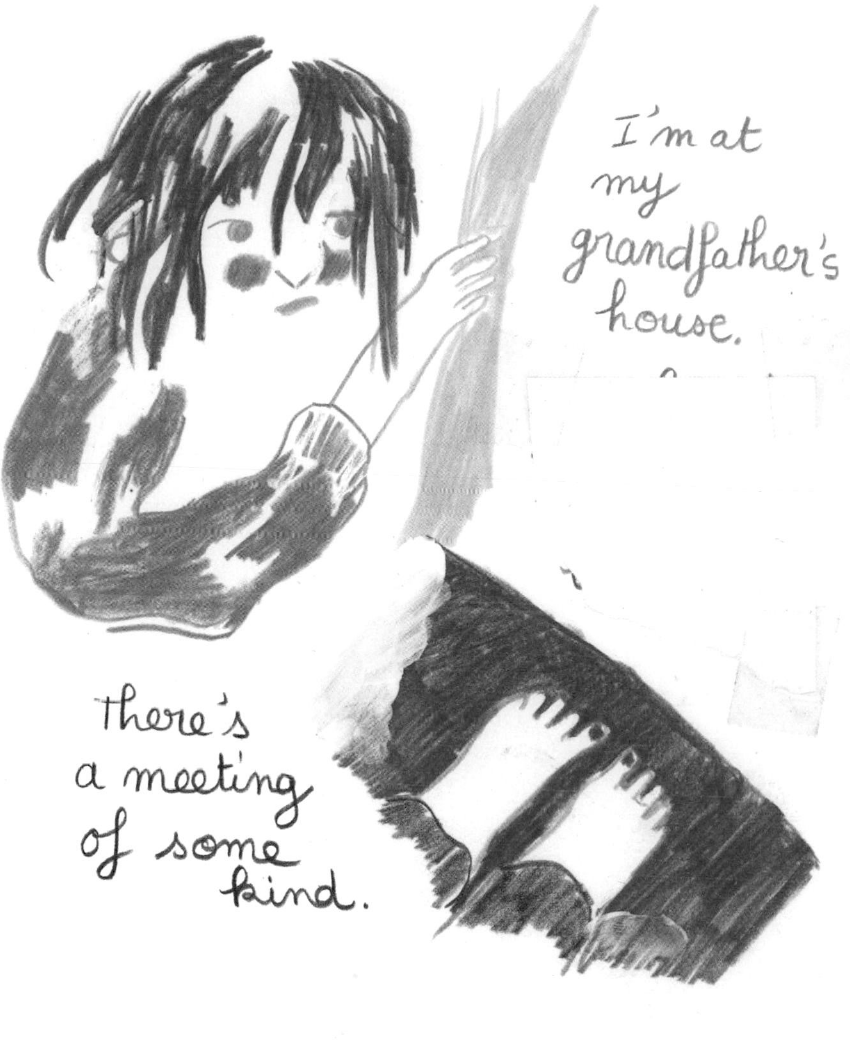
I'm at my grandfather's house.
there's a meeting of some kind.

we need to get the children out of the room

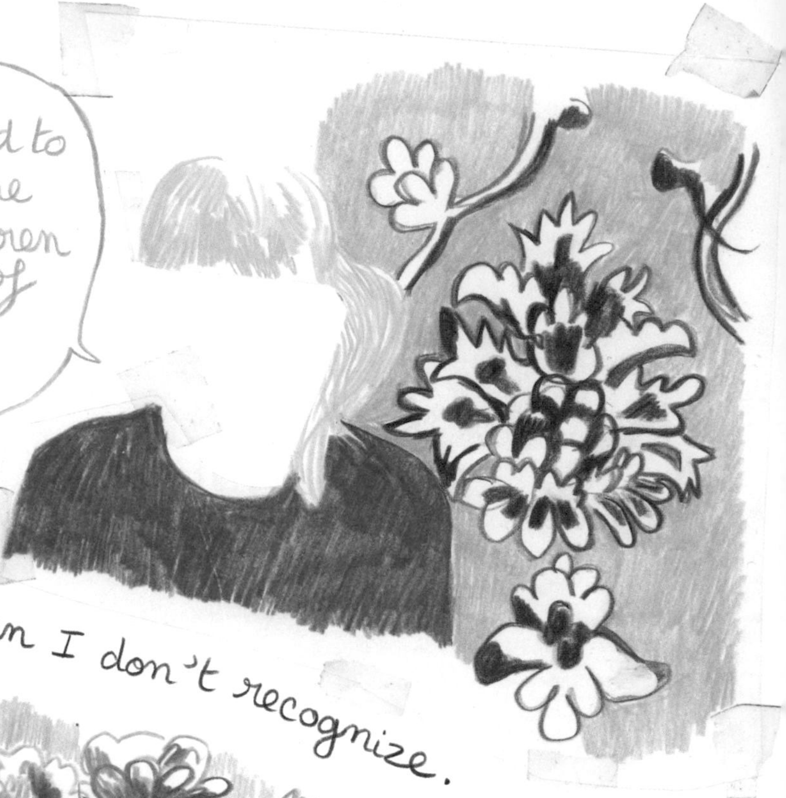

says a woman I don't recognize.

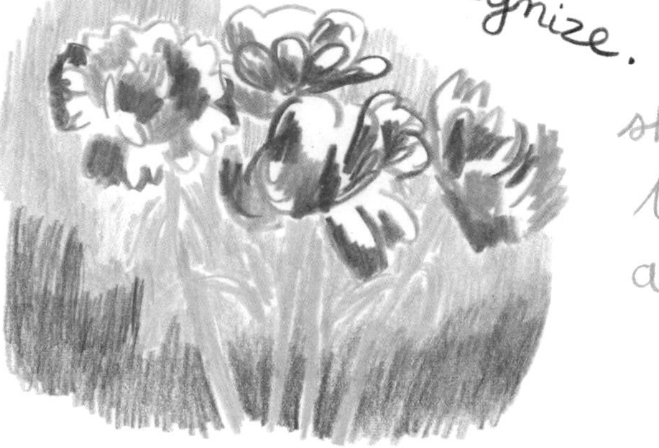

she is going to talk about sexual abuse

my heart is racing, I don't want to be here.

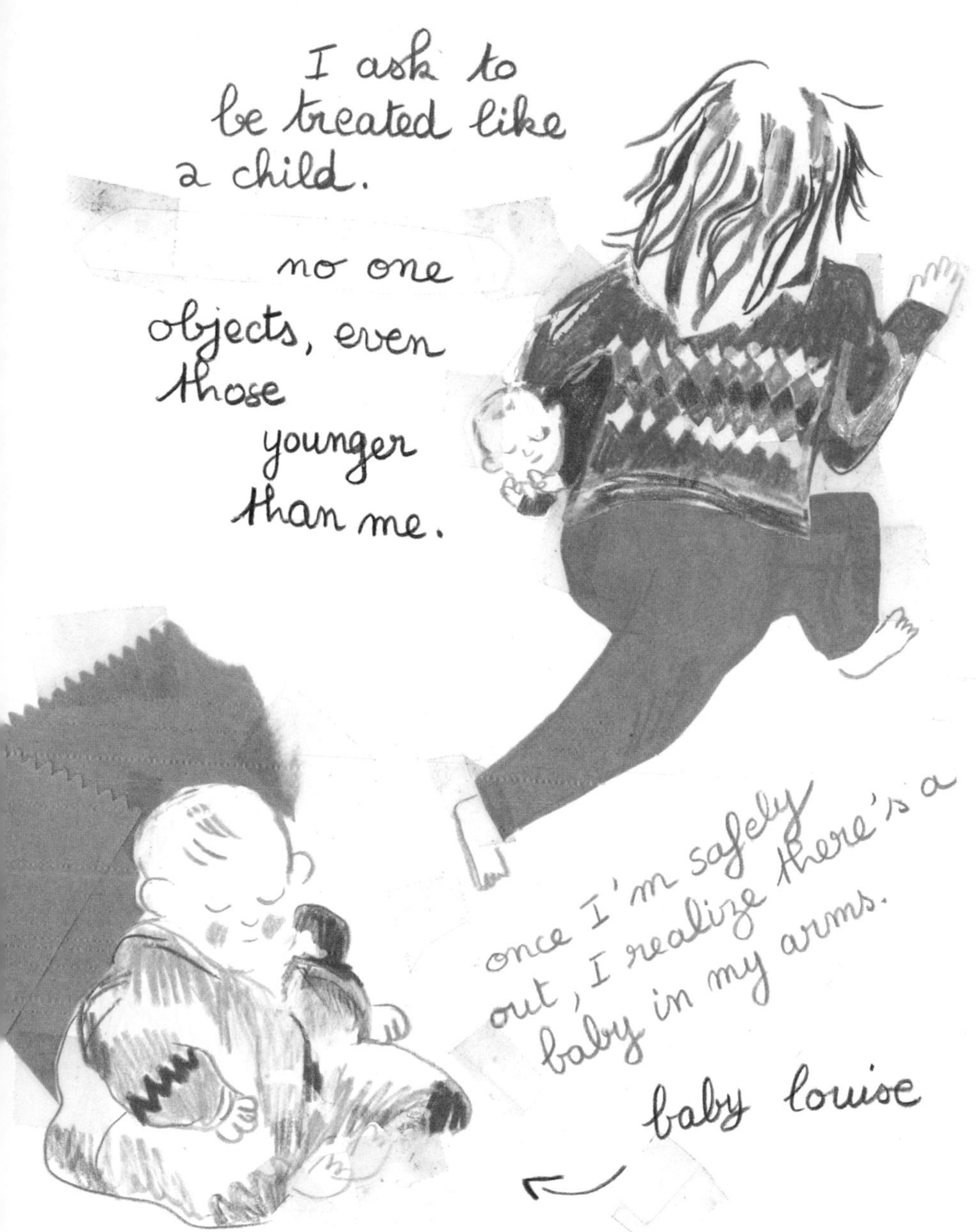
I ask to be treated like a child.
no one objects, even those younger than me.
once I'm safely out, I realize there's a baby in my arms.
baby louise

It's a sweet dream. I take care of Louise and I'm not afraid.

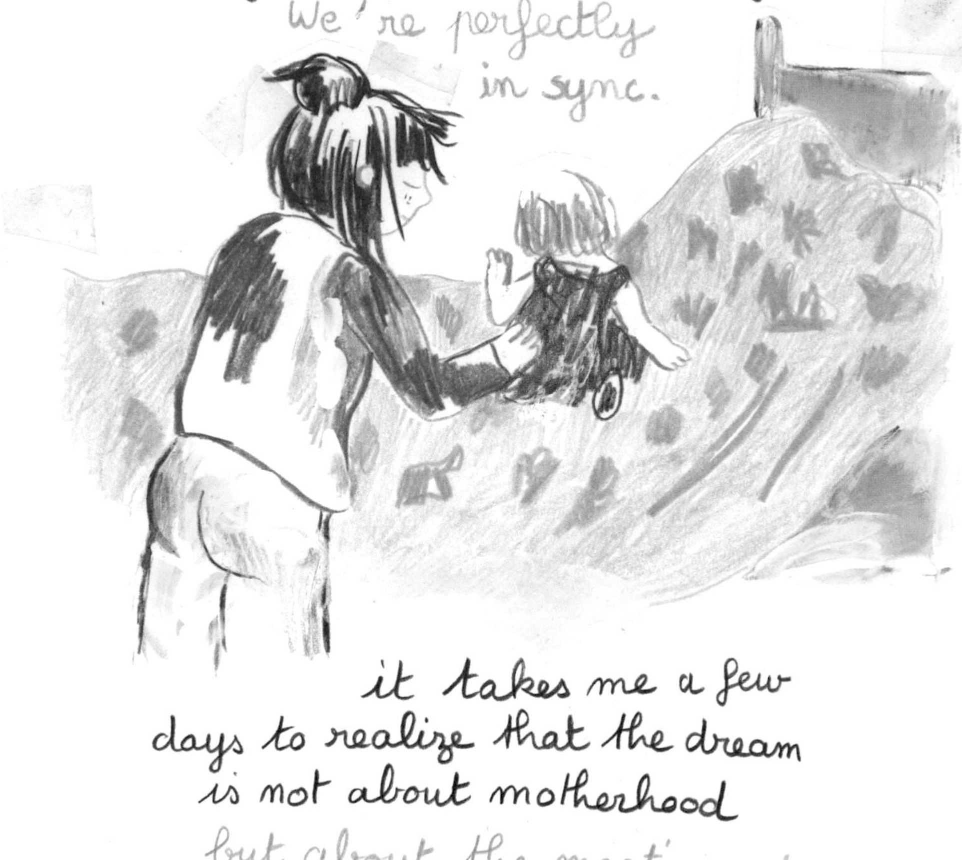
We're perfectly in sync.

it takes me a few days to realize that the dream is not about motherhood

but about the meeting going on downstairs, in my grandfather's living room.

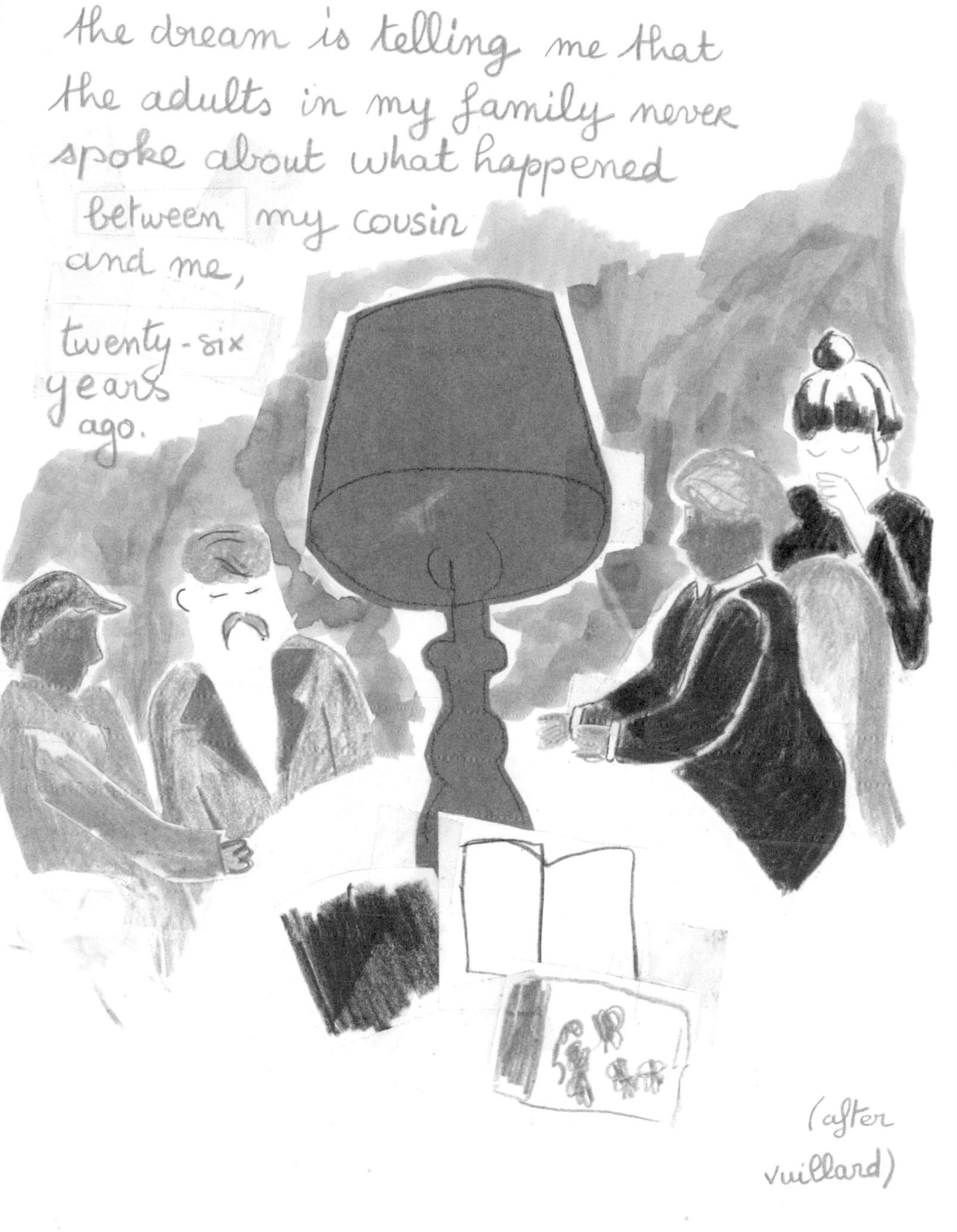
the dream is telling me that the adults in my family never spoke about what happened between my cousin and me,
twenty-six years ago.
(after vuillard)

I often look at my family
tree and wonder:
   which of these women were
                    raped?

léontine

marguerite

camille

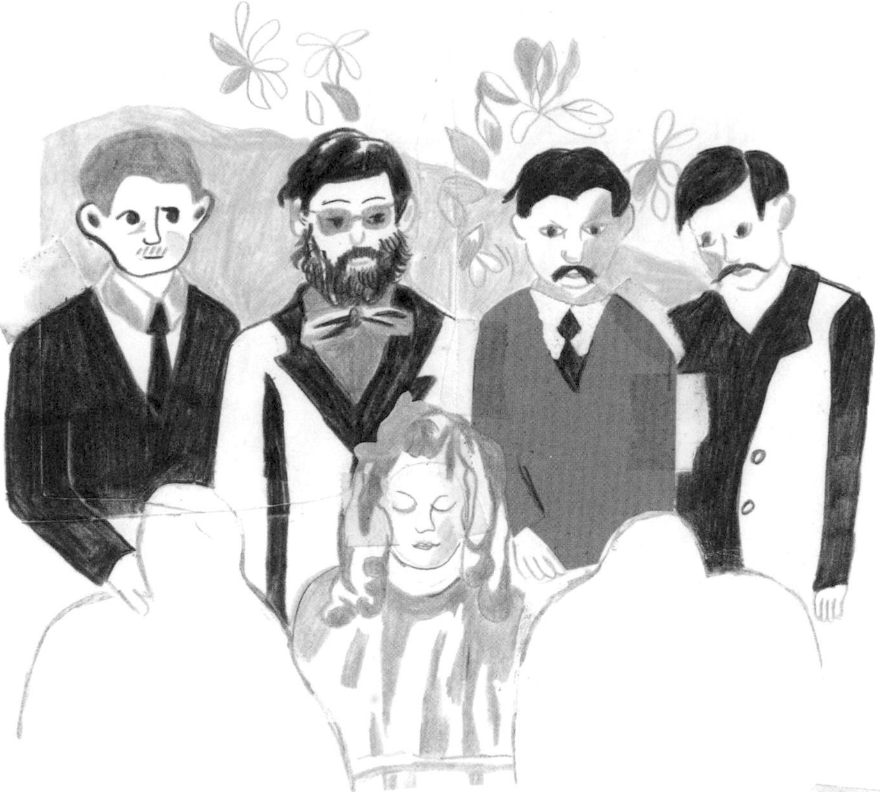

there's a photograph
of my grandmother
surrounded by her
four older brothers.

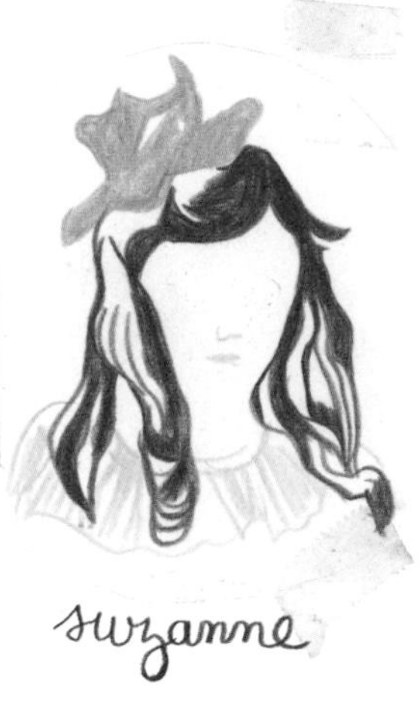

suzanne

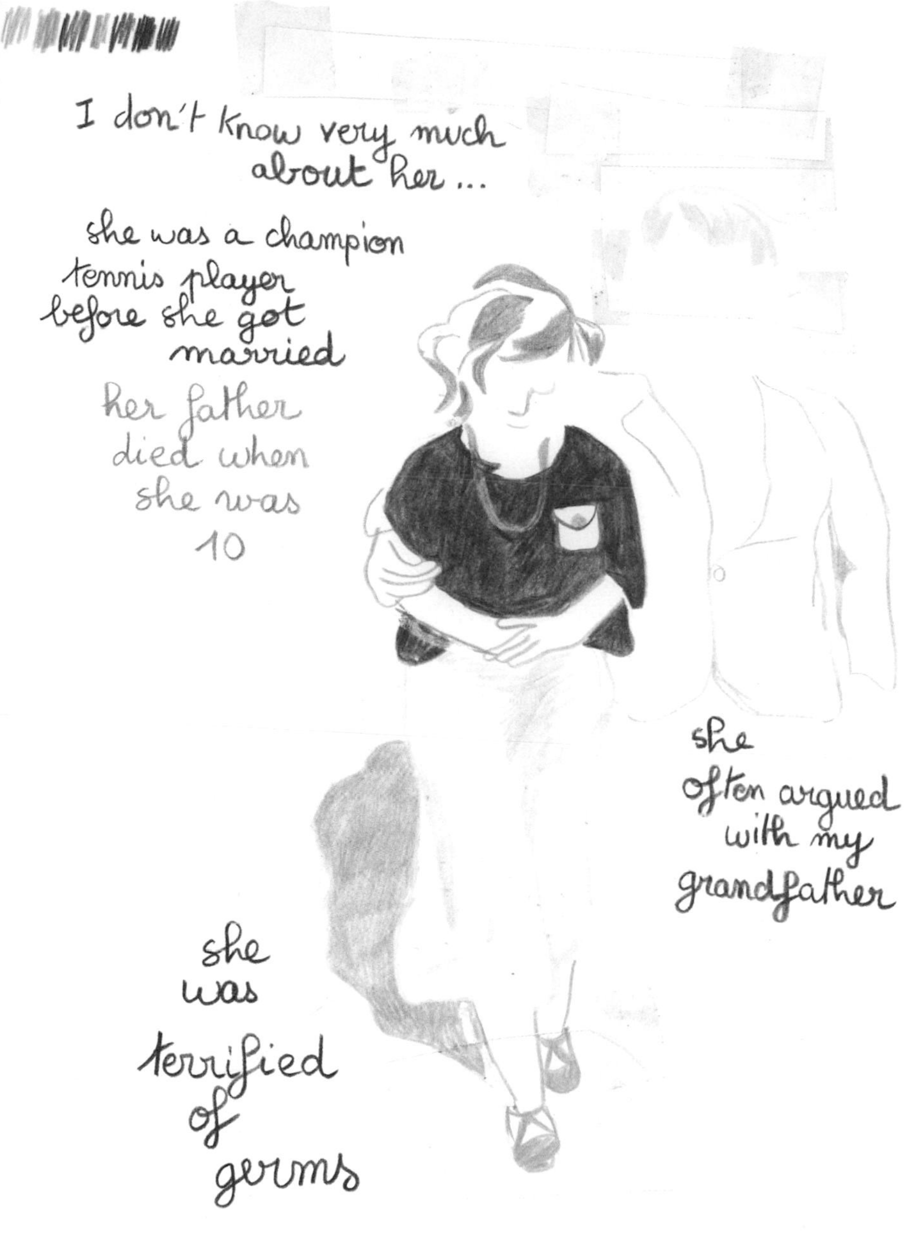
I don't know very much about her...
she was a champion tennis player before she got married
her father died when she was 10
she often argued with my grandfather
she was terrified of germs

Montréal
winter-spring
2016

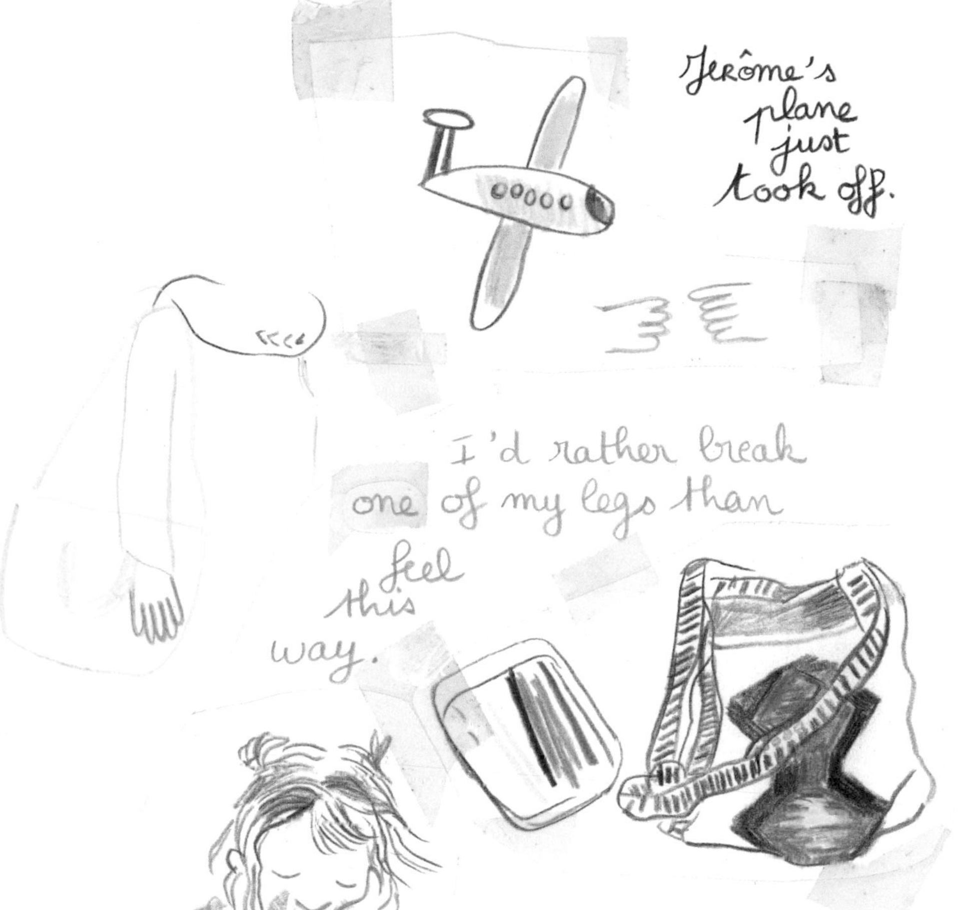
Jérôme's plane just took off.
I'd rather break one of my legs than feel this way.
(when did drawing stop feeling good?)

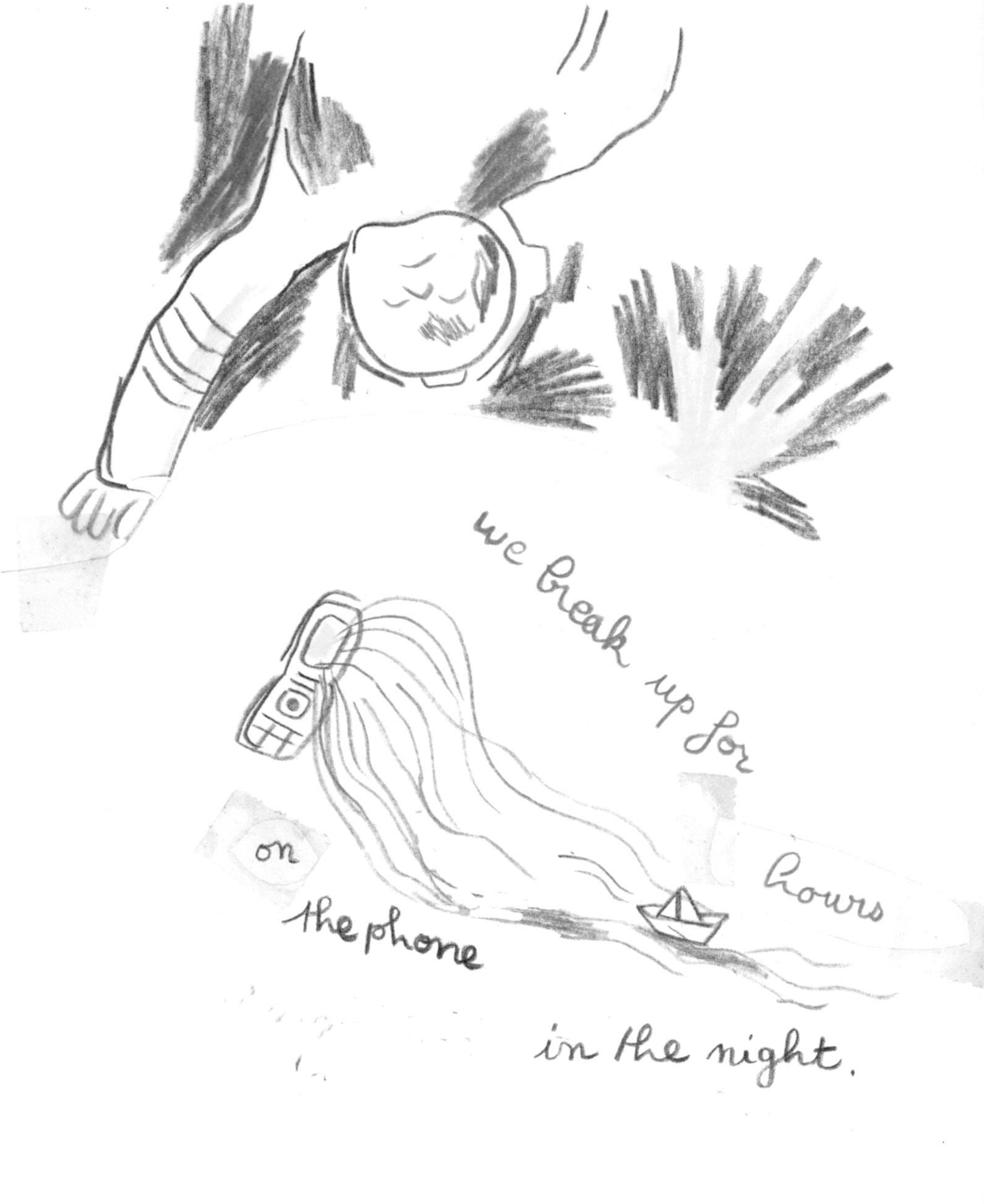
we break up for
hours
on
the phone
in the night.

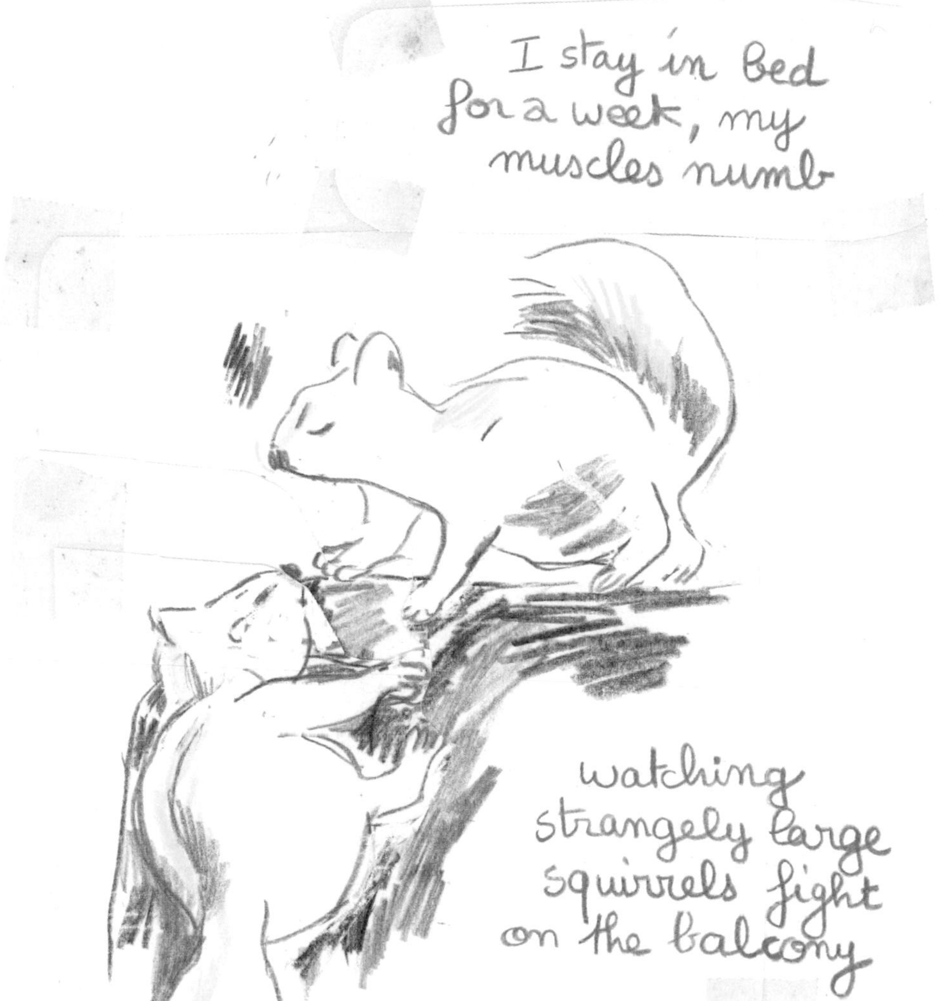
I stay in bed for a week, my muscles numb
watching strangely large squirrels fight on the balcony

I wonder what it feels like
to grow up without
trauma.

"Tender points"

Amy Berkowitz

it's reading
that saves me
(like it did when I was
little)

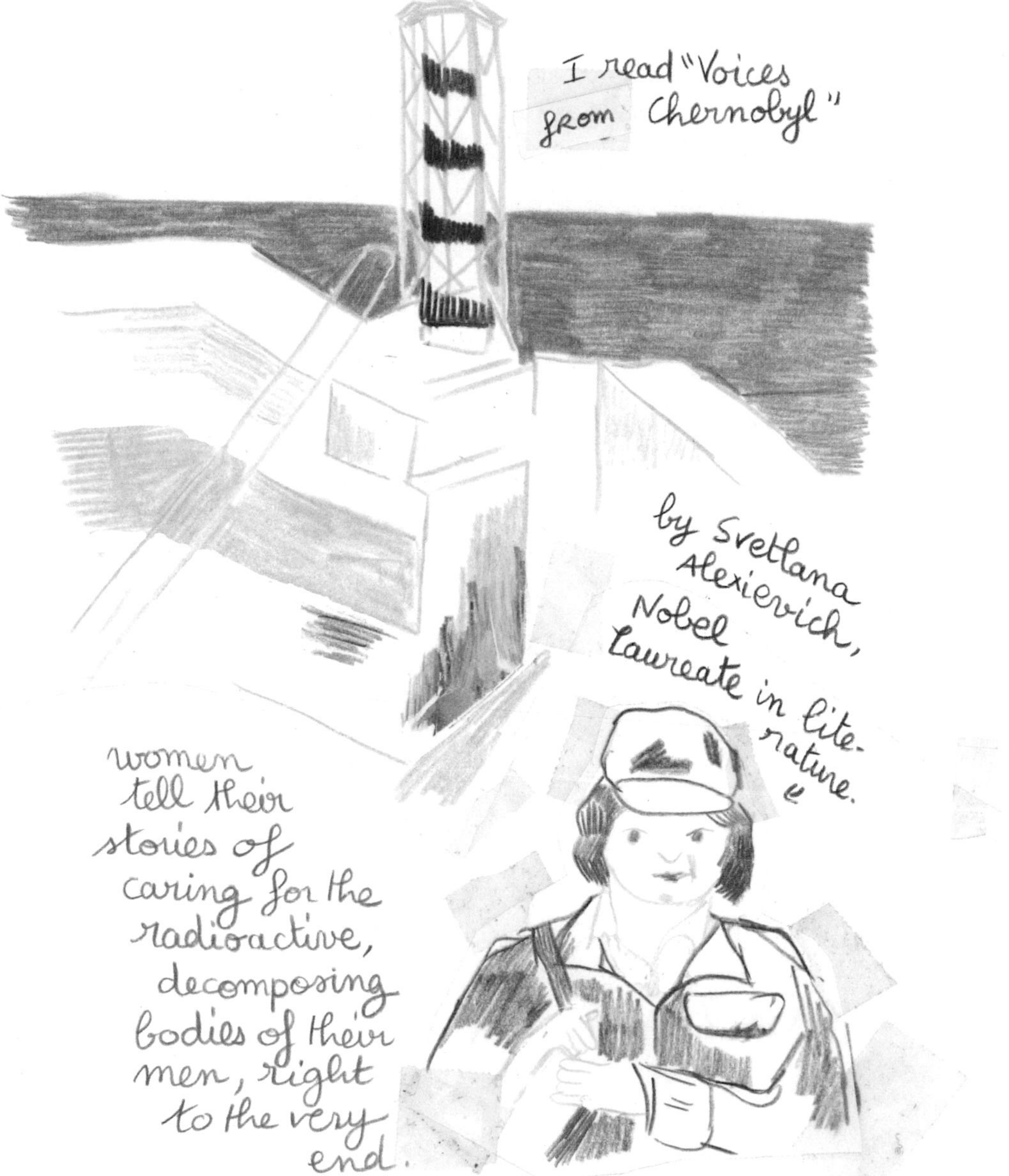
I read "Voices from Chernobyl"
by Svetlana Alexievich, Nobel Laureate in literature.
women tell their stories of caring for the radioactive, decomposing bodies of their men, right to the very end.

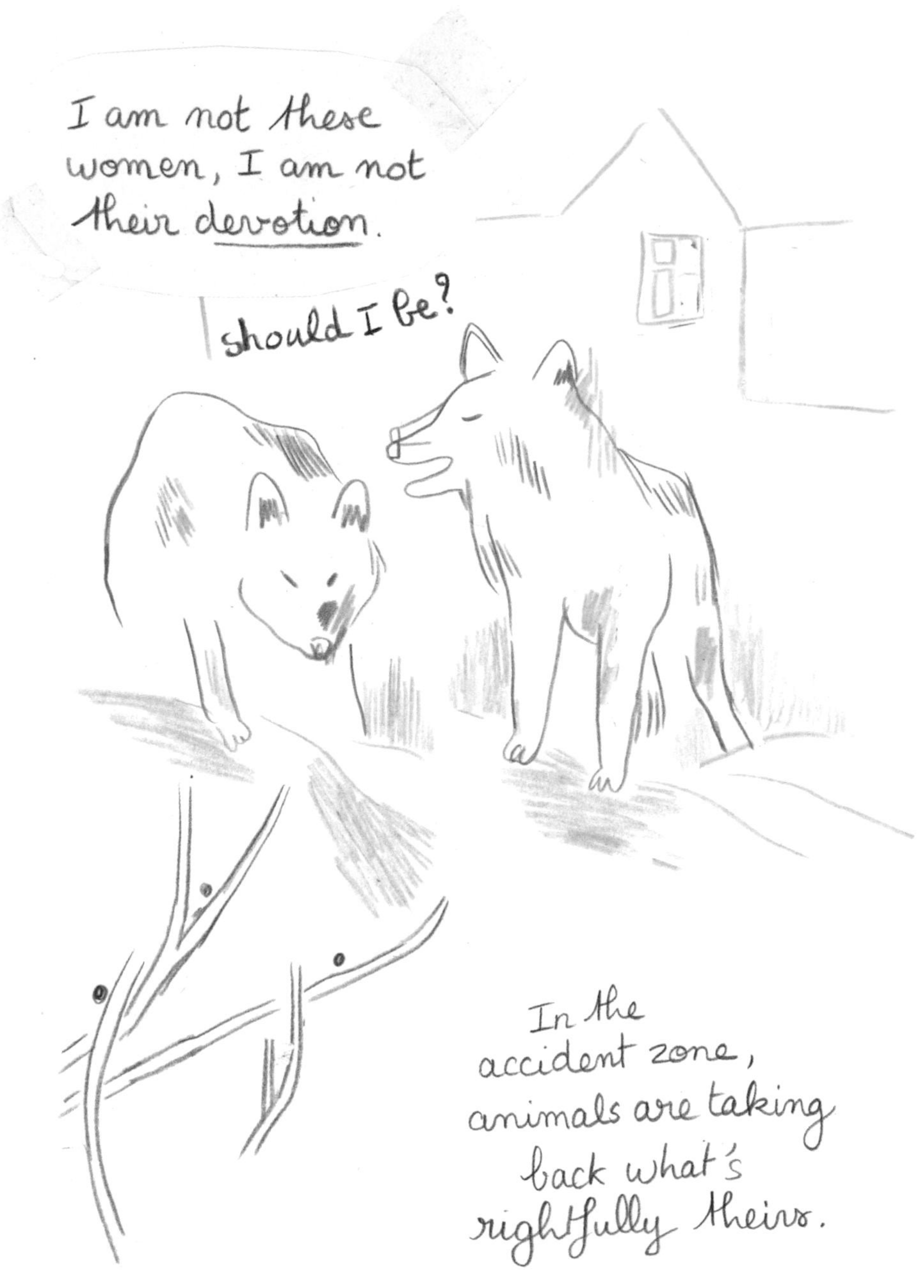
I am not these women, I am not their devotion.
should I be?
In the accident zone, animals are taking back what's rightfully theirs.

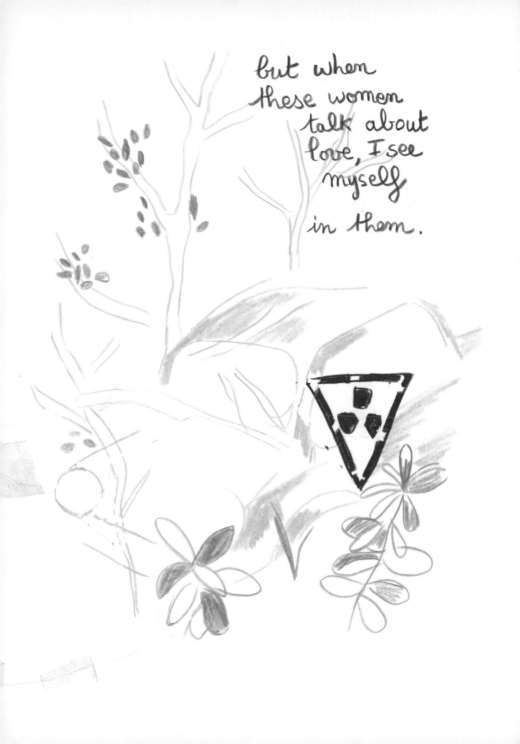

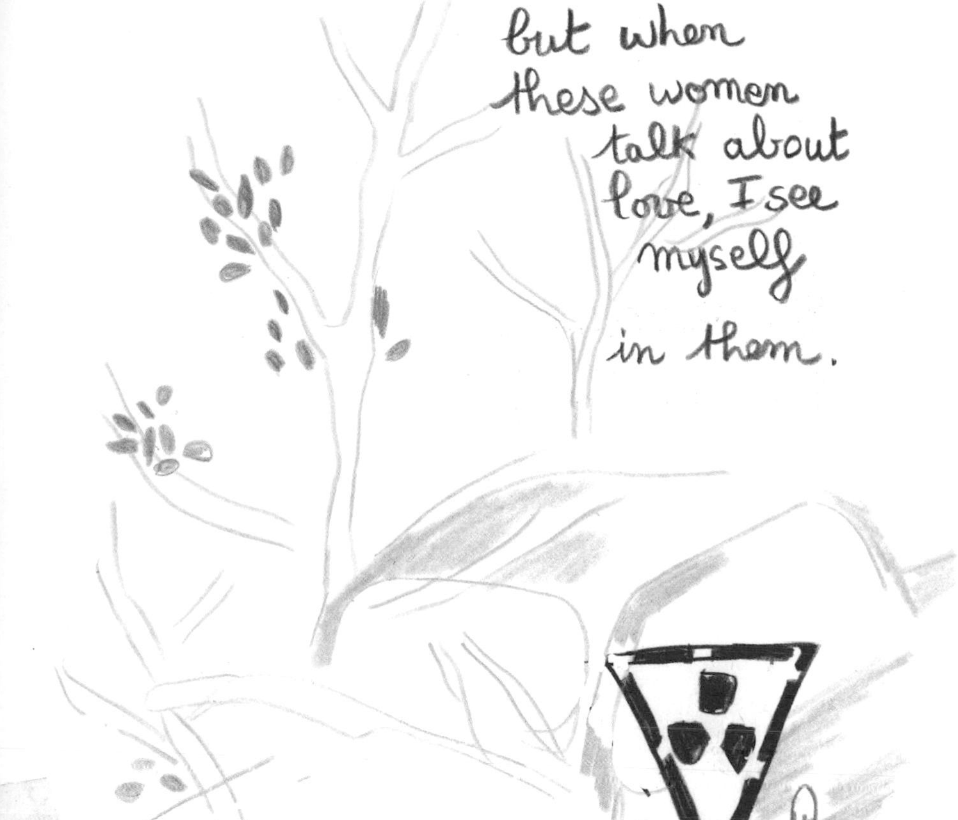
but when these women talk about love, I see myself in them.

richard and I
talk on the phone.

He's at his   house, in the
country...   Be
I want so badly to   like him,
          solitary.

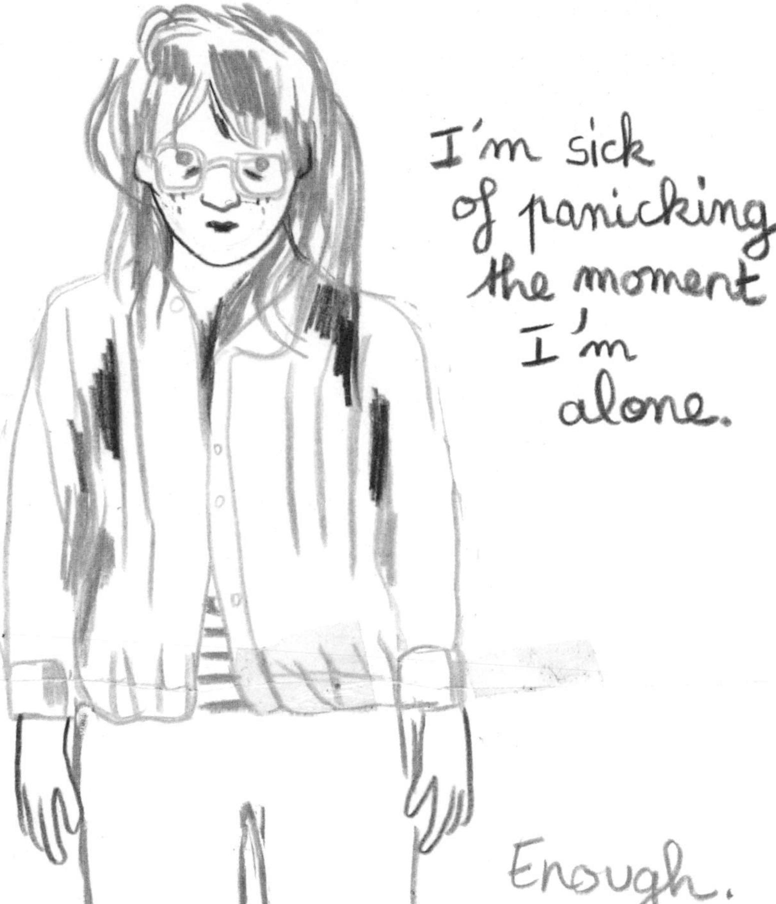
I'm sick of panicking the moment I'm alone.
Enough.

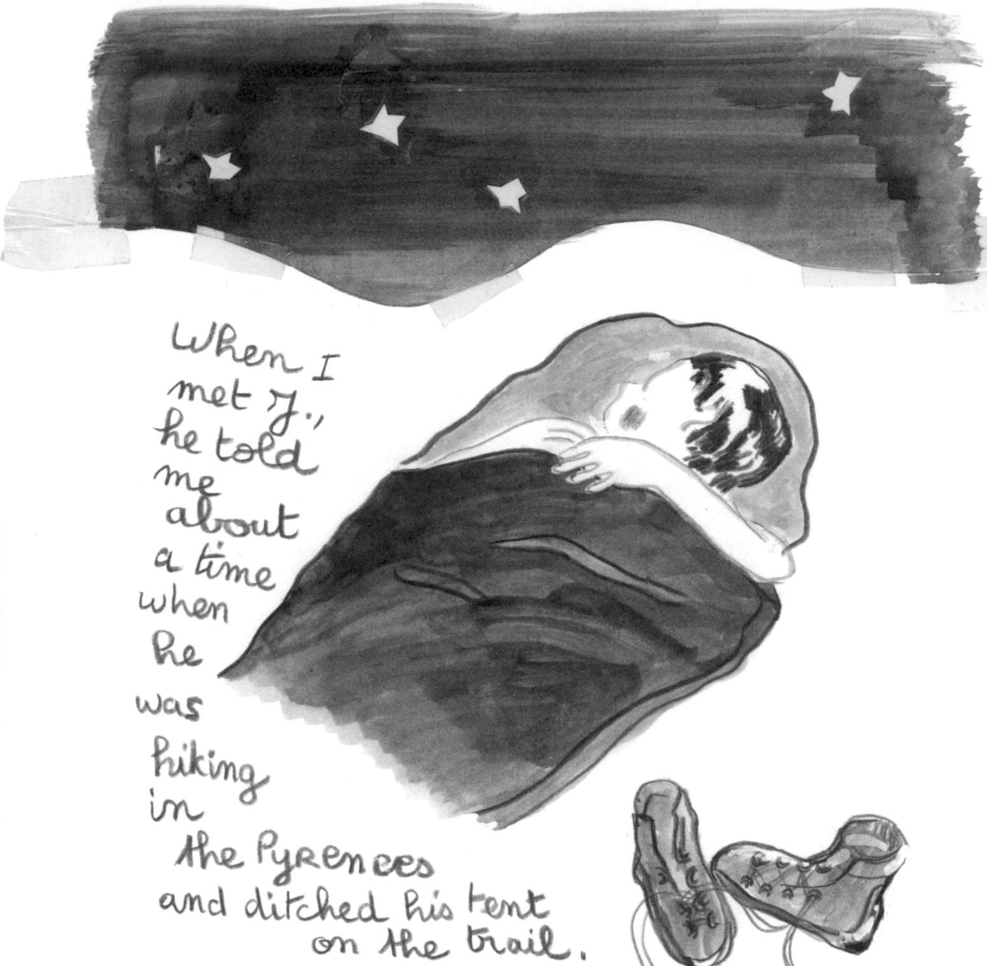
When I met J., he told me about a time when he was hiking in the Pyrenees and ditched his tent on the trail.
I felt so jealous when I heard that story.

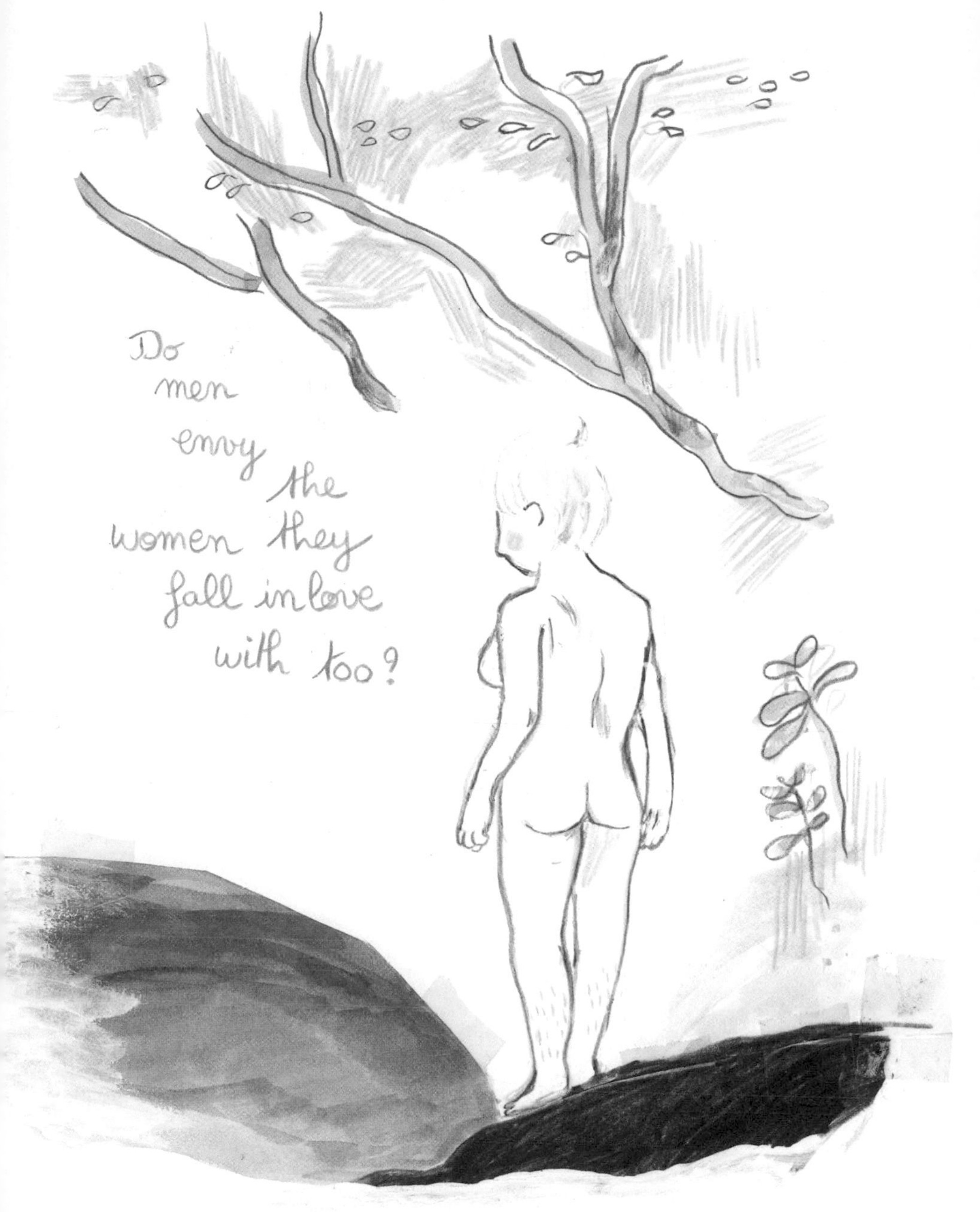
Do
men
envy
the
women they
fall in love
with too?

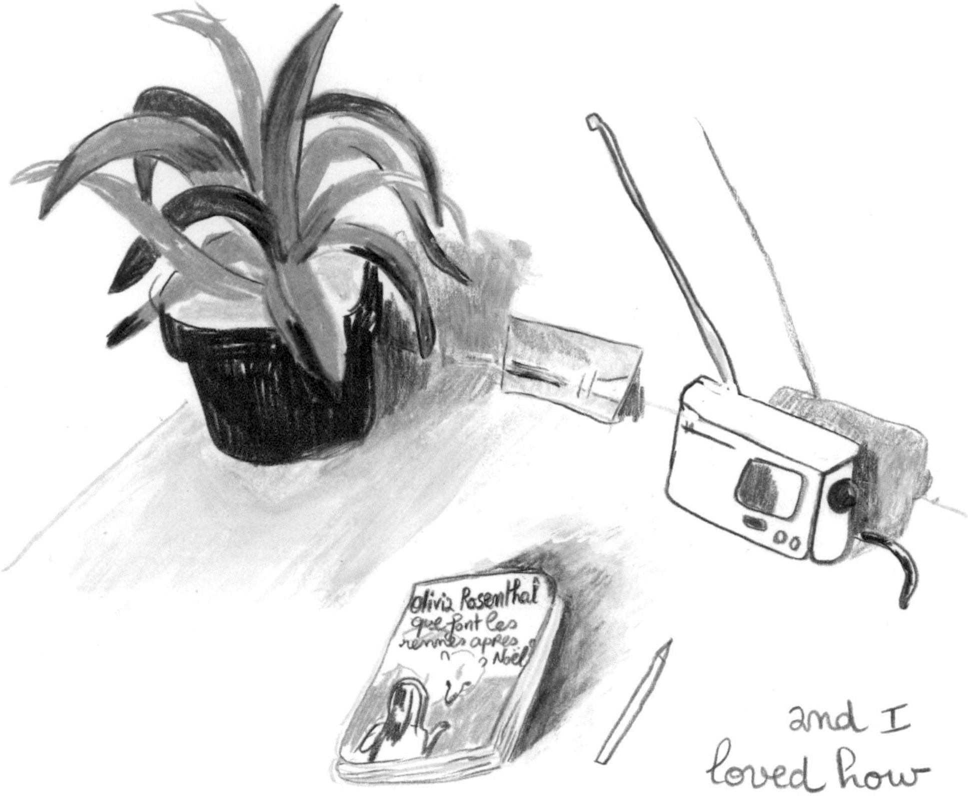
Olivia Rosenthal
que font les rennes après Noël

and I loved how knowledgeable he was

as though I wanted every boy to be my very own dictionary, so I'd be sure to learn something.

(and they could remember all the things I forget)

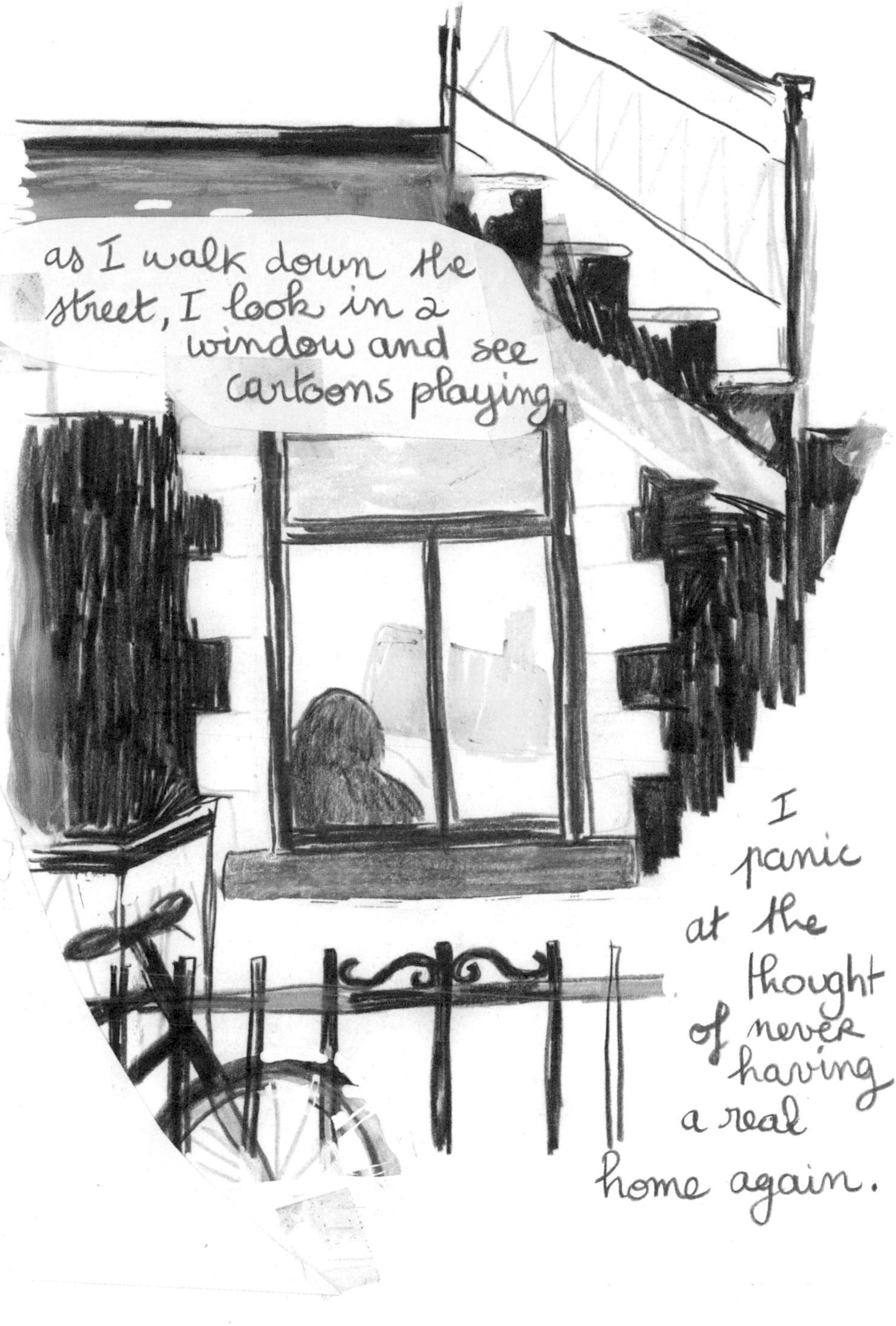
as I walk down the street, I look in a window and see cartoons playing
I panic at the thought of never having a real home again.

the movies
with christophe

there's a jedi on screen and she is a girl!

REY, a self-sufficient woman, on the screen.

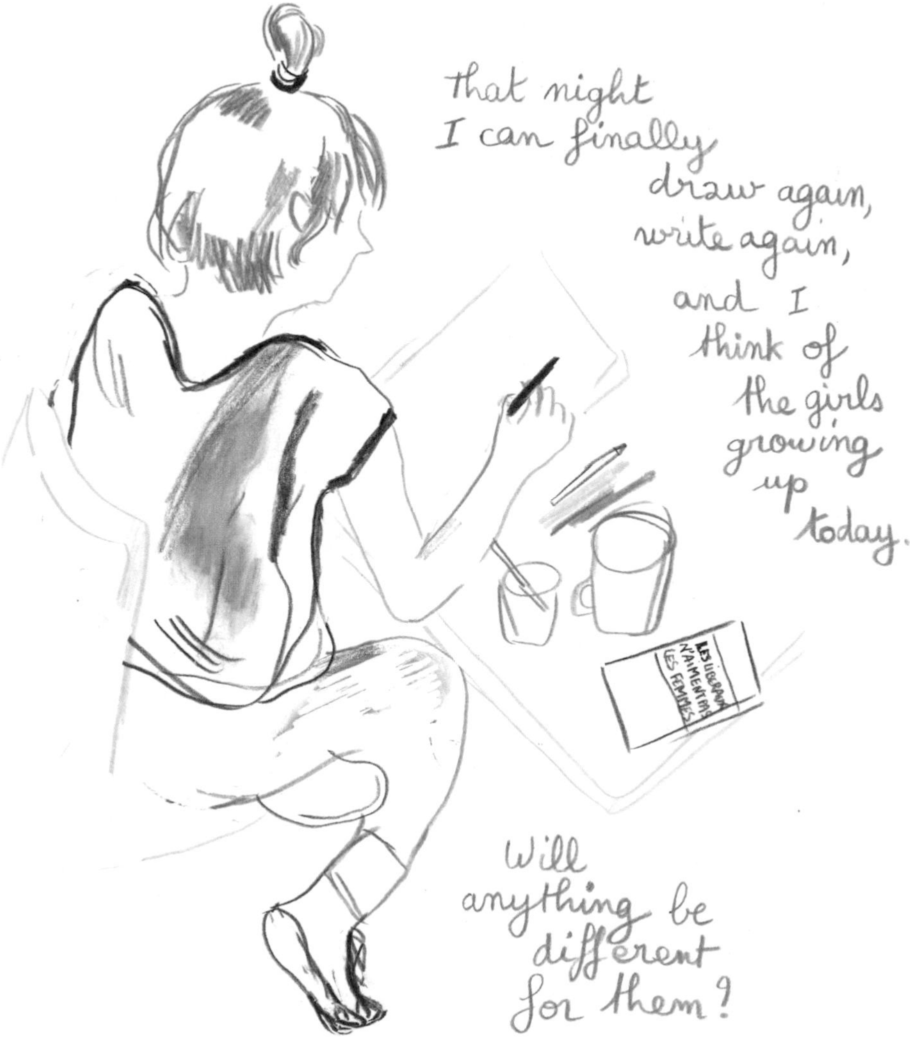
That night I can finally draw again, write again, and I think of the girls growing up today.
N'AIMENT PAS
LES FEMMES
Will anything be different for them?

I only had Jo March*
(Winona Ryder, in 1994)

(she is hiding the ink stains
on her fingers)
I grow up to be an author,
just like her.

* Little Women
Louisa May Alcott (1868)
Winona Ryder, in the
Gillian Armstrong
film adaptation

except you'd think I was
still waiting for the German
professor she marries...

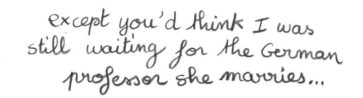

a professor   (like Jérôme)
    who's older than she is...
        she kisses him in the rain
        at the end of the movie.

↲ the wet cat in "Breakfast at Tiffany's"

what are the
    images that hold us

        captive?

overwhelmed at work,
I try to communicate my needs.

clearly I'm going about
things the wrong way.

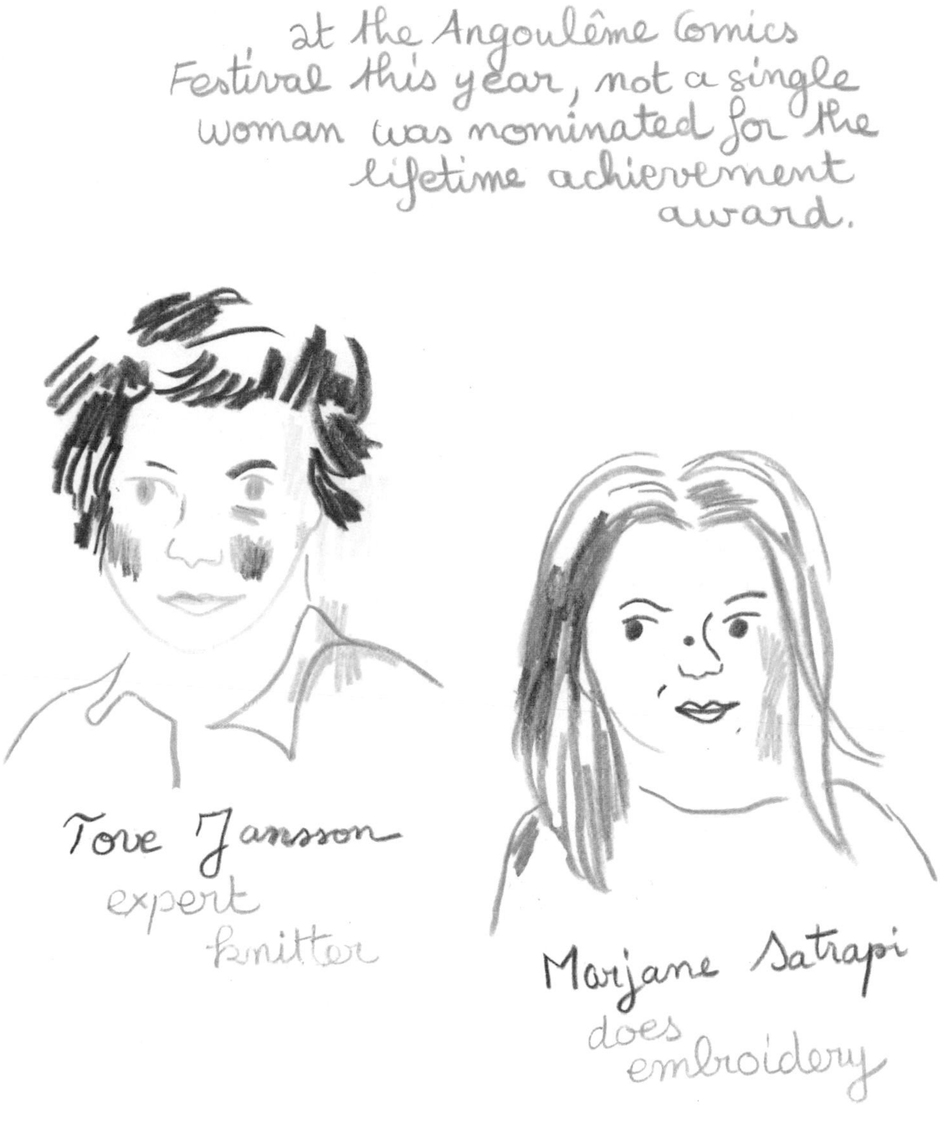
at the Angoulême Comics Festival this year, not a single woman was nominated for the lifetime achievement award.
Tove Jansson
expert knitter
Marjane Satrapi
does embroidery

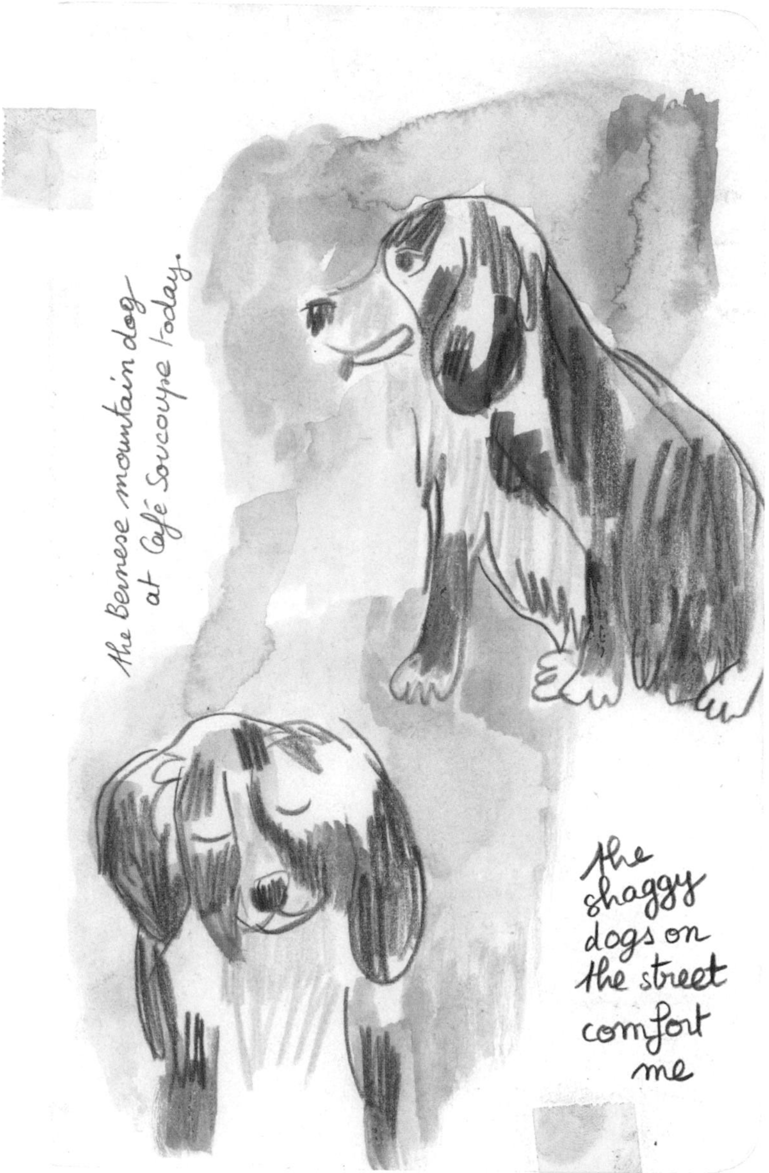
the Bernese mountain dog at Café Soucoupe today.
the shaggy dogs on the street comfort me

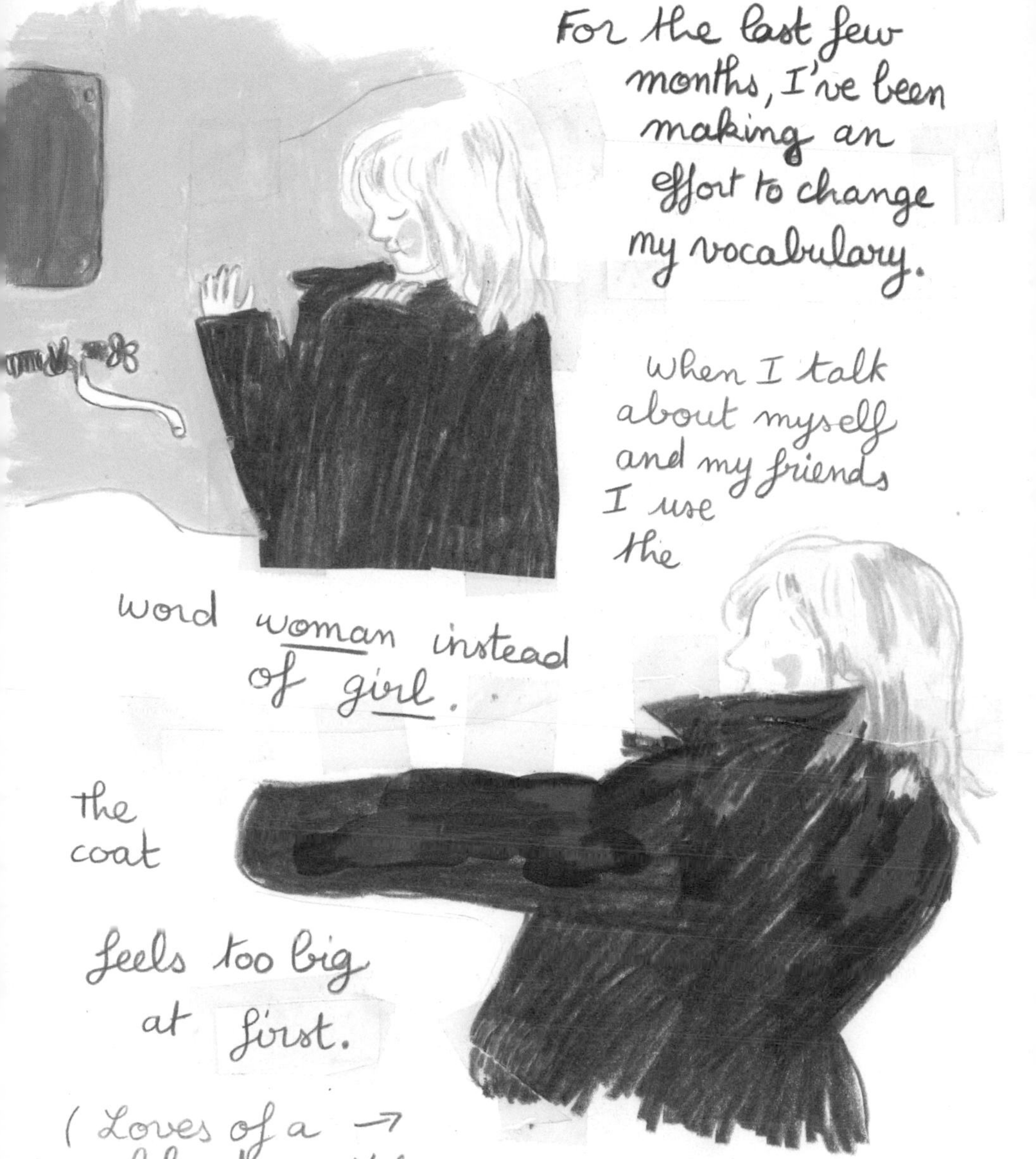
For the last few months, I've been making an effort to change my vocabulary.
When I talk about myself and my friends I use the
word woman instead of girl.
the coat
feels too big at first.
(Loves of a → blonde, Milos Forman)

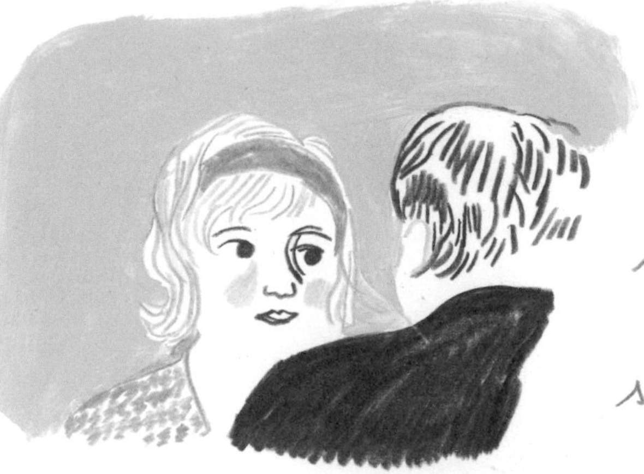

When you use the word, you can feel something take root inside you.

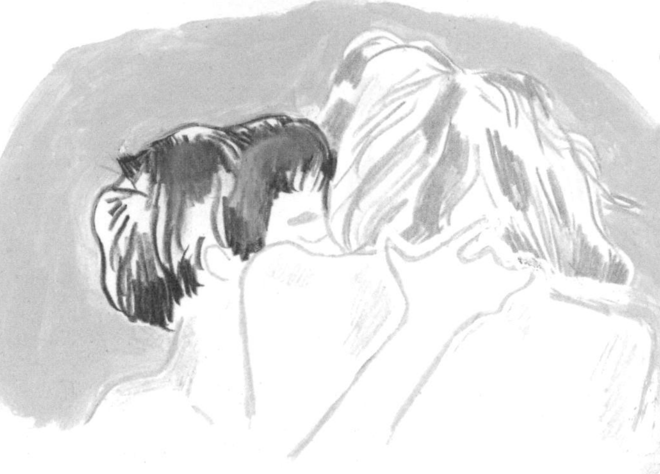

But lately the word "man" sticks in my throat.

I date "*boys*."

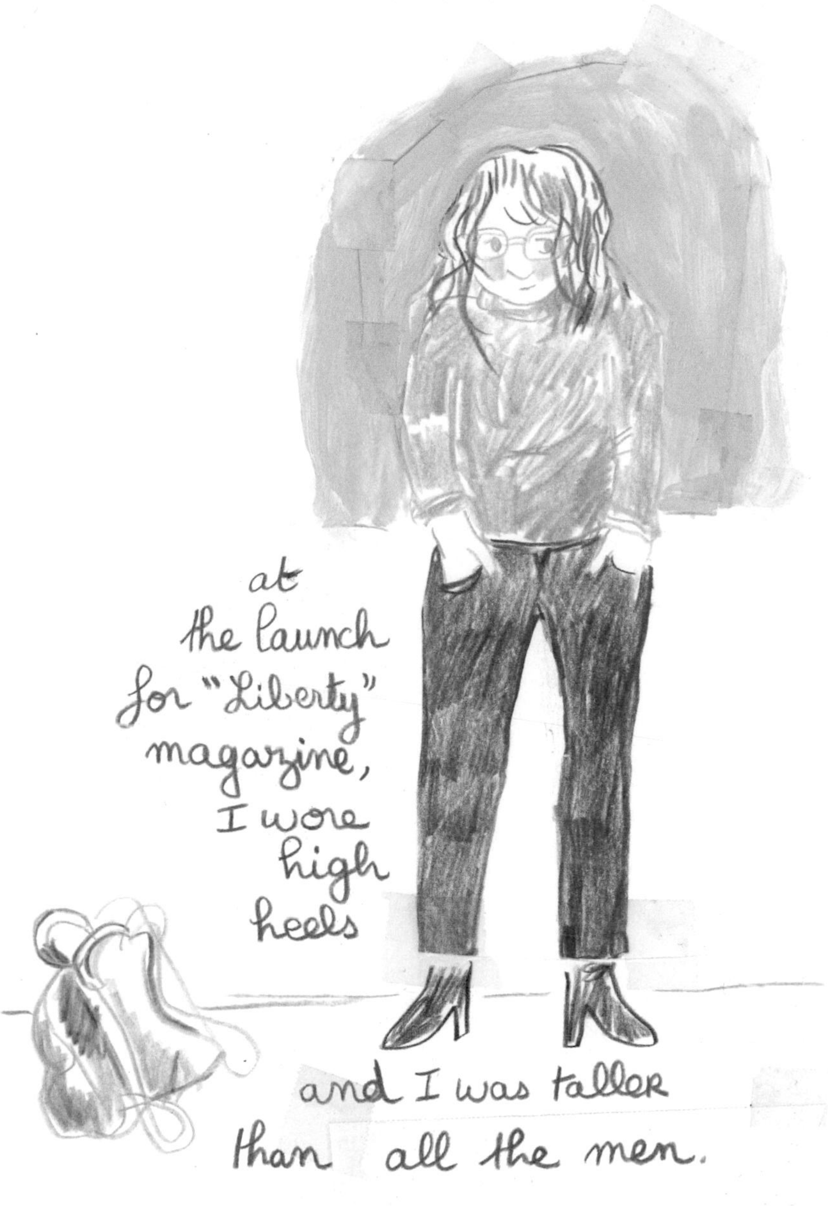
at the launch for "Liberty" magazine, I wore high heels
and I was taller than all the men.

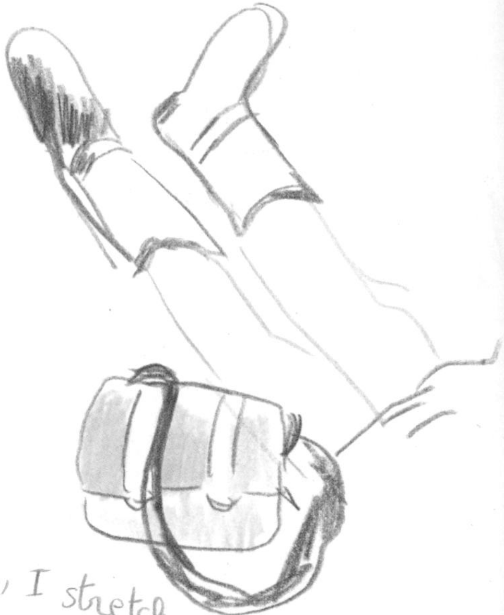

in New York, I stretch out on the floor and a cacophonous Ravel washes over me.

(an Anri Sala video)

and I don't know how to stop thinking about My's death.

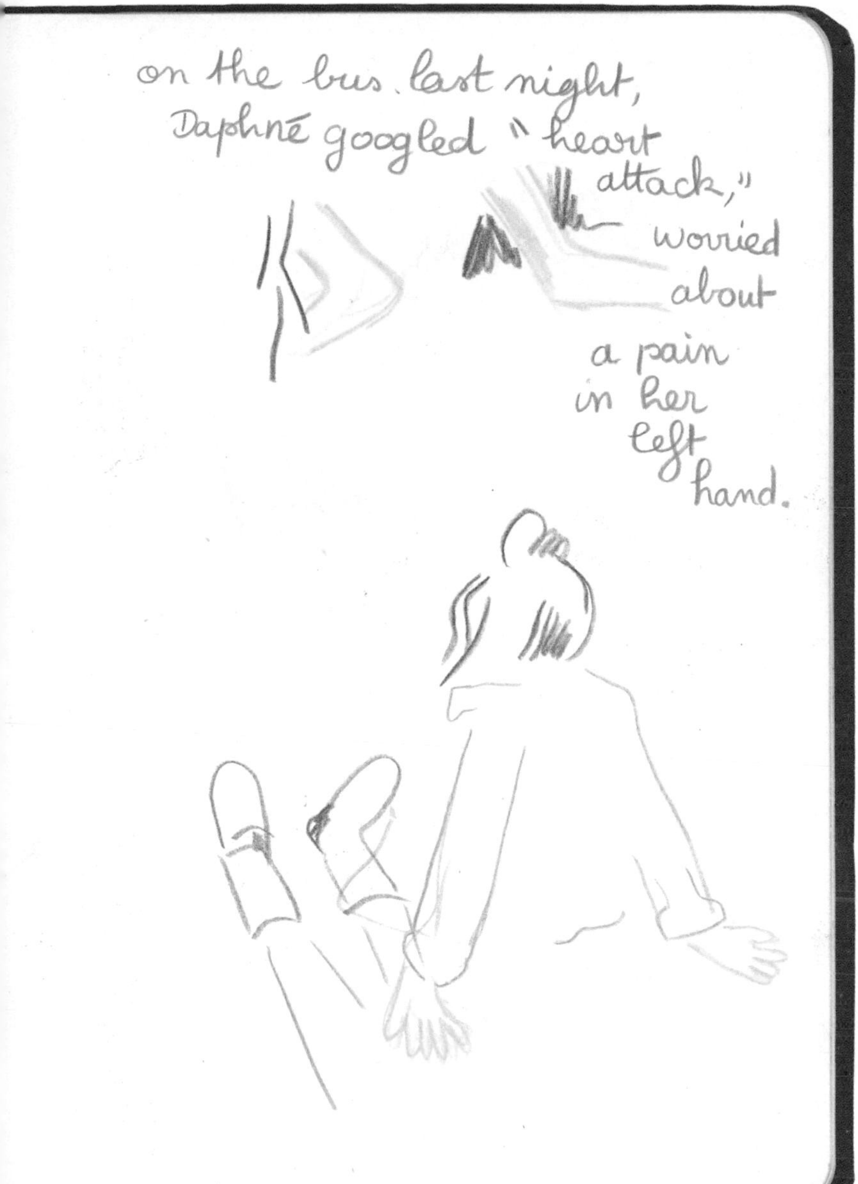
on the bus last night,
Daphné googled "heart attack,"
worried about
a pain in her left hand.

* My Allegrim, an illustrator killed at the age of thirty in the March 2016 terrorist attacks in Brussels.

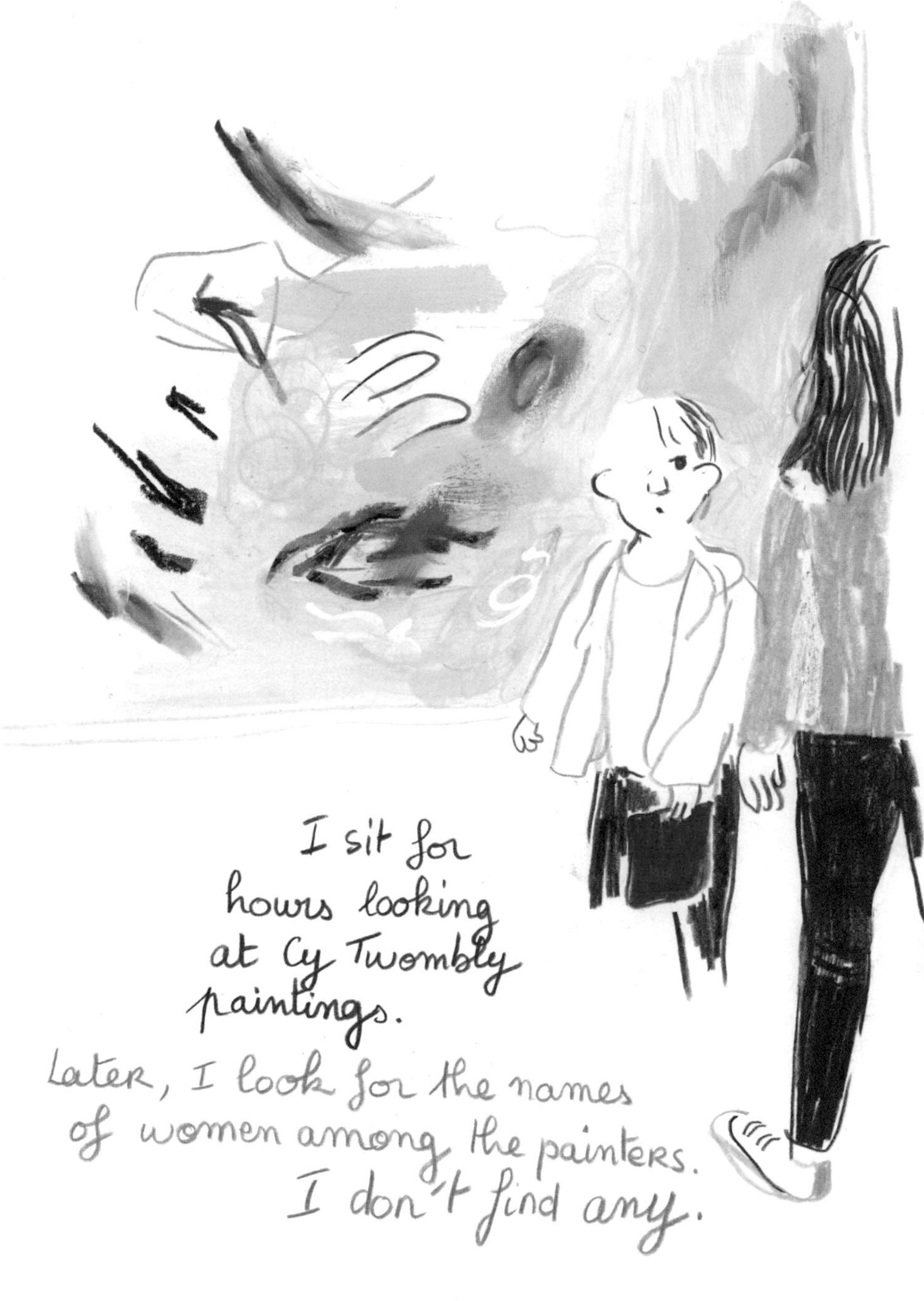
I sit for hours looking at Cy Twombly paintings.
Later, I look for the names of women among the painters. I don't find any.

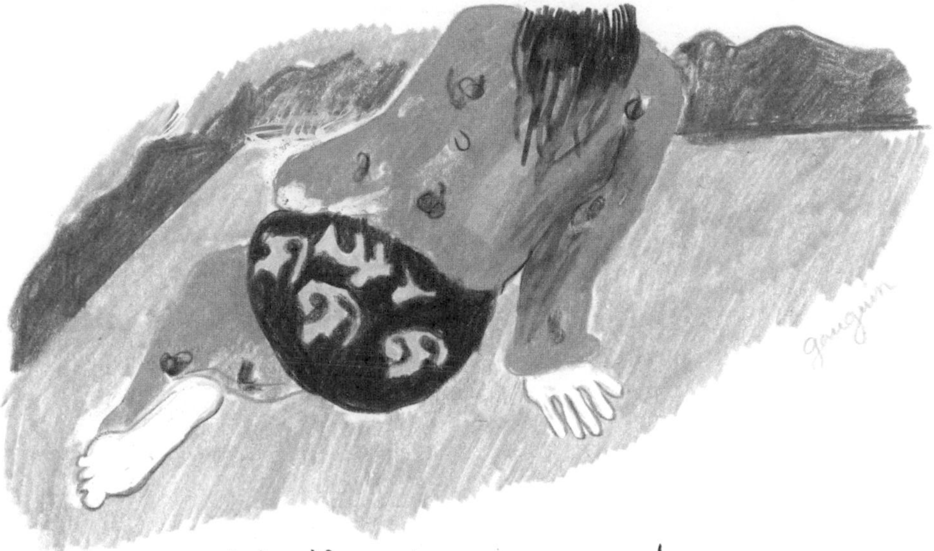
gauguin

Yet they're everywhere:
their bodies, their
faces.

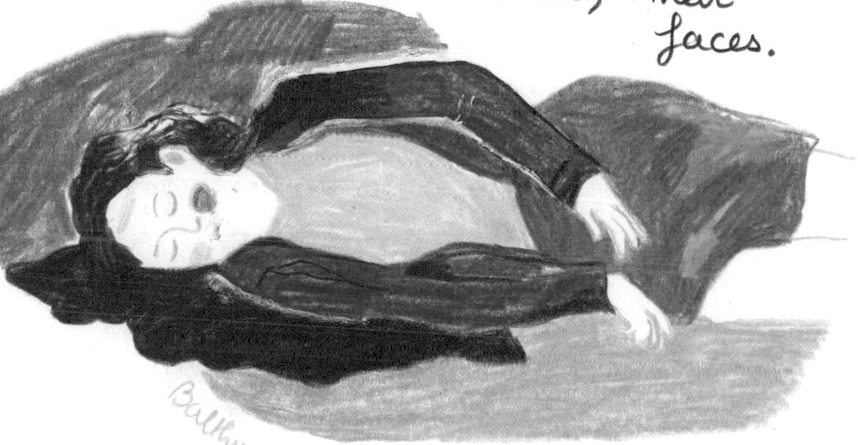
Balthus

naked or draped.
Omnipresent.

after paula M. becker

Si je m'ai pas de
tendresse pour mes
dessims,
qui em aura ?

if I don't love my drawings
who will ?

I'm tired of trying
to sort things out
with Jérôme.

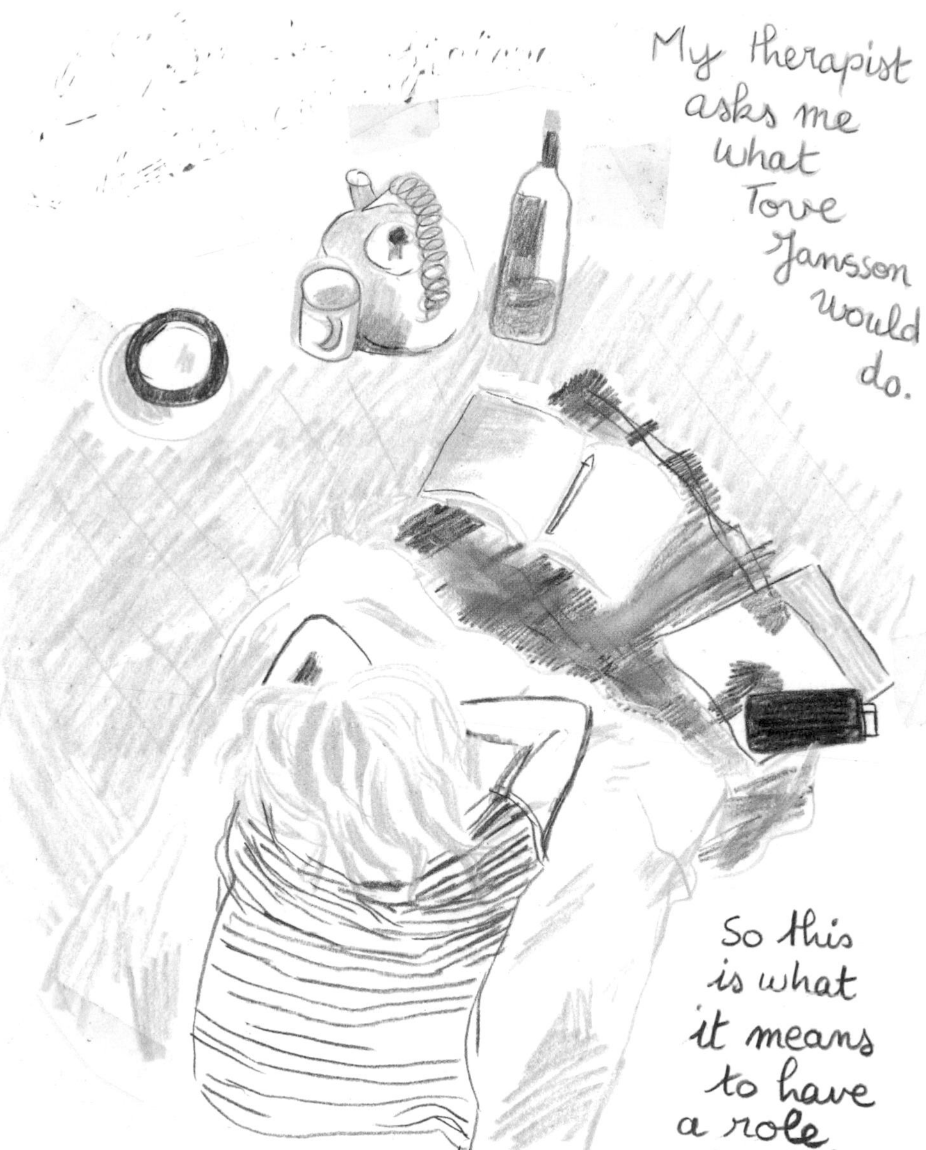
My therapist asks me what Tove Jansson would do.
So this is what it means to have a role model...

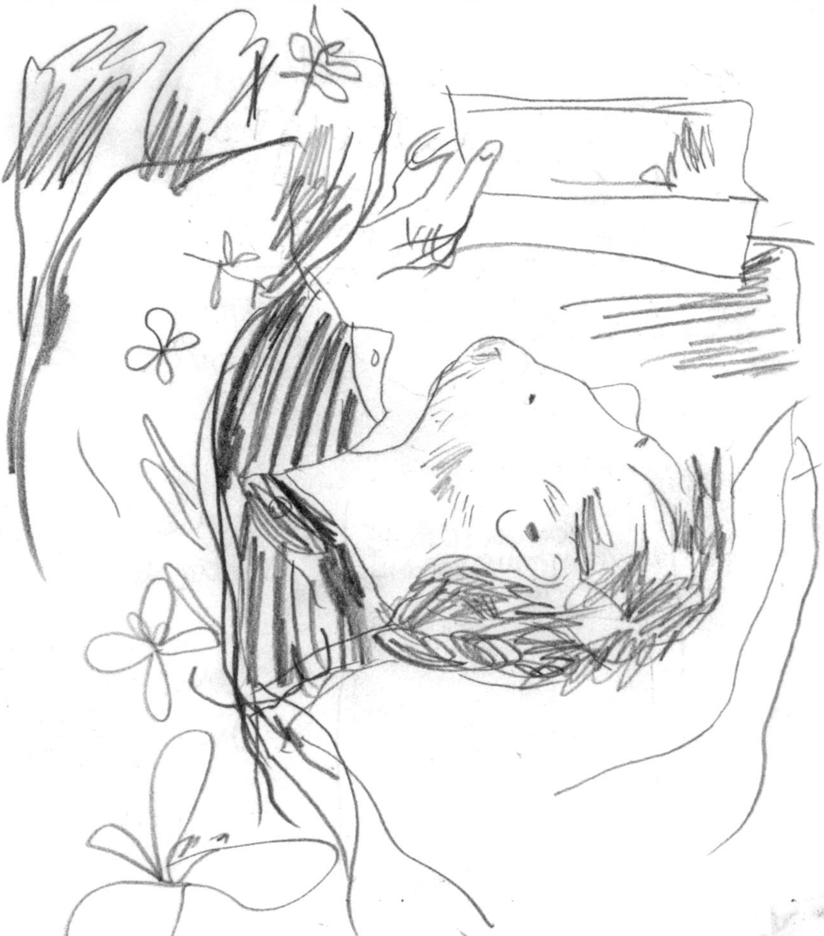

What do men want from me?

↑ Jérôme in bed, last year.

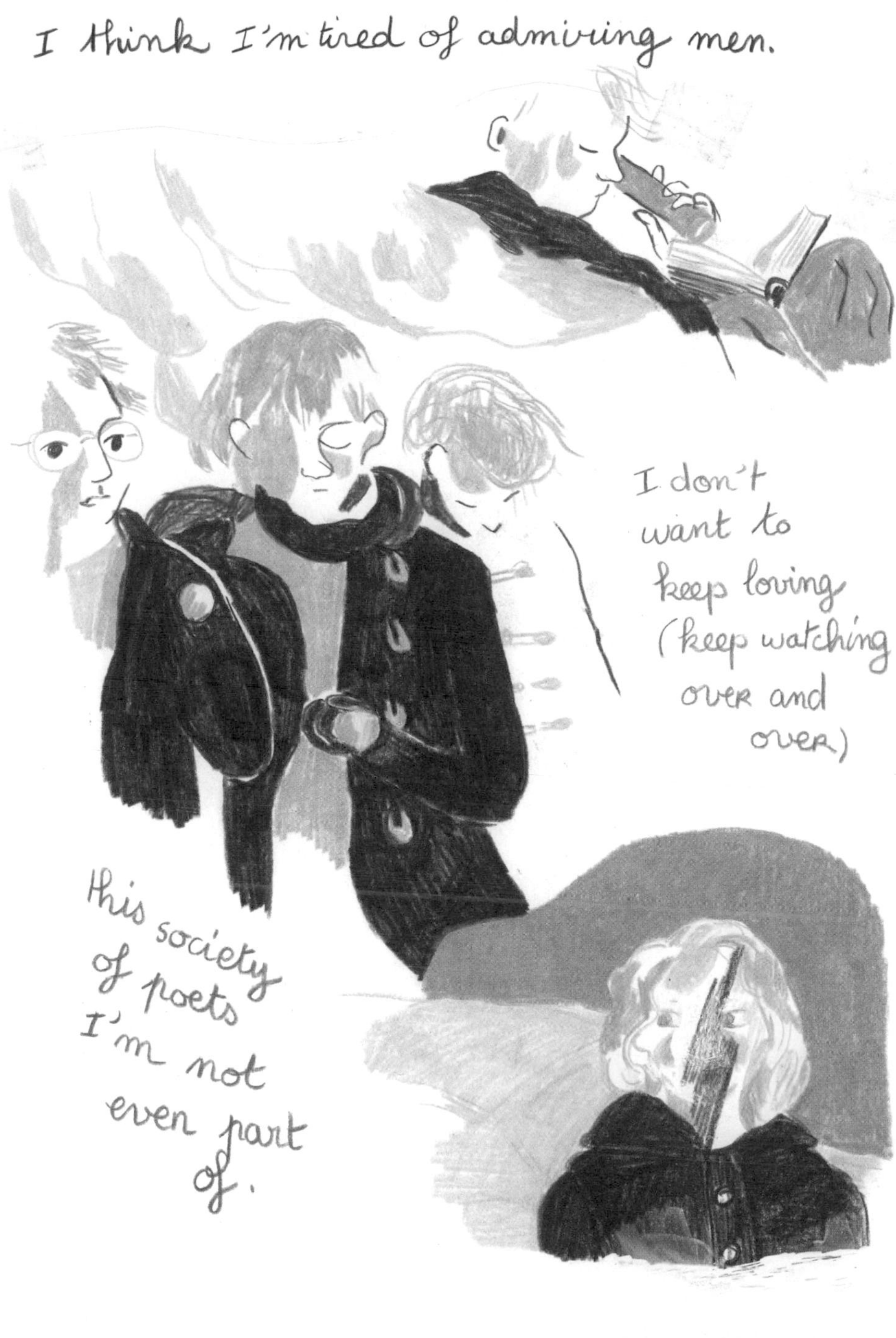
I think I'm tired of admiring men.
I don't want to keep loving (keep watching over and over)
this society of poets I'm not even part of.

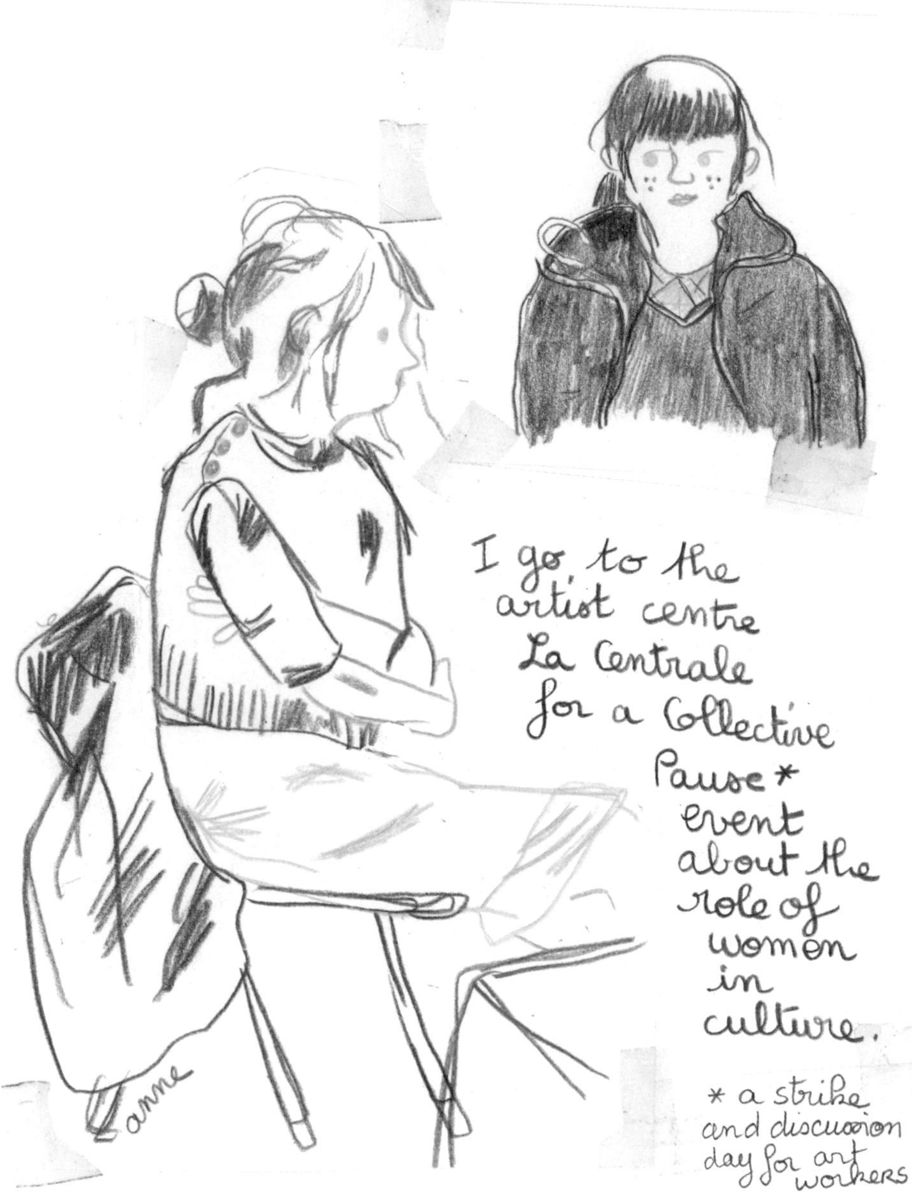
I go to the artist centre La Centrale for a Collective Pause* event about the role of women in culture.
* a strike and discussion day for art workers
anne

we read some statistics together. I barely notice the pay gap:

$13 681 Average earnings of women artists in the visual arts, compared with $21 180 for their male counterparts

Hill Strategies. Statistical Profile of Artists in Canada, based on the 2011 census.

($45 400 Average earnings of Canada's overall labour force.)

instead, the numbers that really anger me are these:

4.2   Average number of additional hours spent per week on studio practice by men in the visual arts, compared with their female counterparts

I see in them my own inability to concentrate on my work (my book).

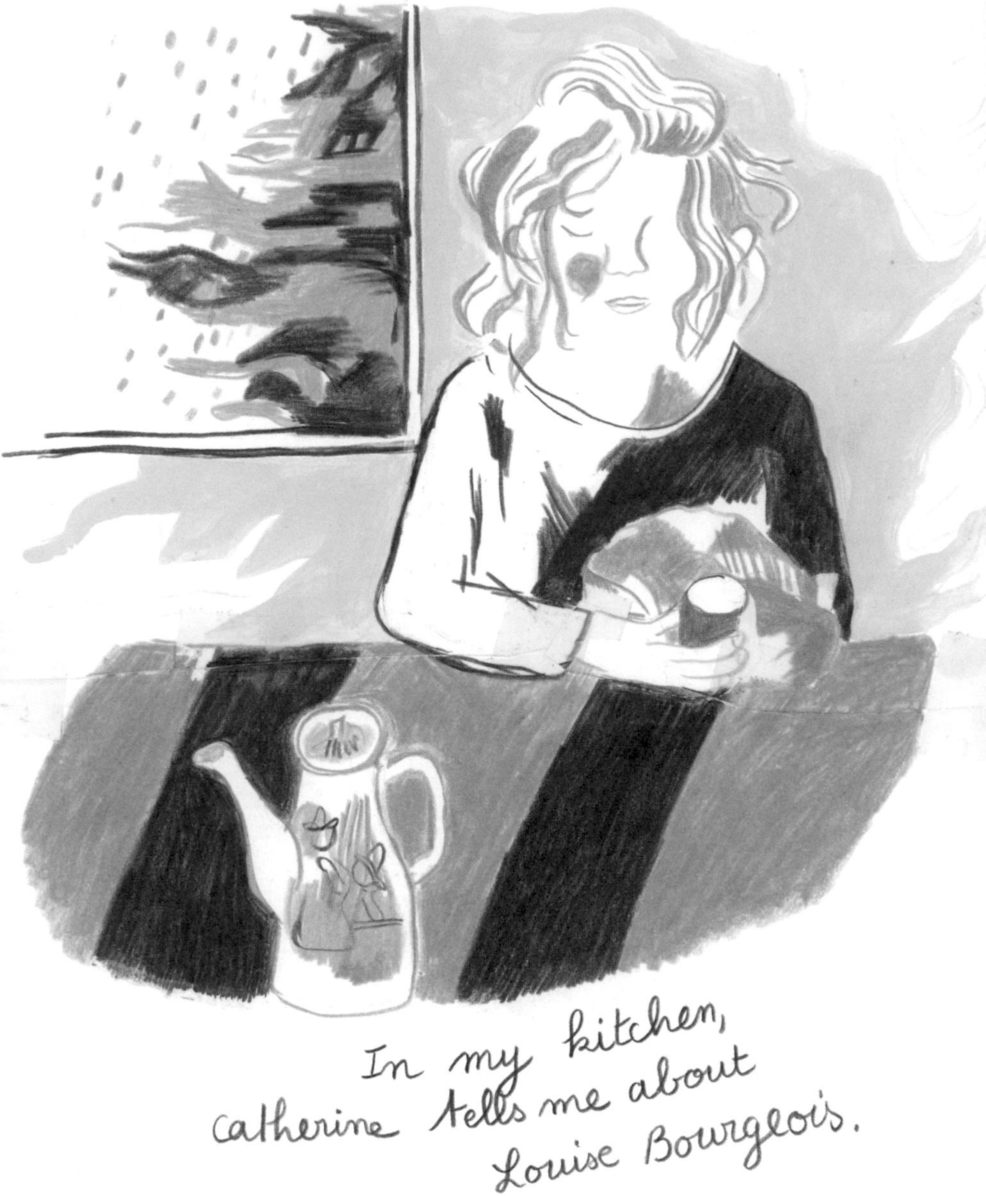

In my kitchen,
Catherine tells me about
Louise Bourgeois.

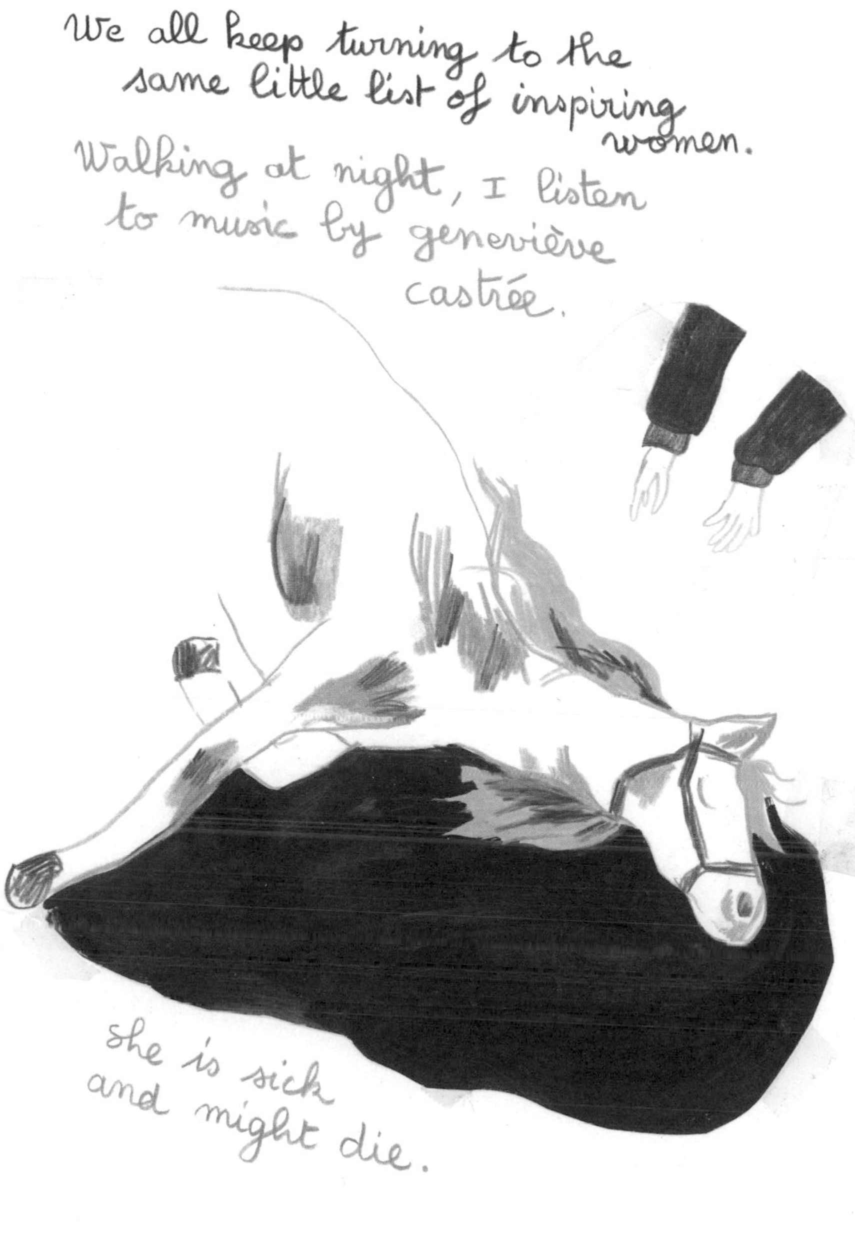
We all keep turning to the same little list of inspiring women.
Walking at night, I listen to music by geneviève castrée.
she is sick and might die.

And I reread
Jo Manix's journals.*
There's a page where
she's on the beach at St. Malo,
in 1998.

(* Joëlle Guillevic,
cartoonist, 1966-2001)

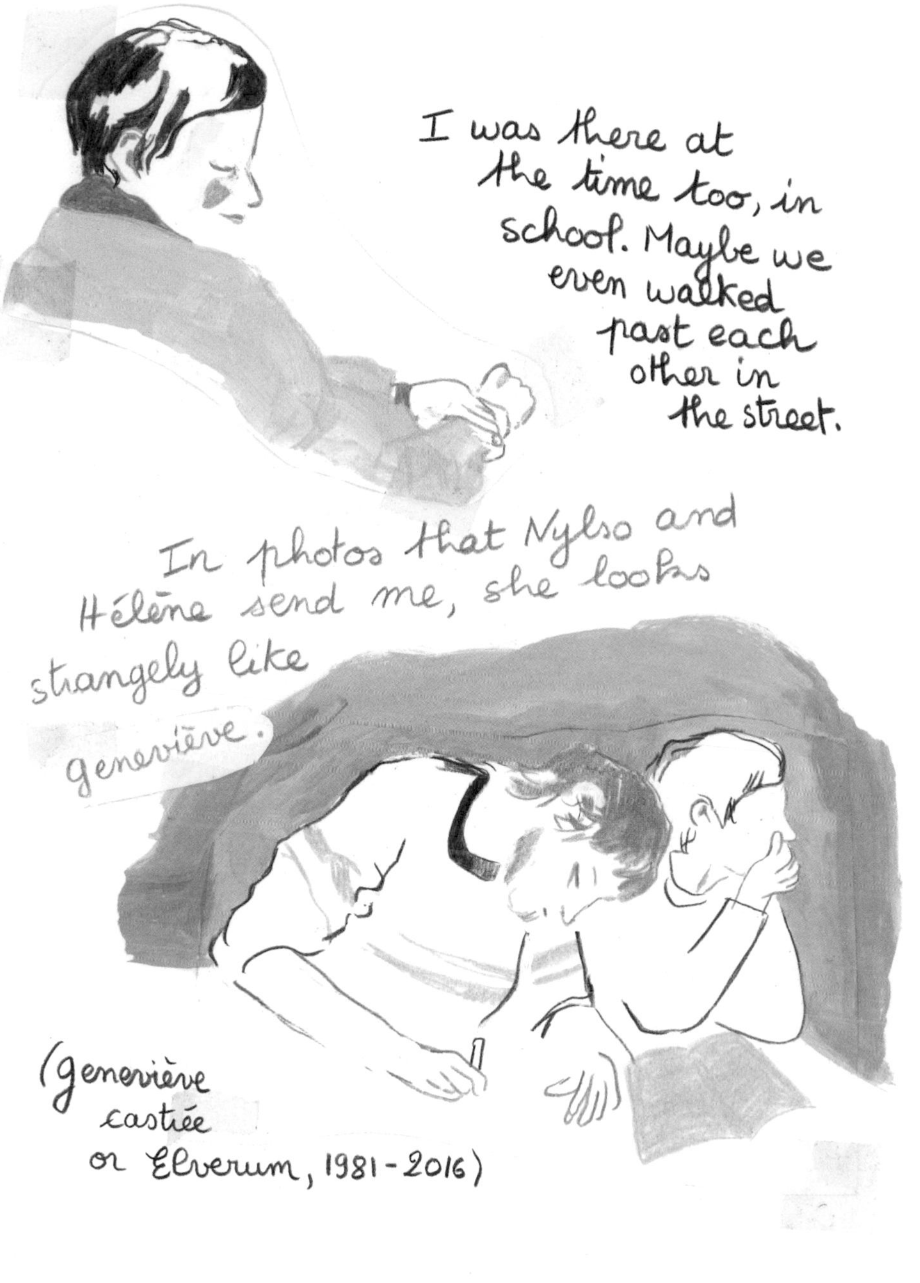
I was there at the time too, in school. Maybe we even walked past each other in the street.
In photos that Nylso and Hélène send me, she looks strangely like
geneviève.
(geneviève castrée or Elverum, 1981-2016)

It seems women will never have enough time to make art.

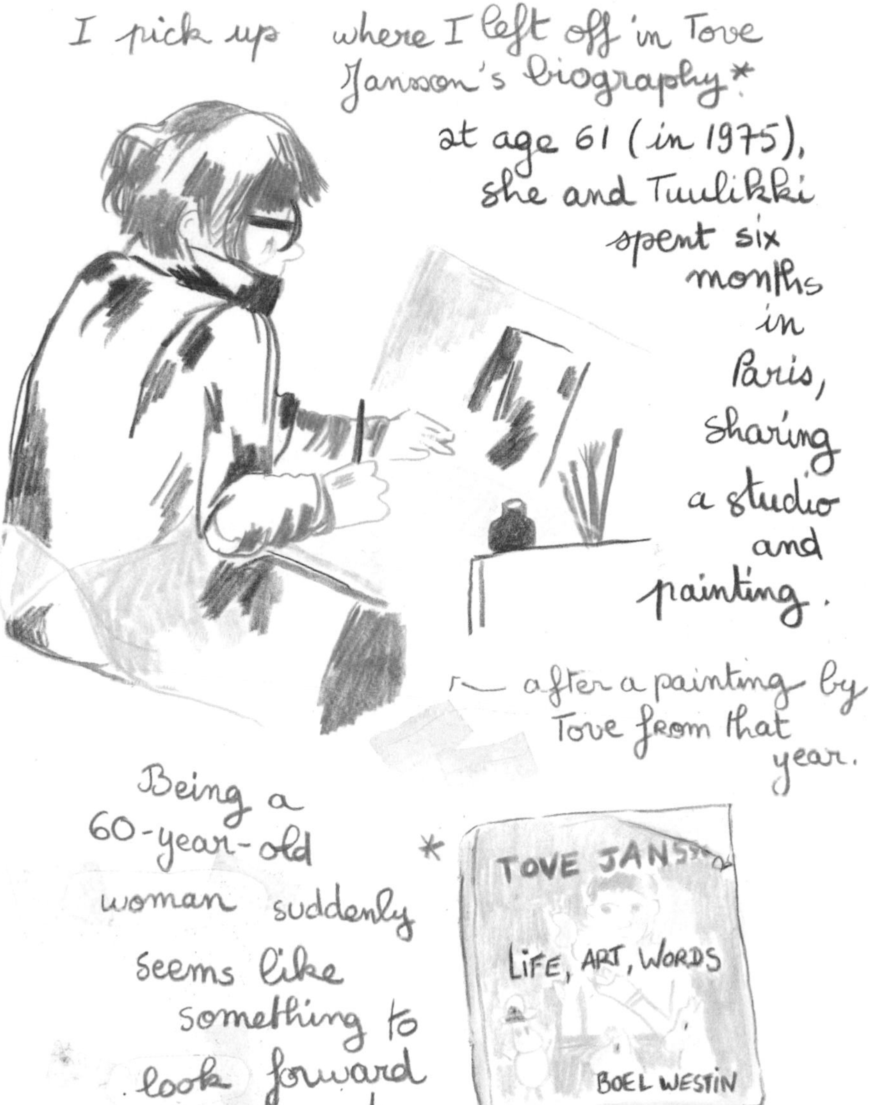
I pick up where I left off in Tove Jansson's biography*
at age 61 (in 1975), she and Tuulikki spent six months in Paris, sharing a studio and painting.
← after a painting by Tove from that year.
Being a 60-year-old woman suddenly seems like something to look forward to.
*
TOVE JANS
LIFE, ART, WORDS
BOEL WESTIN

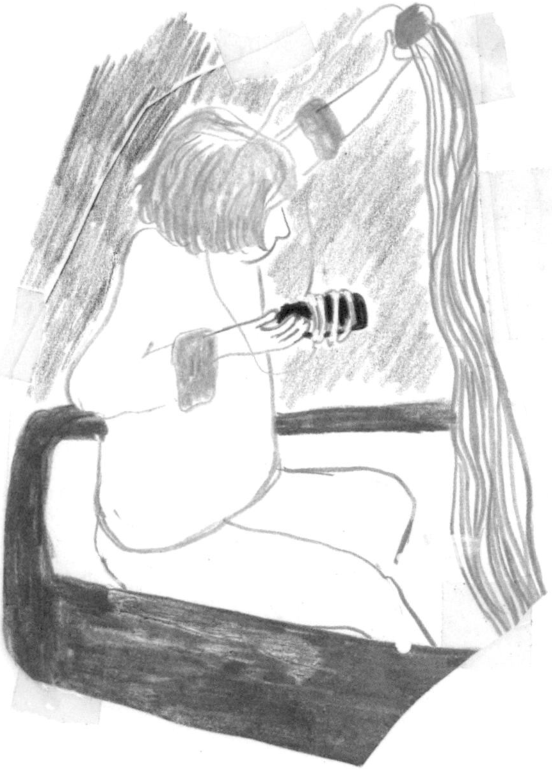

Photos show the two of them fishing and travelling ...

But Tove's diairies

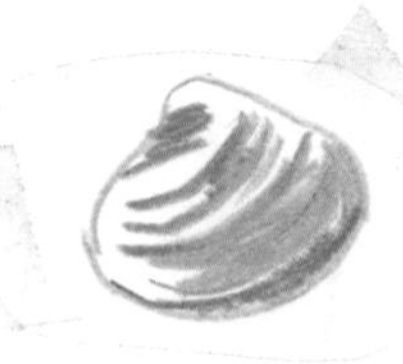

tell us that they spent most of their time *working*.

I never considered that I might still be making relevant art at that age...

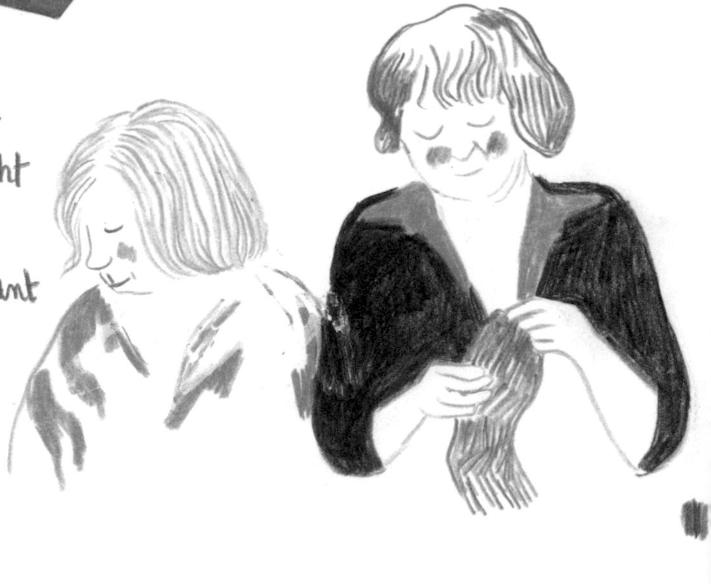

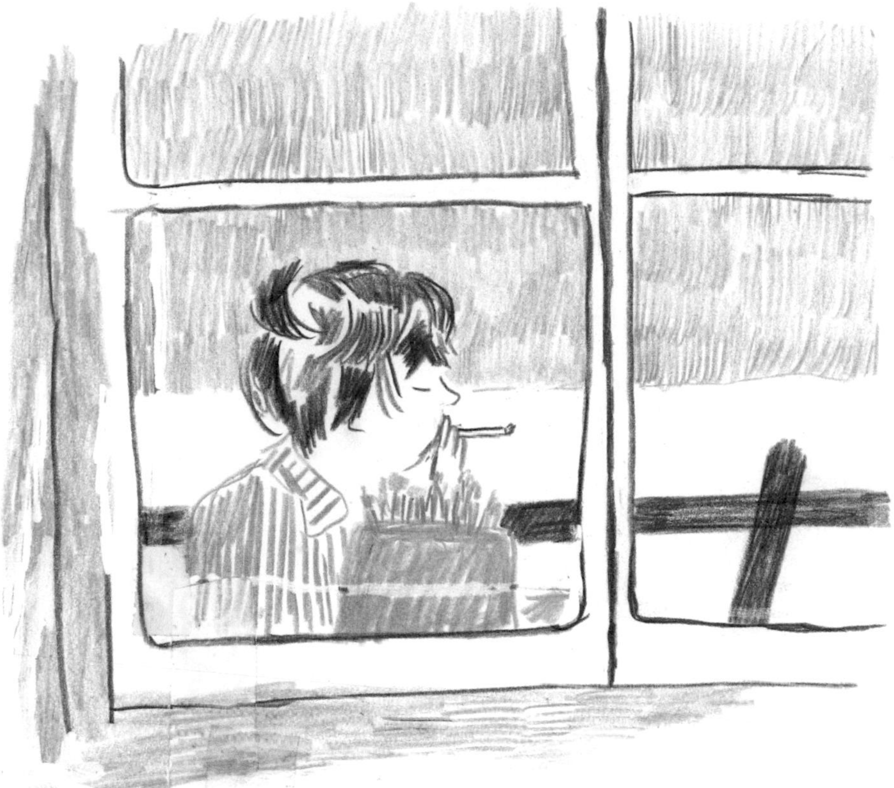

As though I'd
be totally obsolete once
men no longer desired me

(after they'd long
since left me for
younger women)

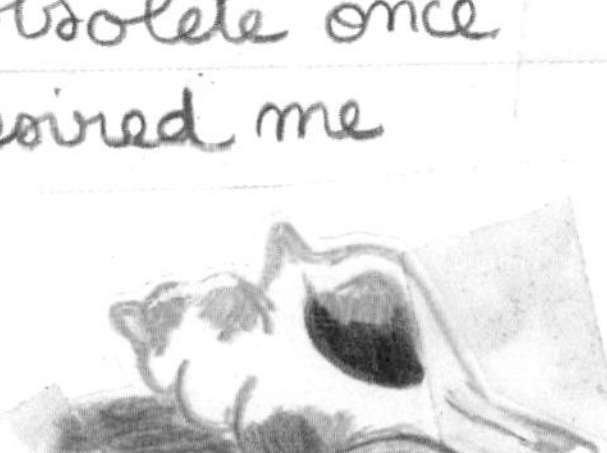

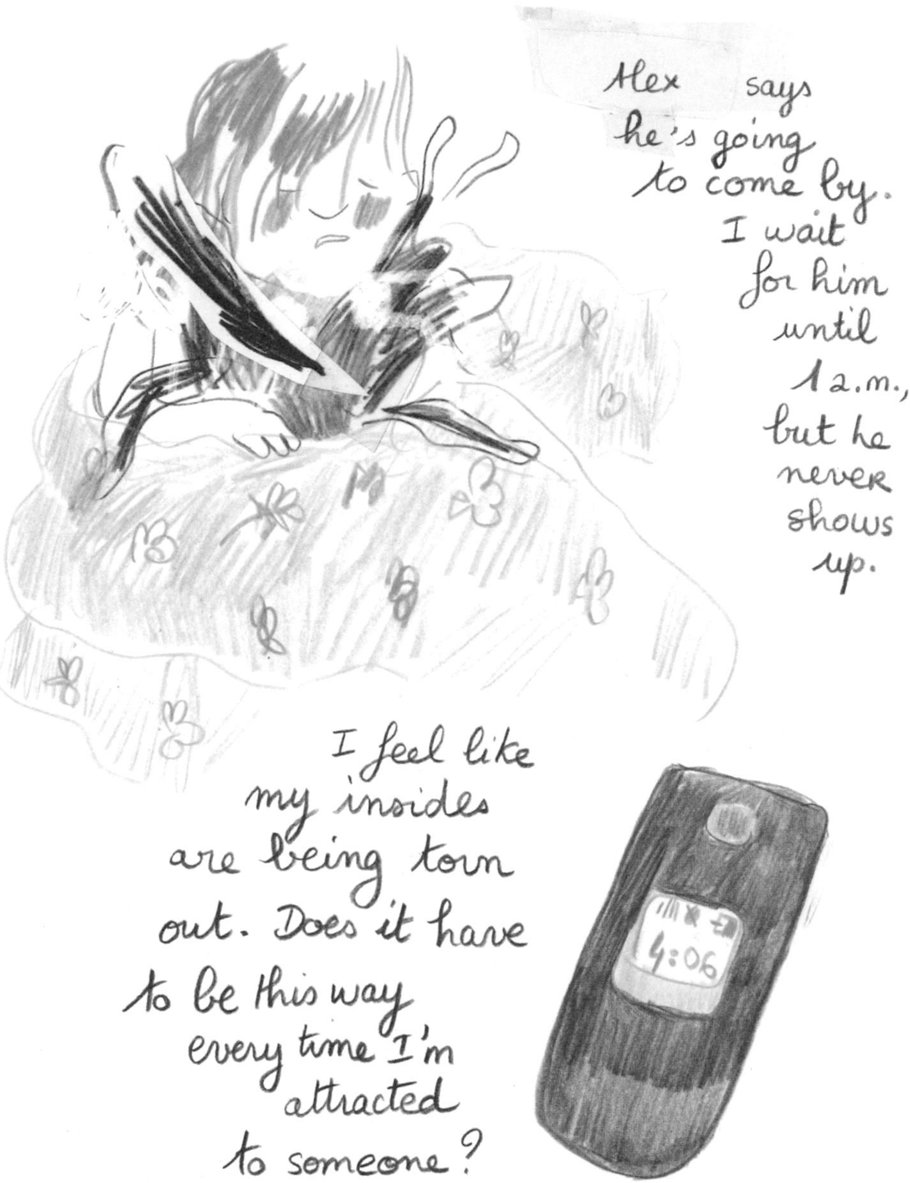
Alex says he's going to come by. I wait for him until 1 a.m., but he never shows up.
I feel like my insides are being torn out. Does it have to be this way every time I'm attracted to someone?
4:06

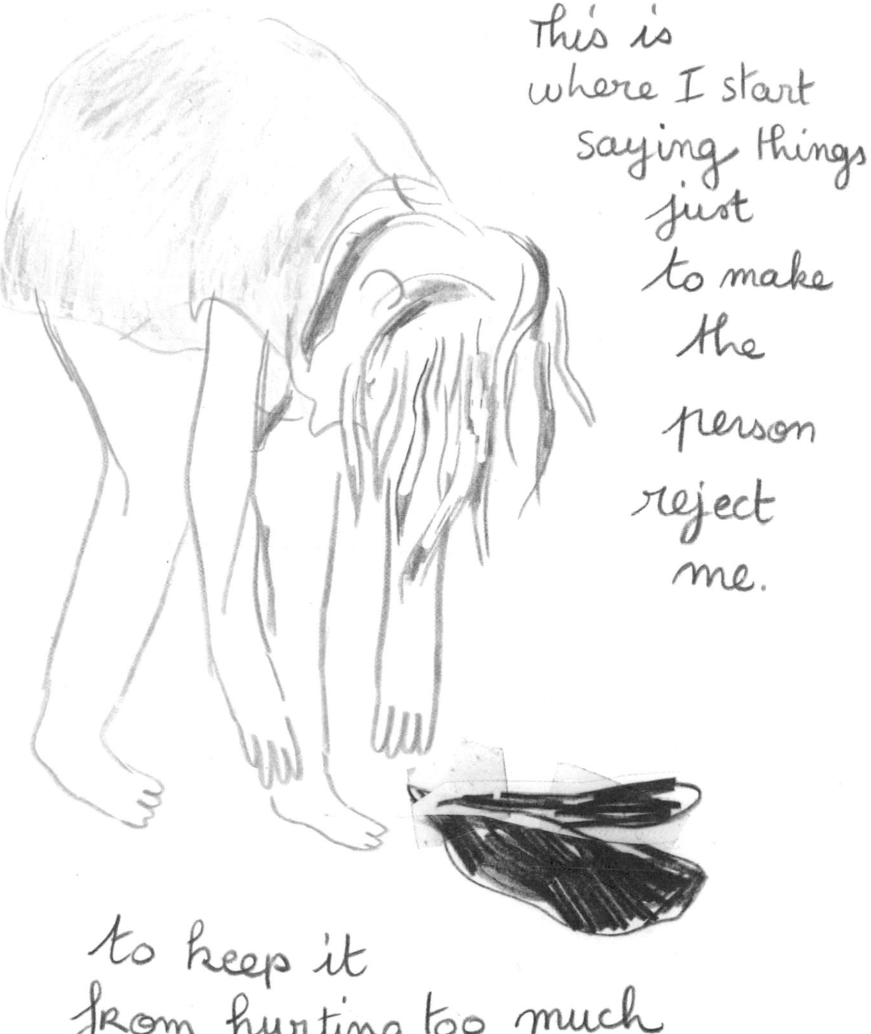
This is
where I start
saying things
just
to make
the
person
reject
me.
to keep it
from hurting too much

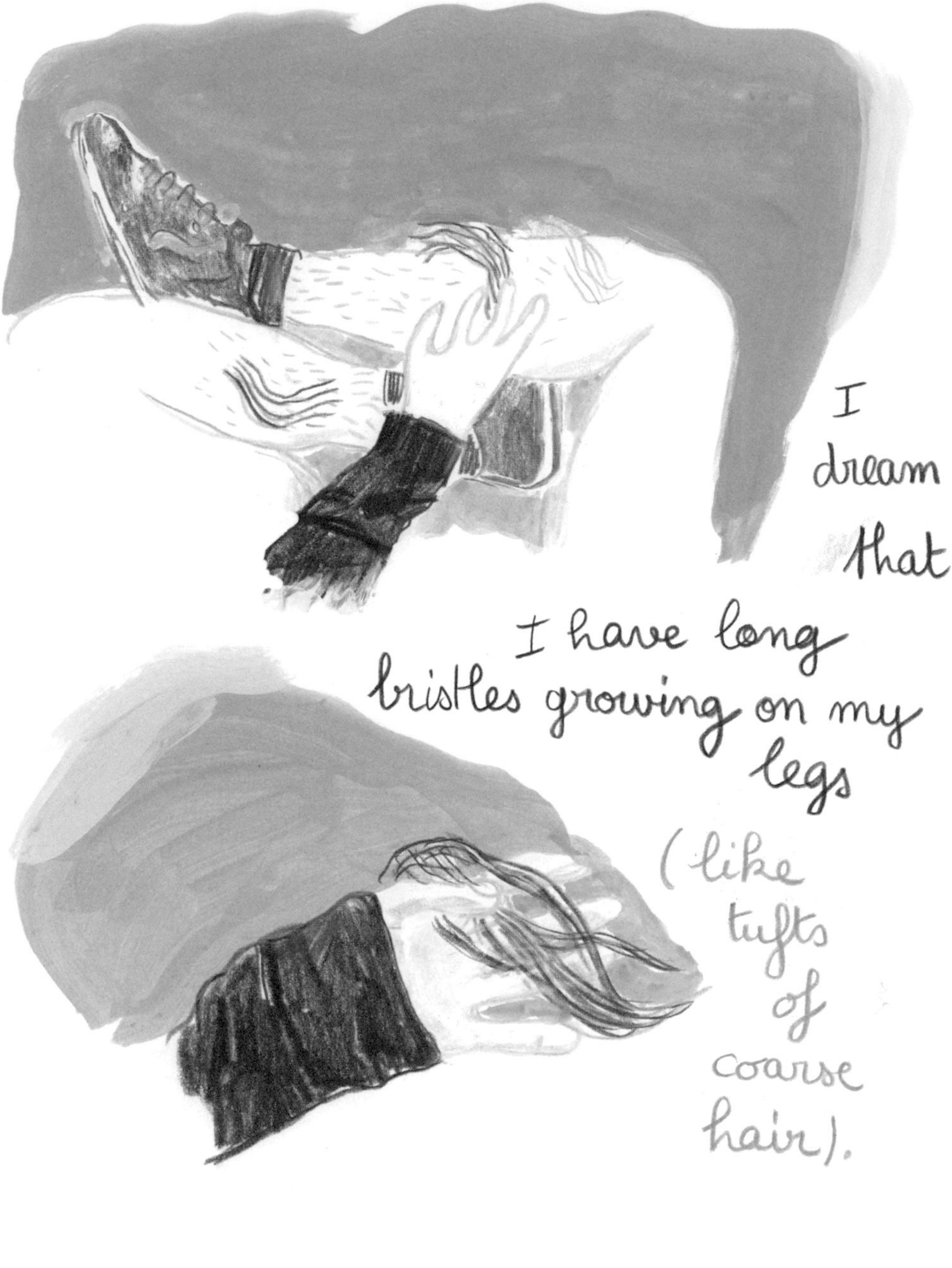
I dream that
I have long bristles growing on my legs
(like tufts of coarse hair).

and
that
I
bumped
into
Alex,
who seems
to be
laughing at me.

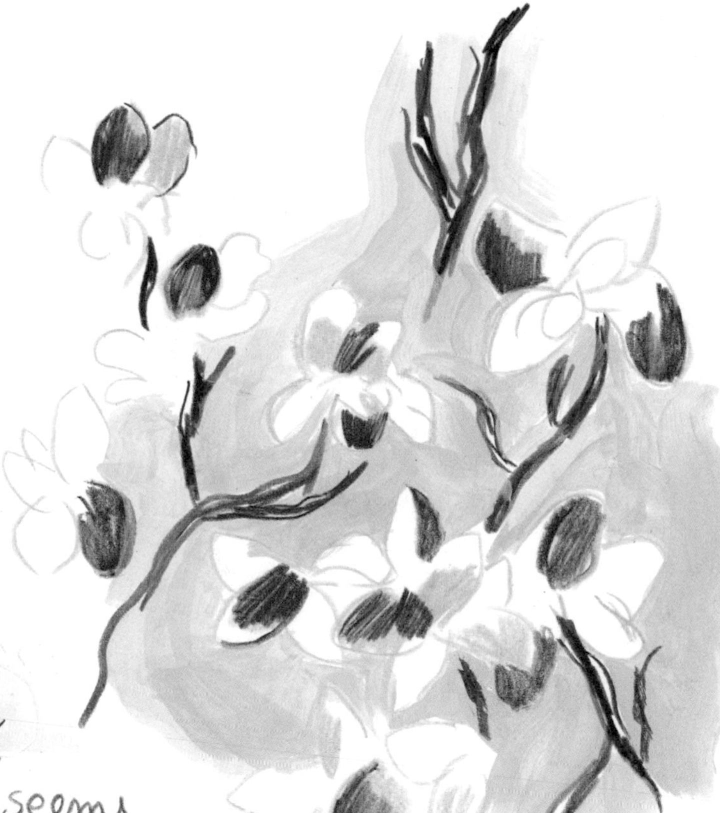

should I
shave and forget about
my politics?

I think about Chantal Akerman*

who didn't survive her mother's death.

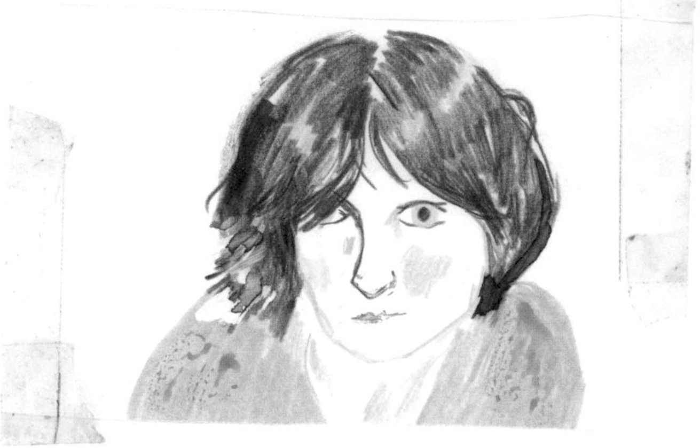

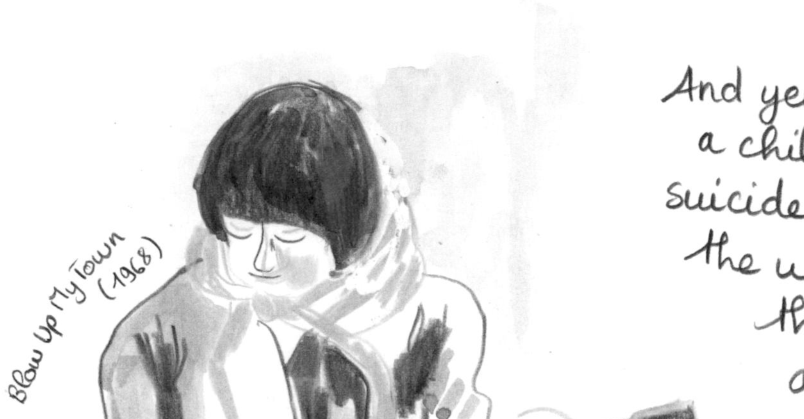
Blow Up My Town (1968)

And yet a child's suicide is the worst thing any mother could imagine.

* Belgian filmmaker (1950-2015)

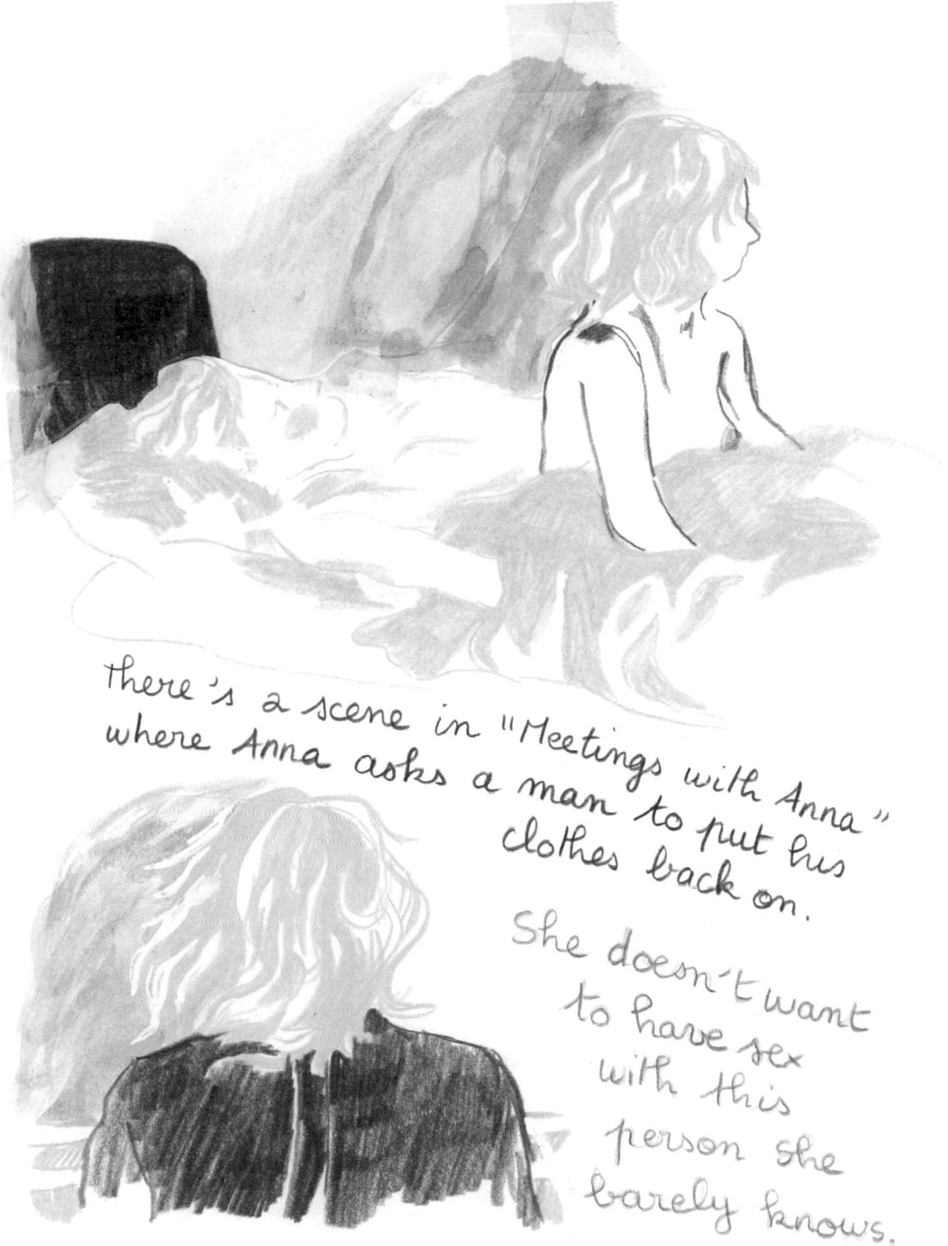
there's a scene in "Meetings with Anna" where Anna asks a man to put his clothes back on.
She doesn't want to have sex with this person she barely knows.

No, she tells herself, there's nothing magic about it.

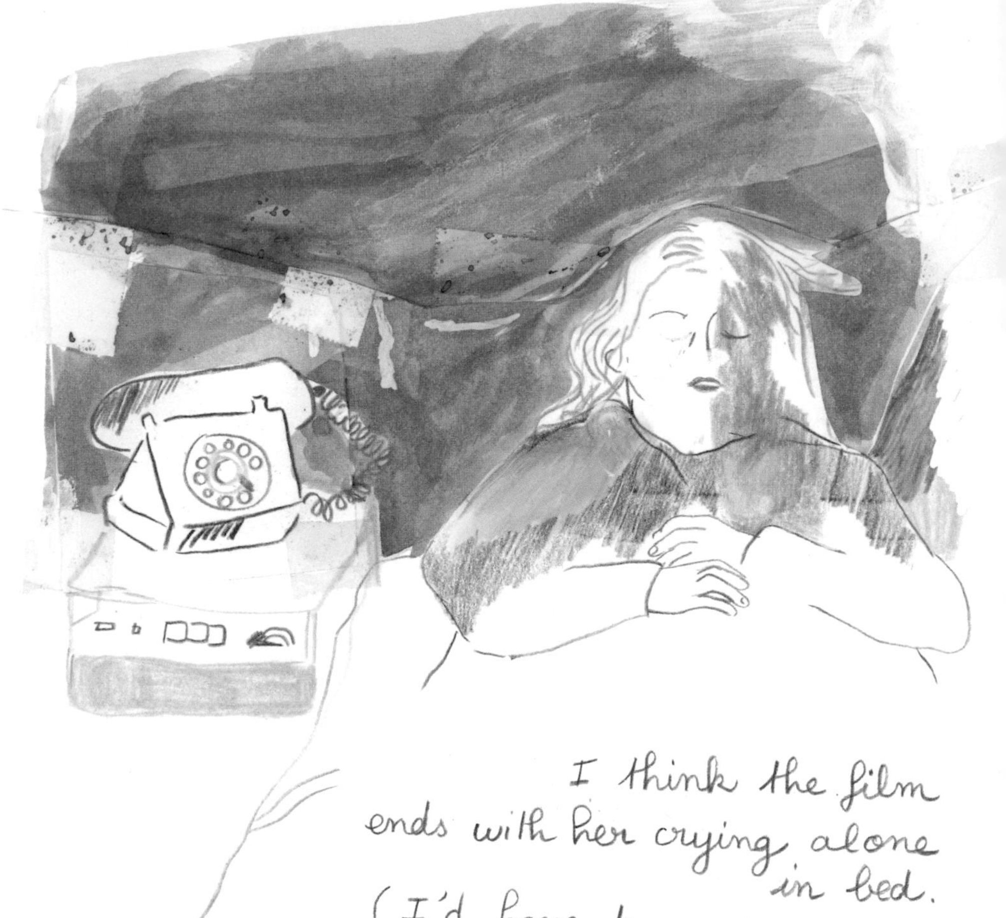
I think the film ends with her crying alone in bed.
(I'd have to see it again)

about her films,
she said:

" I want people to feel the
passage of time in their bodies. That
way I won't have robbed them of
two hours, they'll have lived them."

In August,
I go camping
on my own, on
an island in the middle of the
St. Lawrence.

There's nothing special to report,
that's how easy it is.
I put up my tent.
I heat water over the fire
and use it to wash
myself.

Everything
tastes
better
than it
does
in
the
city.

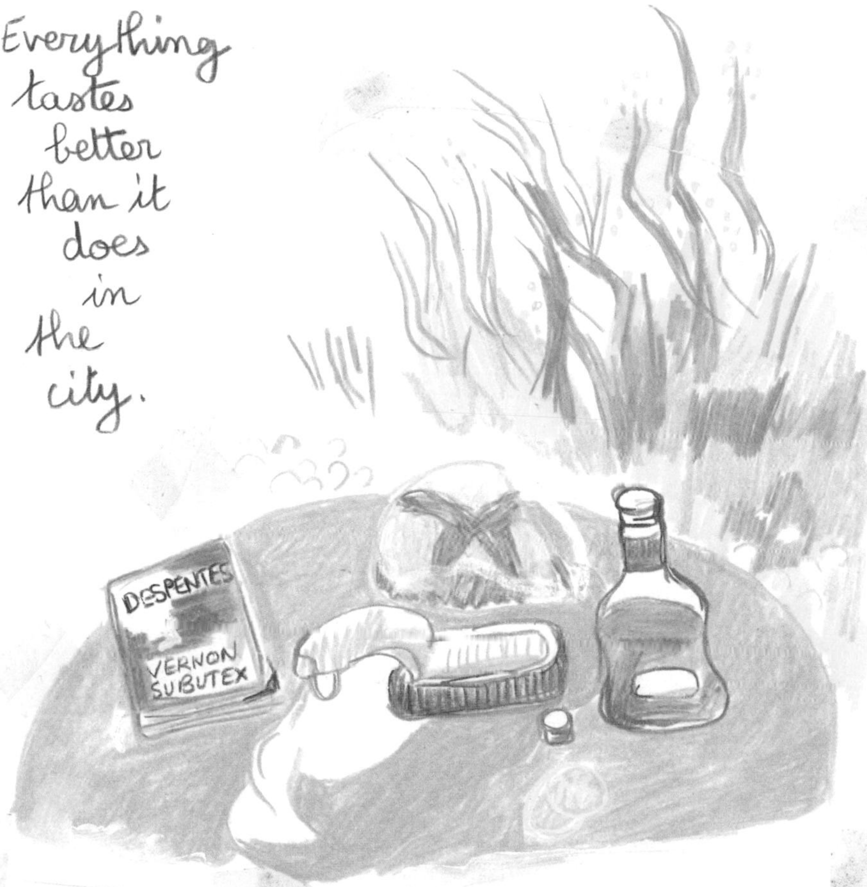
DESPENTES
VERNON
SUBUTEX

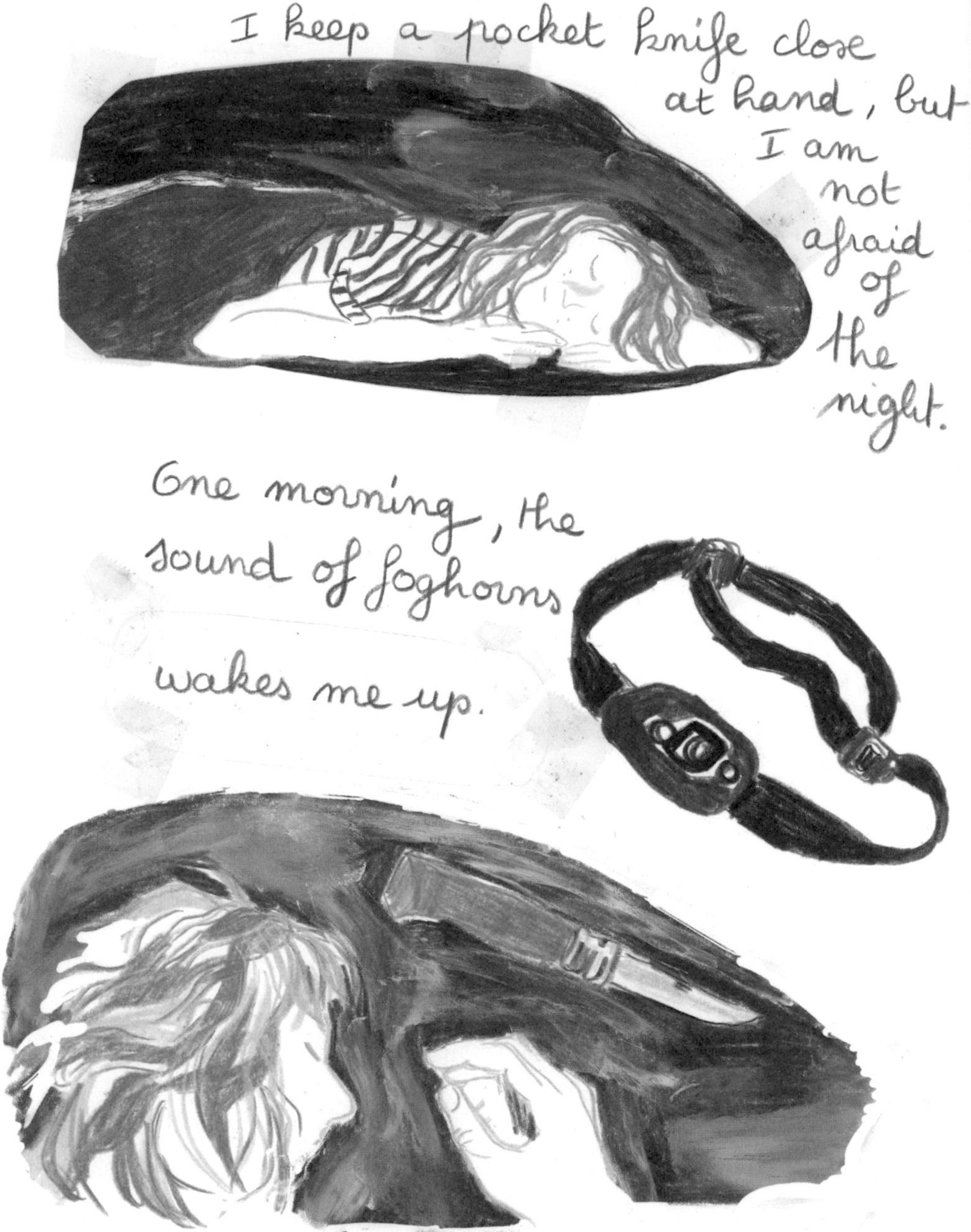
I keep a pocket knife close at hand, but I am not afraid of the night.
One morning, the sound of foghorns wakes me up.

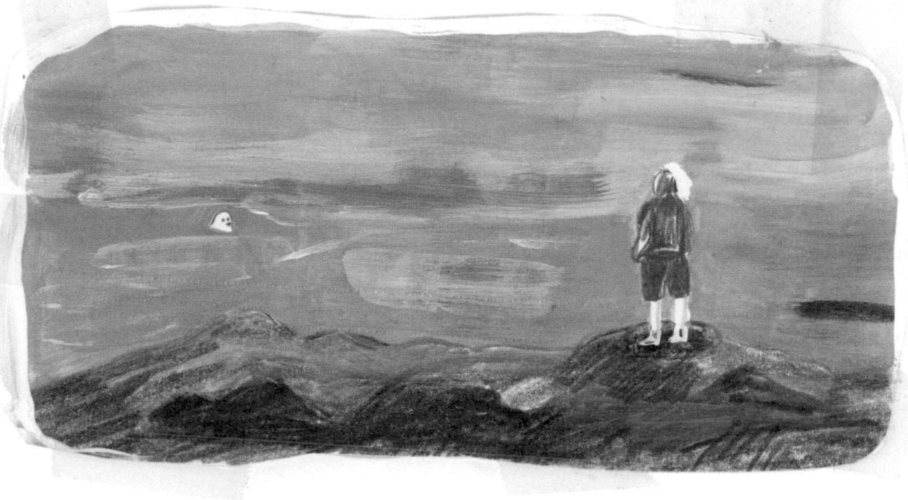

Outside I can't see anything, except the small head of a seal.

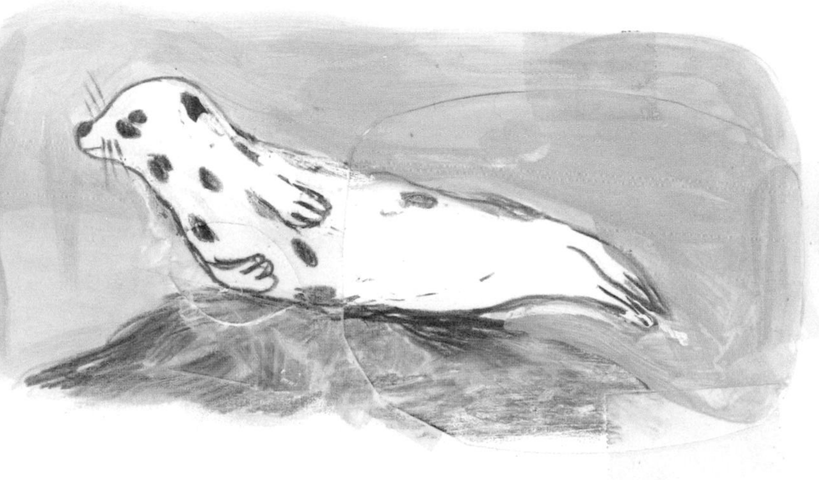

The bear
dream

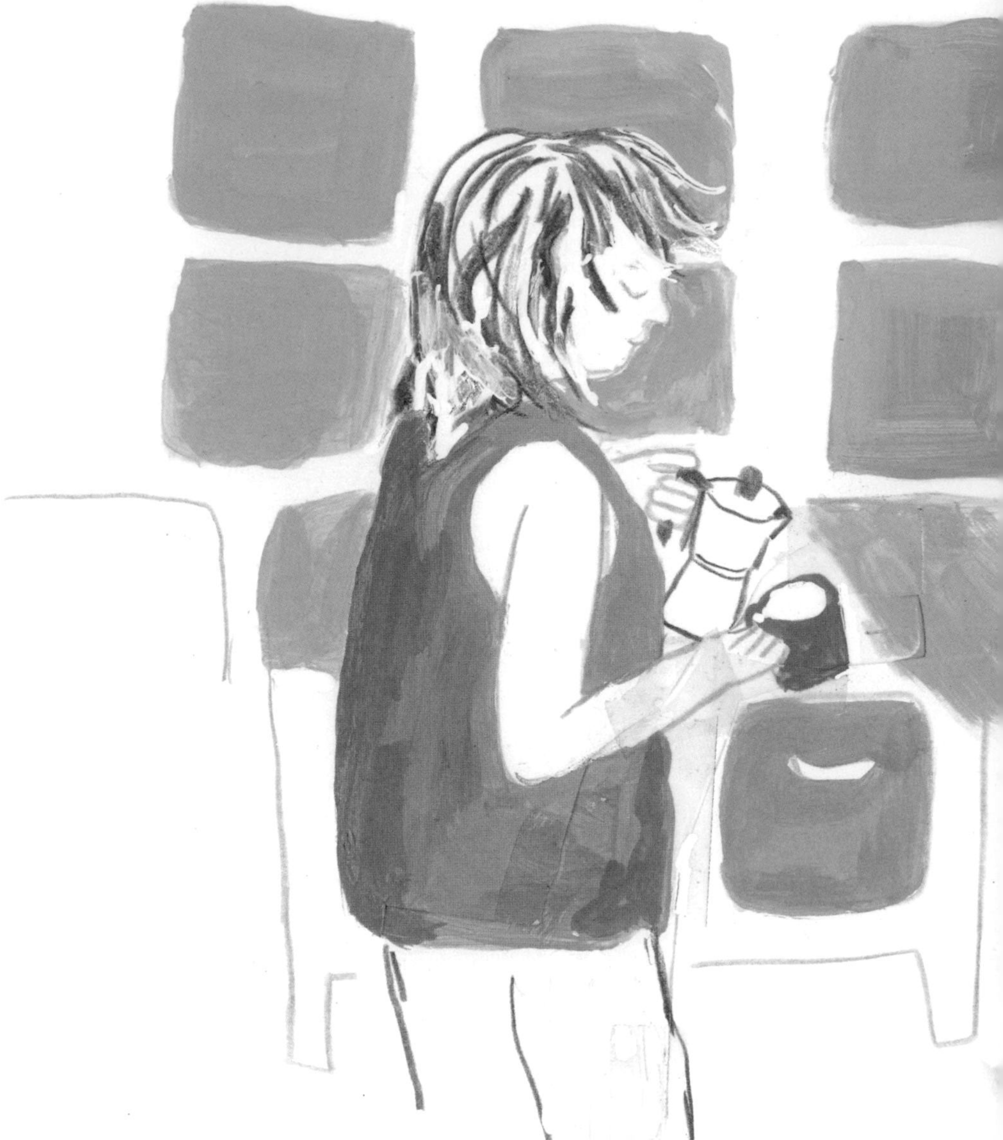

We
rent
a house
on a
rocky
shore,
by
the ocean.

suddenly,
polar bears
attack

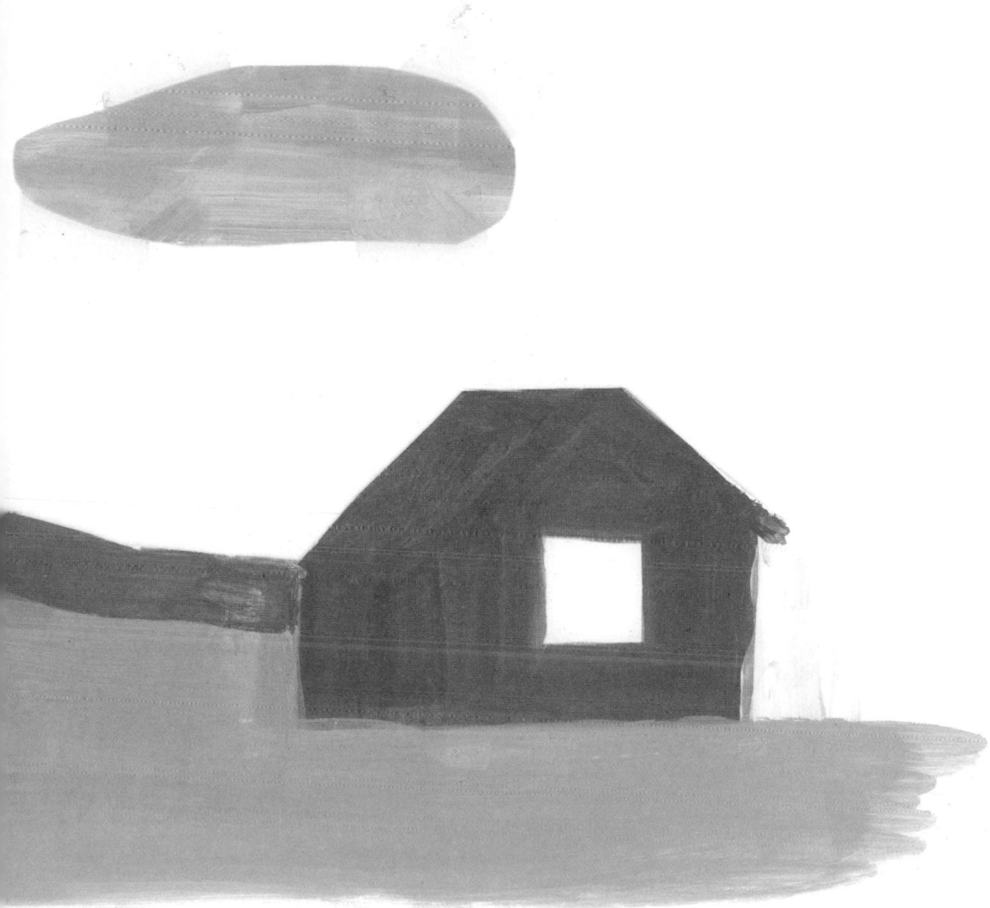

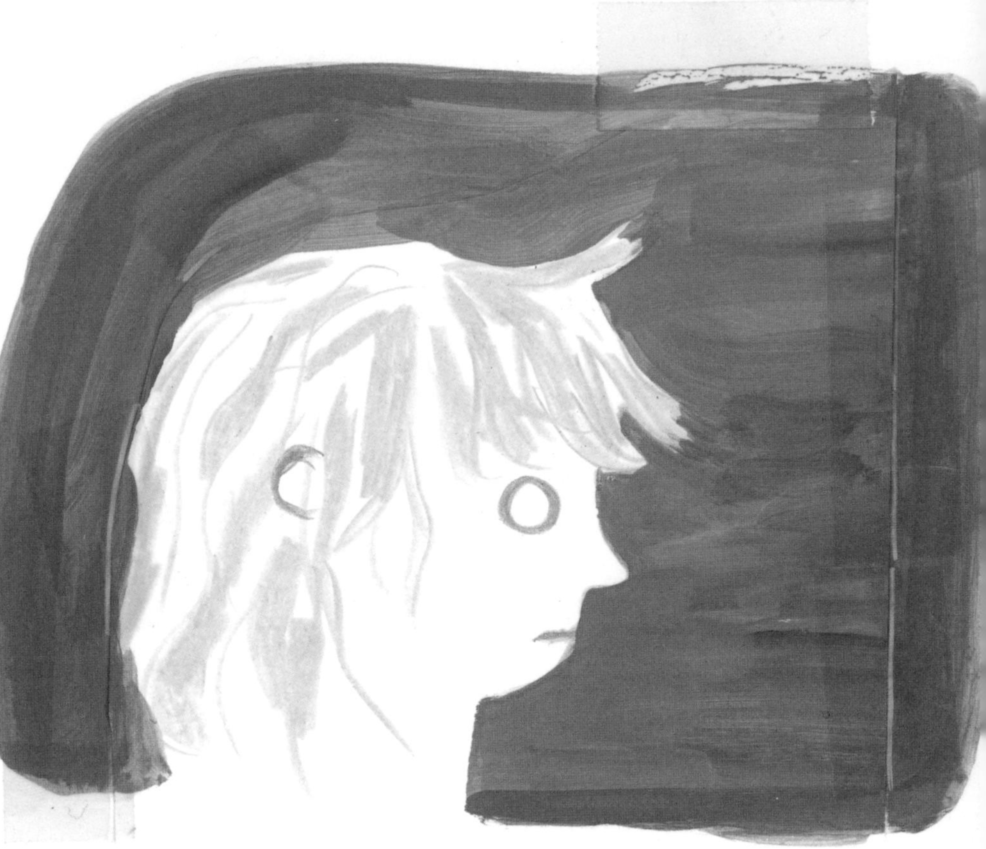

they press
themselves up
against the
large window

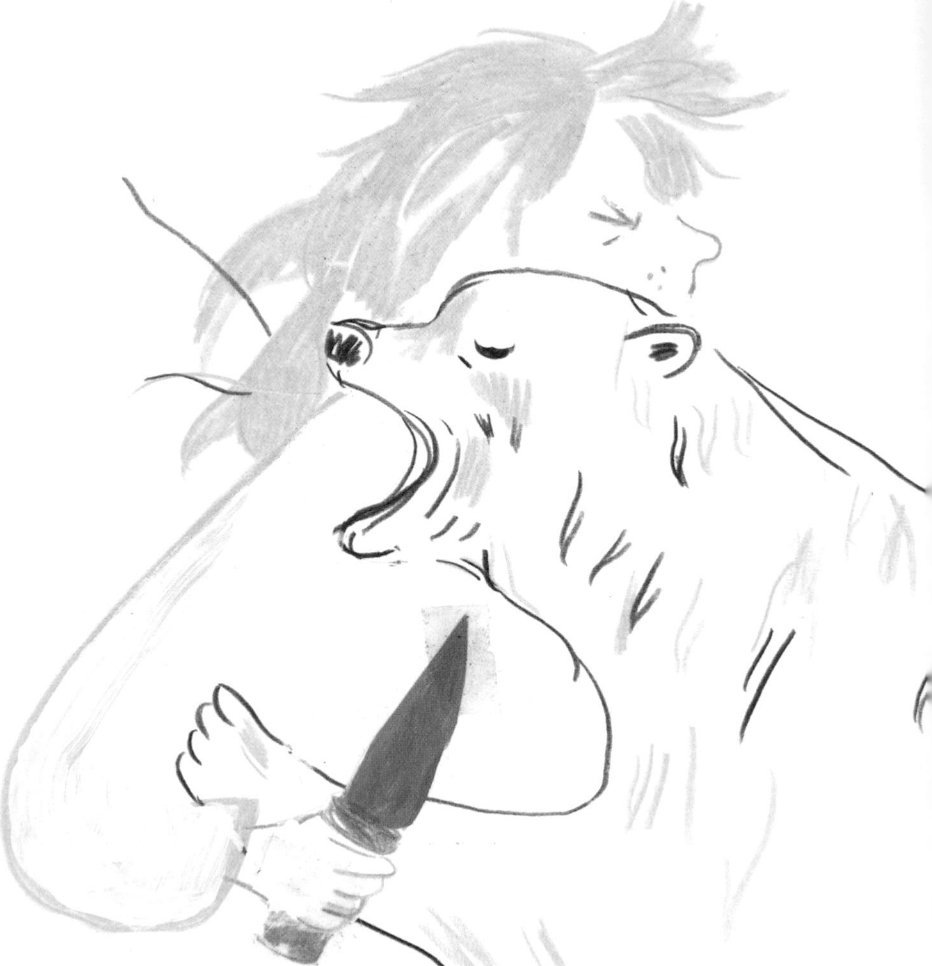

one comes into
the house

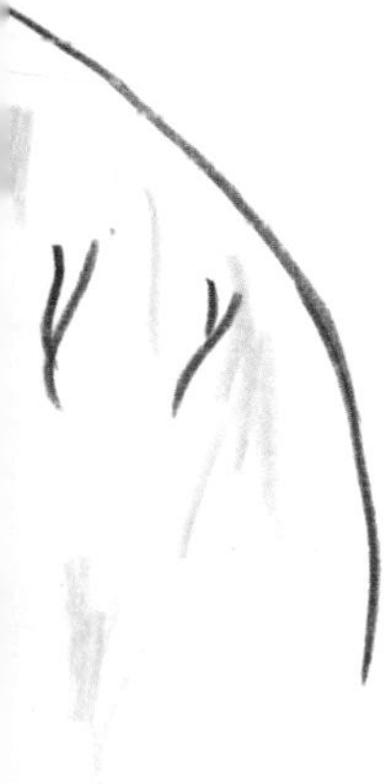

I brandish
my knife
and plunge
it into
the bear's
heart.

I kill
him to save
my life

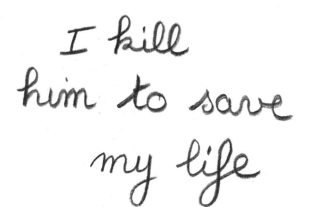

it makes me so
sad

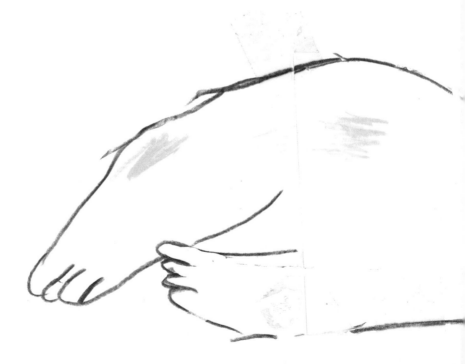

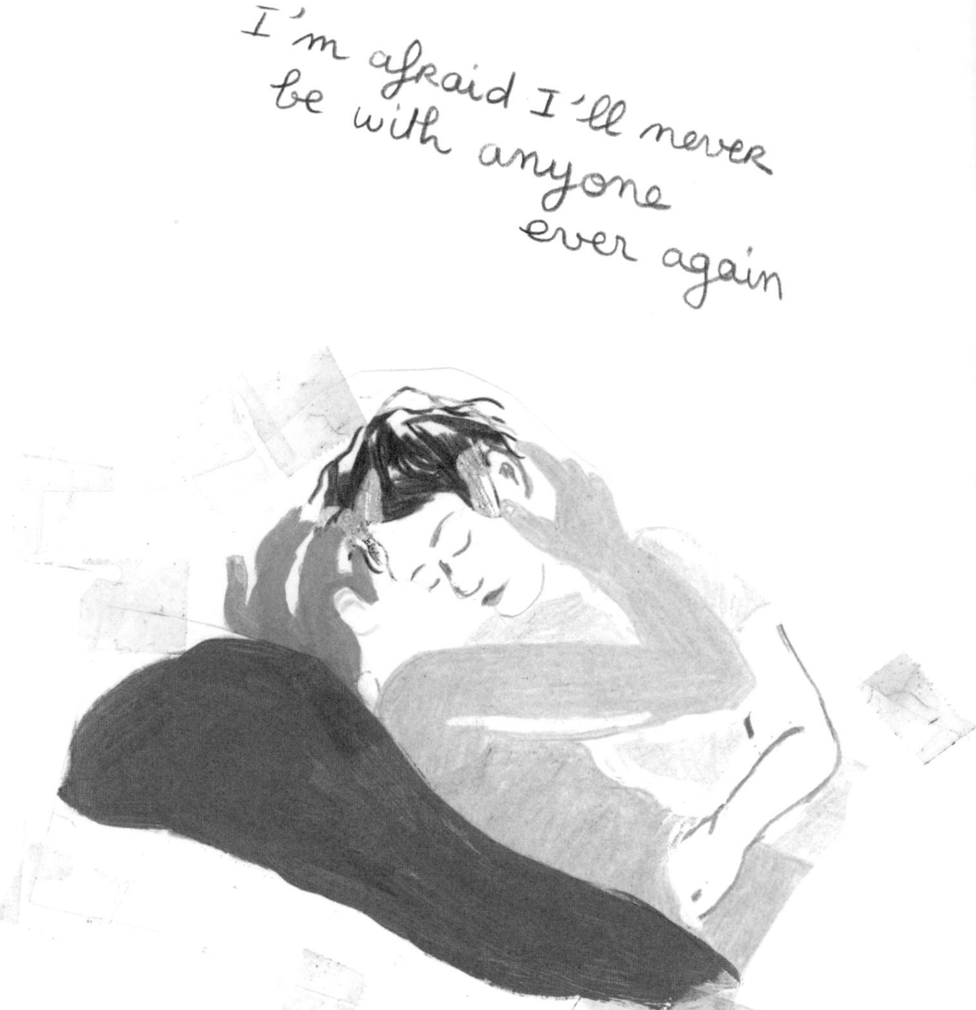
I'm afraid I'll never be with anyone ever again

what man would be
able to live with a feminist?

what man would I be
able to live with?

Greece
Summer 2016

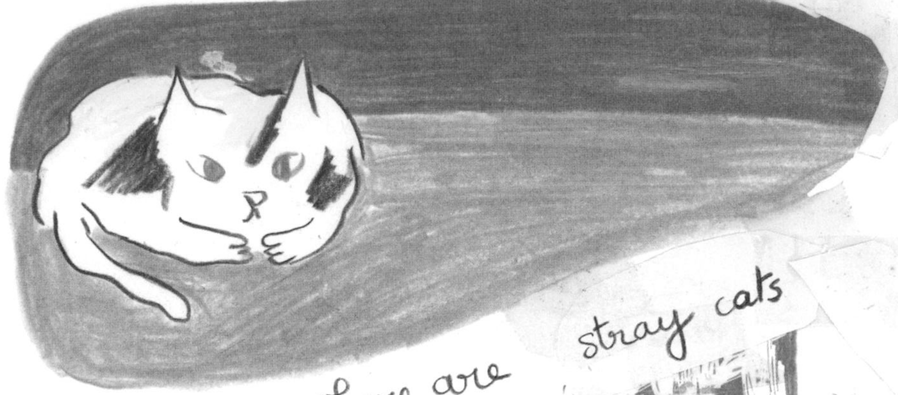

there are stray cats
everywhere.

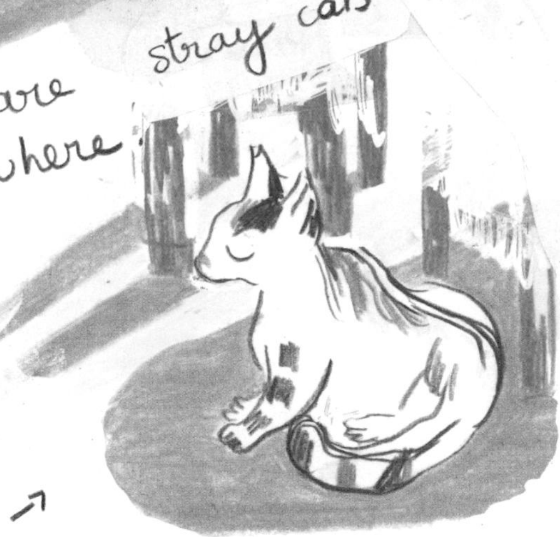

this one
is waiting for
my leftover fish ↗

I am moved at the sight of a
little black bowl more than
5000
years
old.

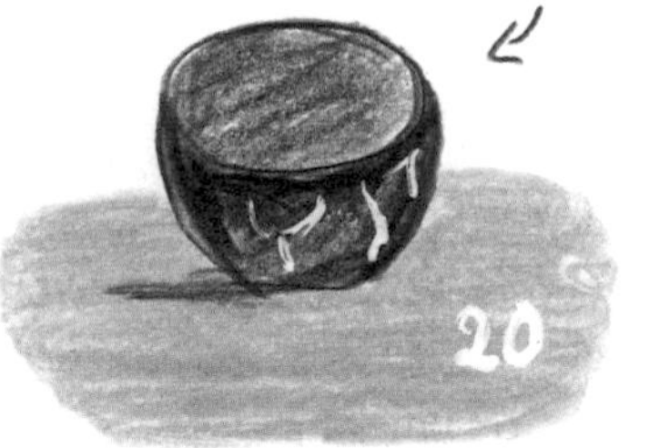
20

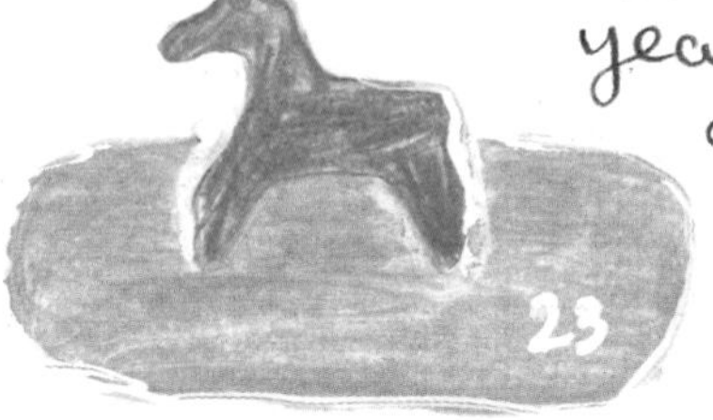
23

It's so beautiful on the mountain that I don't feel like I'm really there.

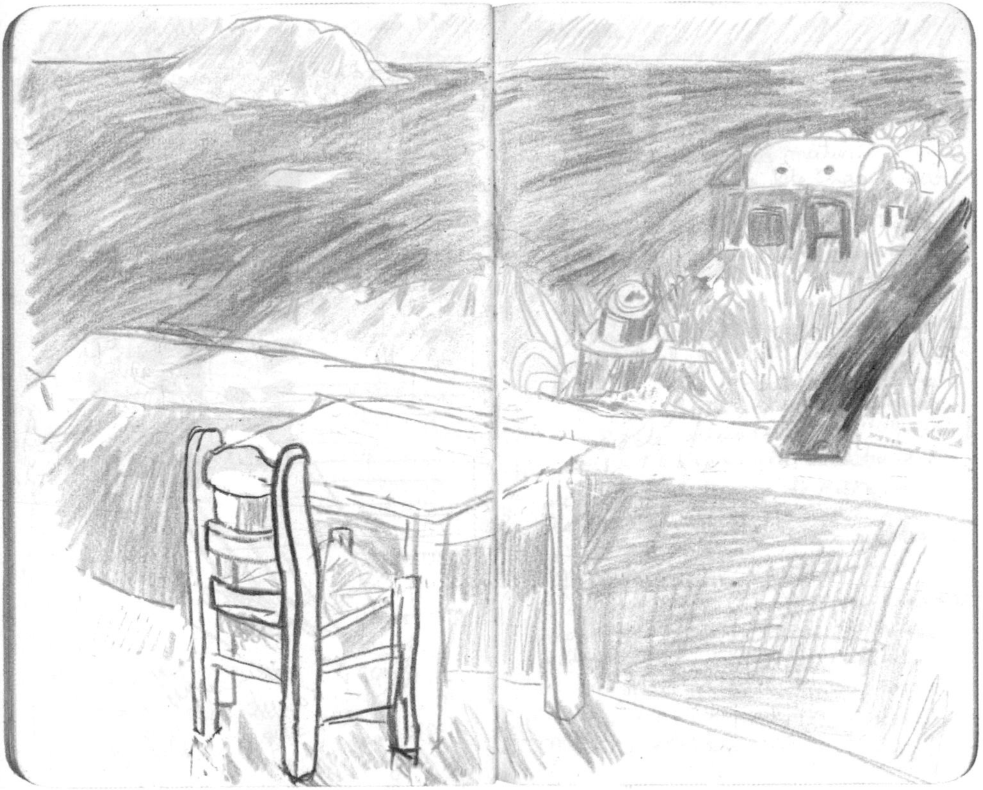

(it's only after I've left the place that the landscape comes alive for me.)

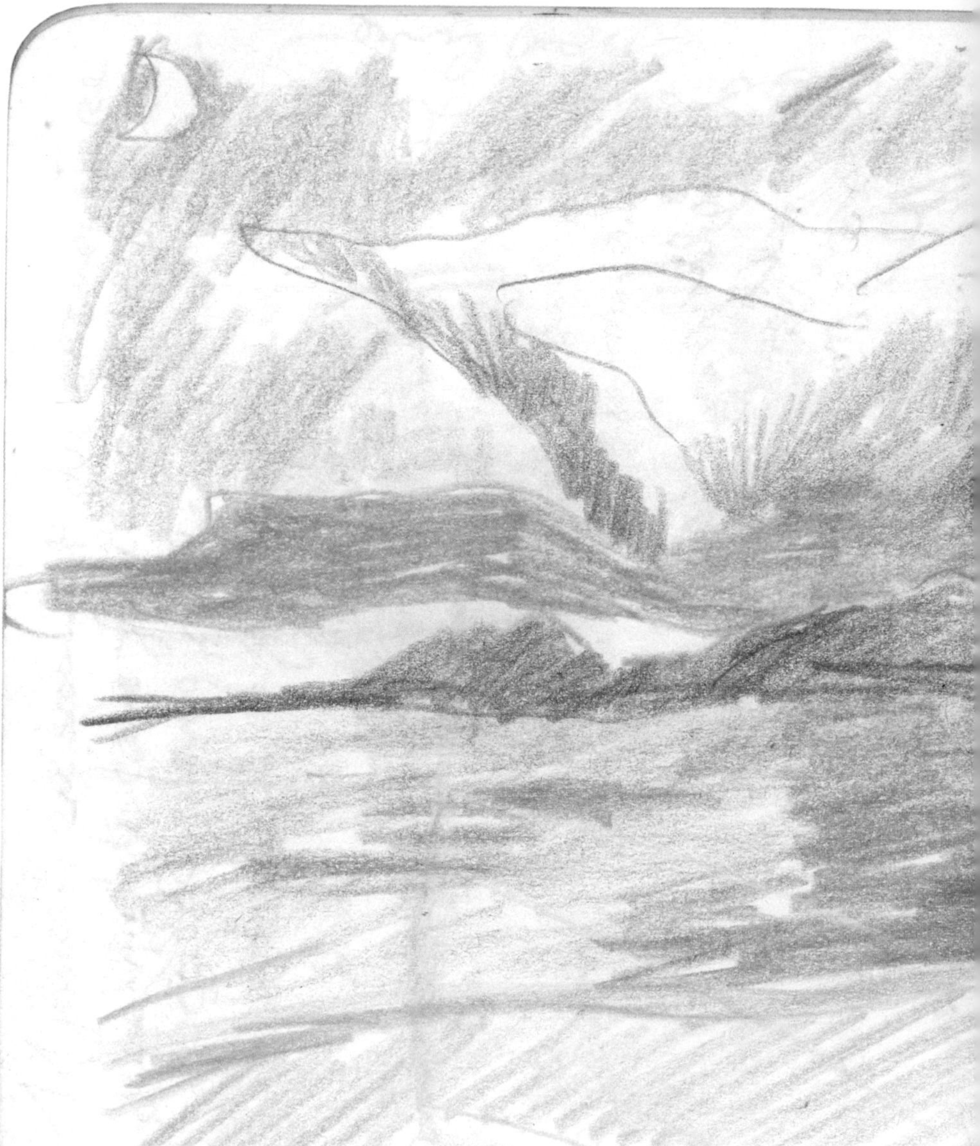

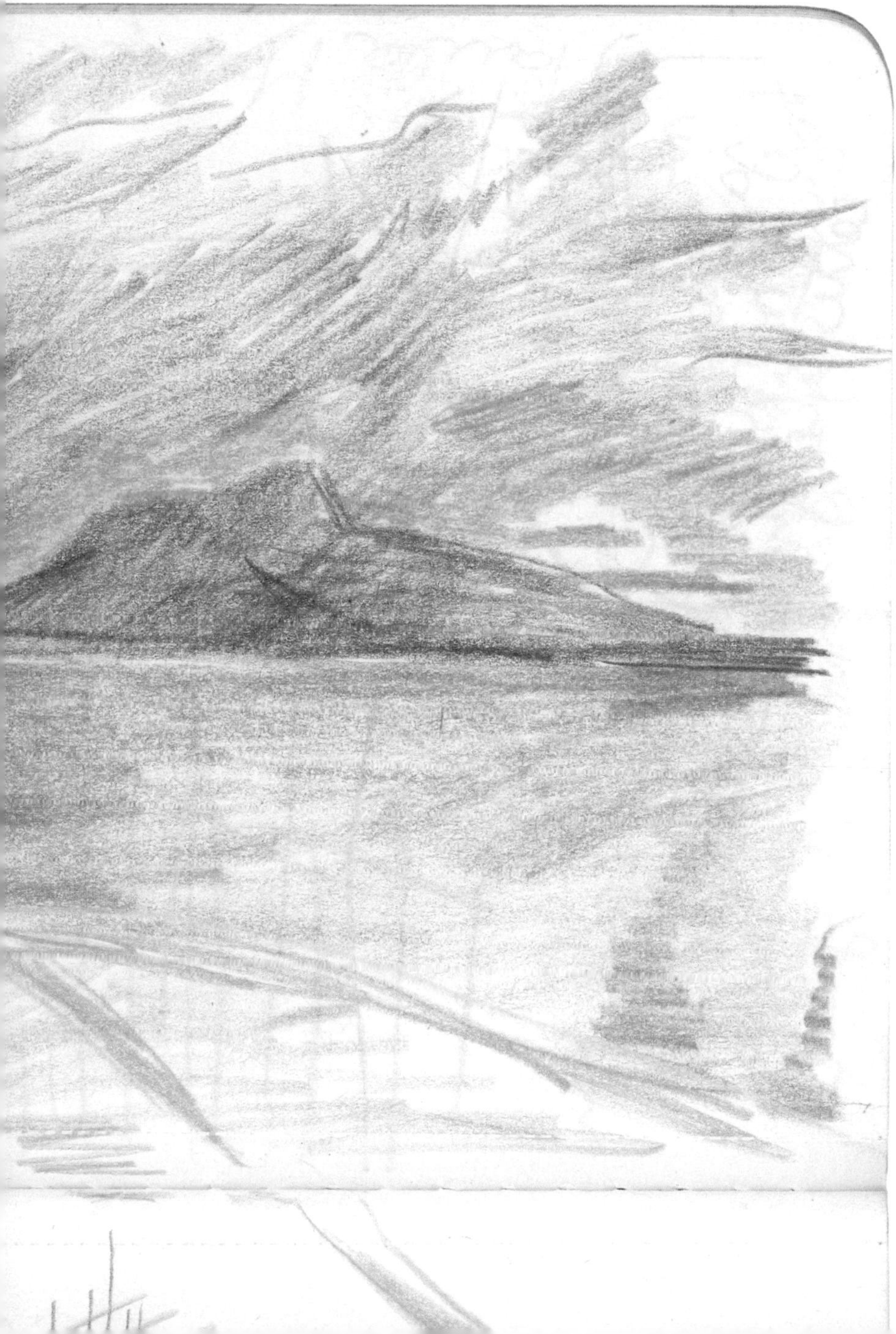

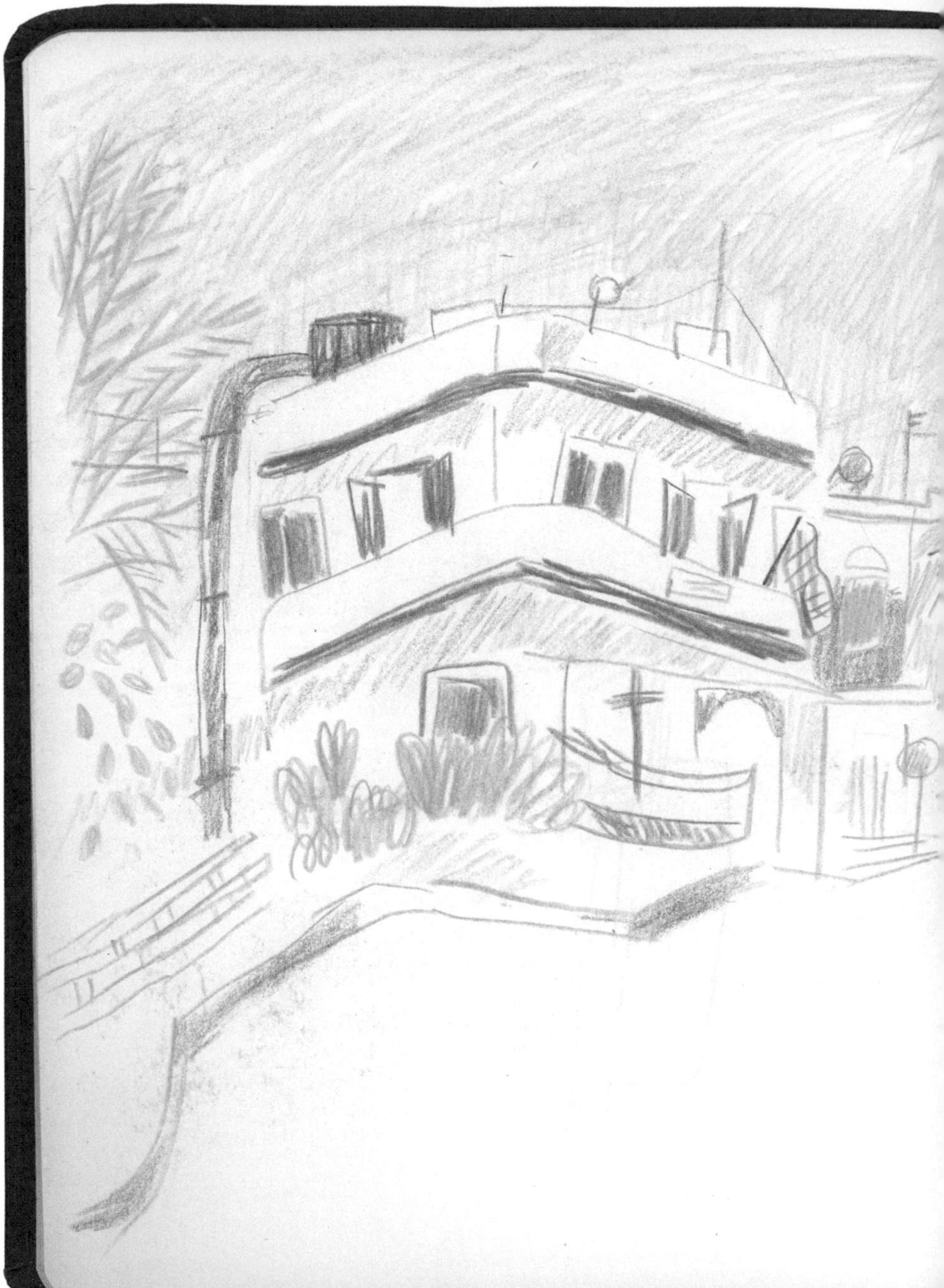

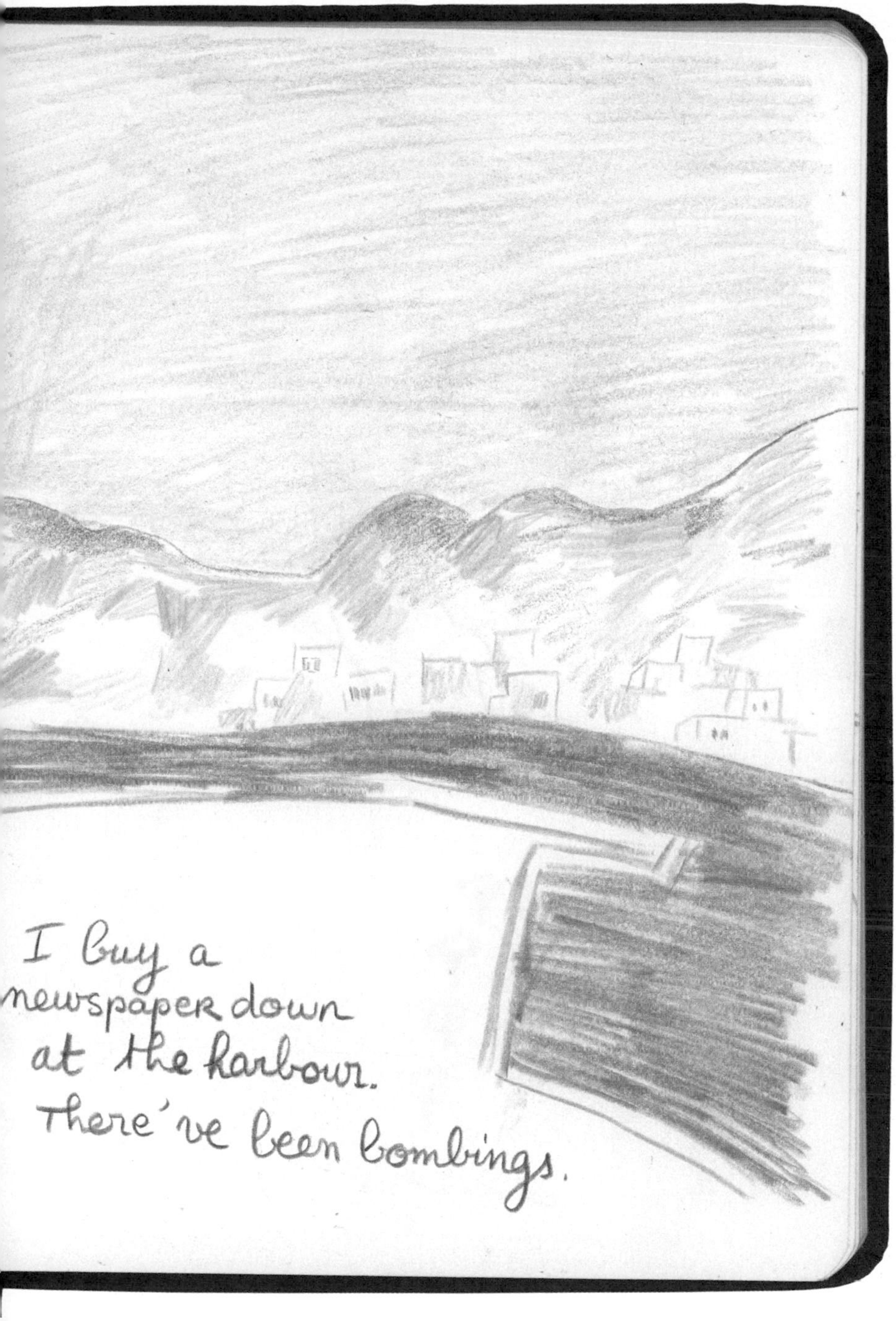
I buy a newspaper down at the harbour. There've been bombings.

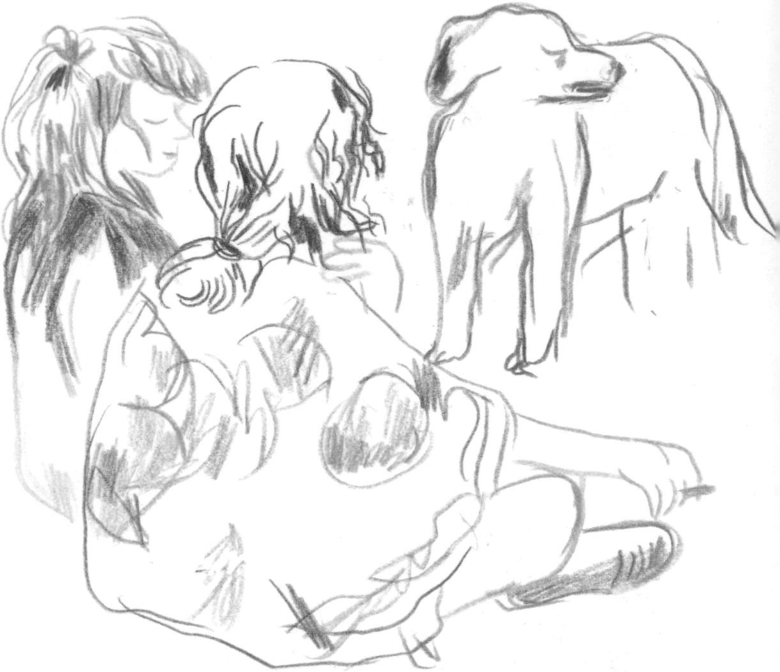

Doing nothing at all,
Watching time go by,
this seems like the
only way to keep death
from closing in.

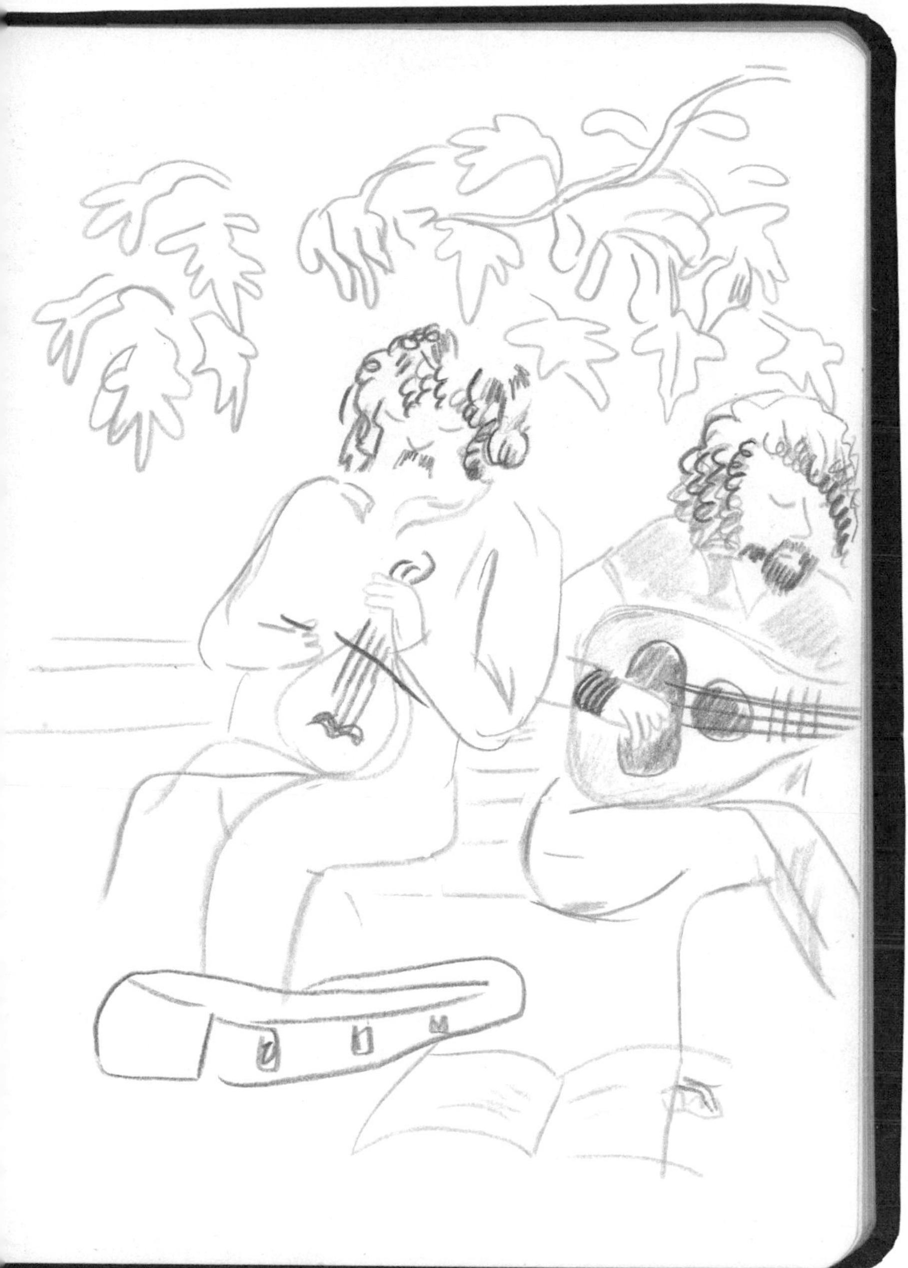

"It feels safe to be on a little island, a bit like being at home"

Tove Jansson wrote to her mother in 1959.

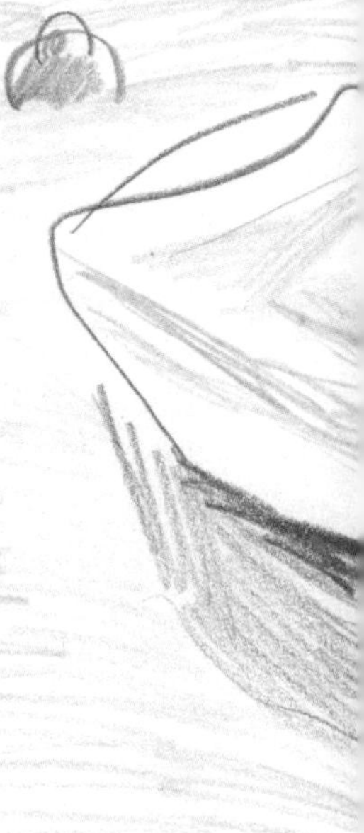

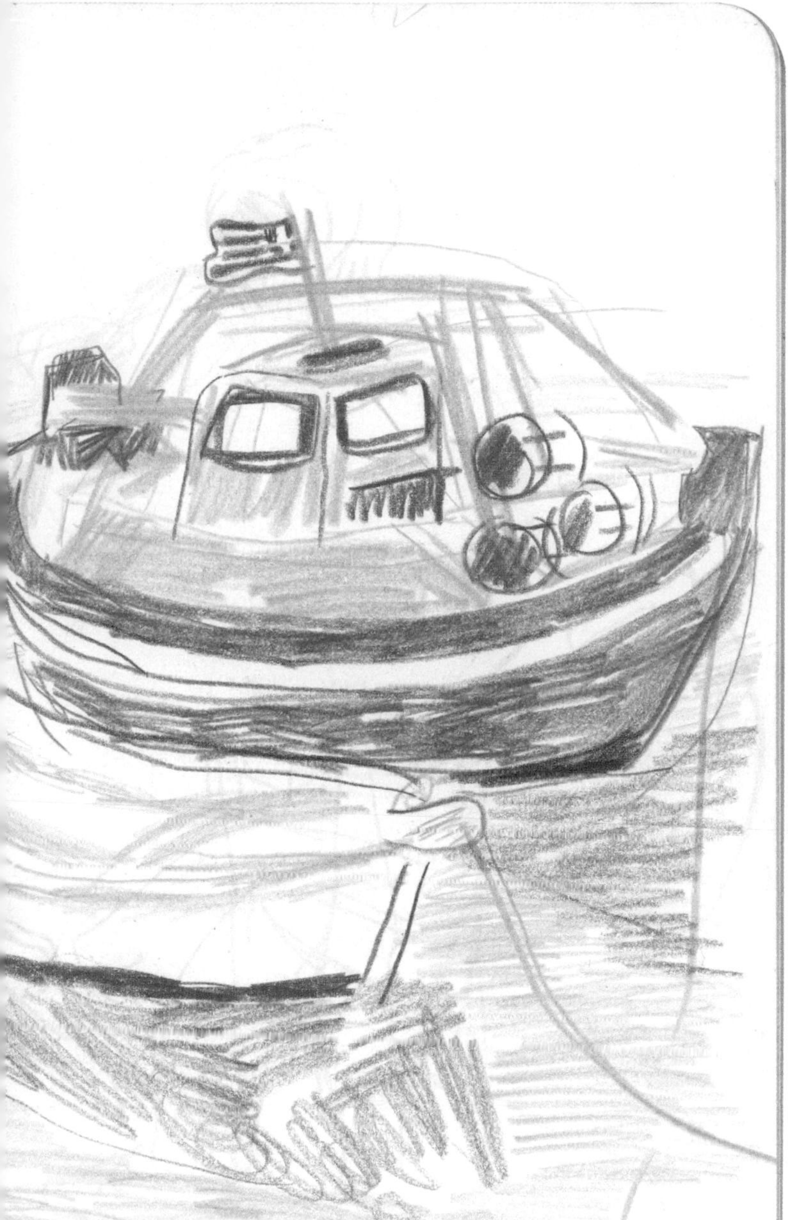

She was in Mykonos, on the
Cyclades, a few kilometres from
where I am now. (I read some letters
she wrote that I find translated
into English on the internet).

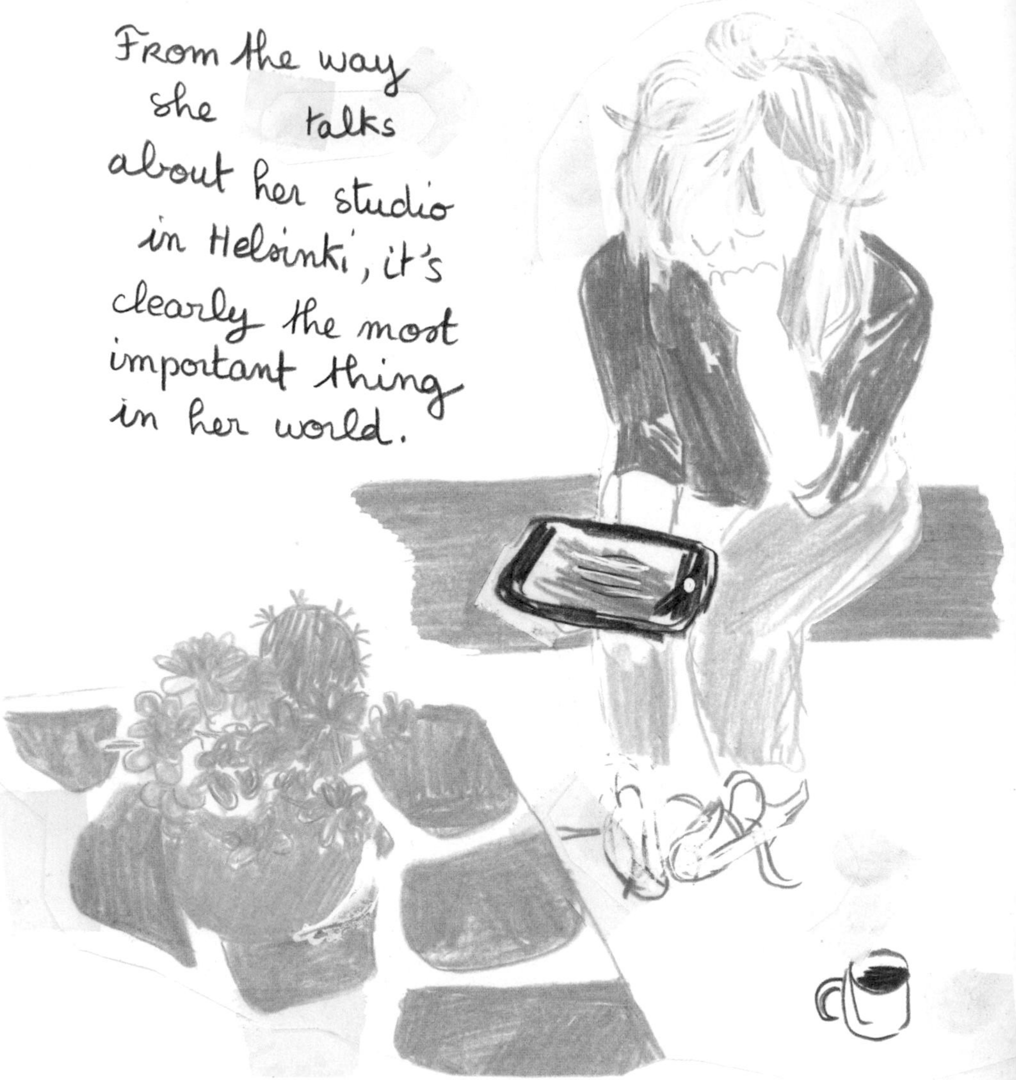
From the way she talks about her studio in Helsinki, it's clearly the most important thing in her world.

her partner at the time (a man named Atos) comes second.

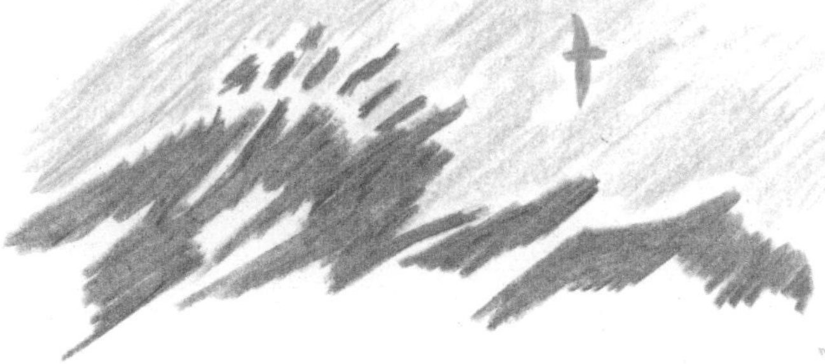

Tove also made several trips to Brittany, where I grew up.

Brittany and Finland look alike, with all their islands and lighthouses.

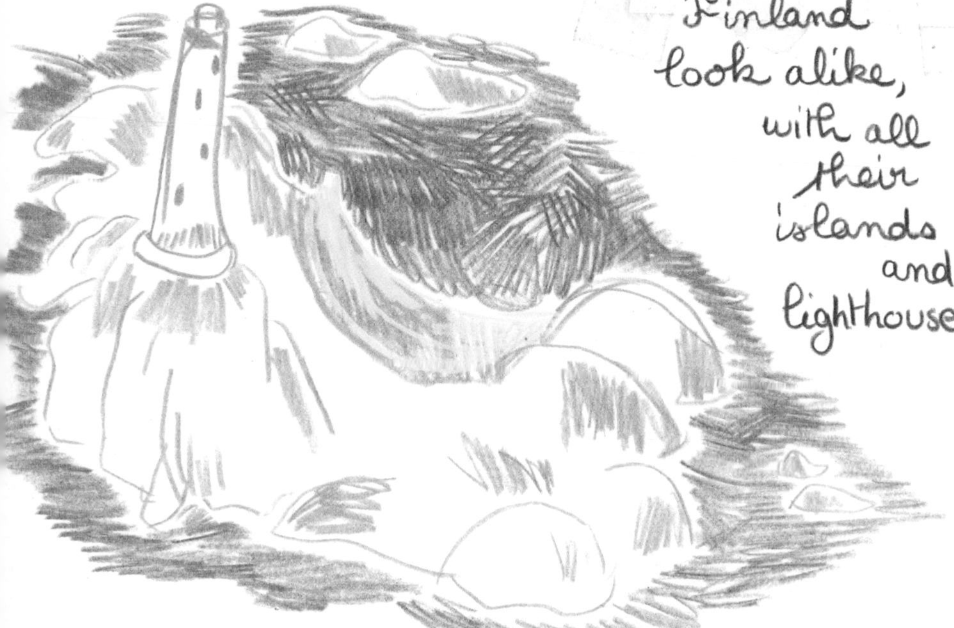

When I met Charlotte Airas* in
Montréal, she told me that Tove
had a lover during her first trip
to Brittany
in
1938.

He was a sailor. She was 24 and
travelling alone to paint.

* director of a documentary on Tove's
work as a visual artist.

Ten years later in the harbour of Saint-Pierre (Finistère), she wrote to Atos:

"Right now your still faithful Tofsla is sitting in Bar de l'Océan near the fishing harbour and drinking absinthe"

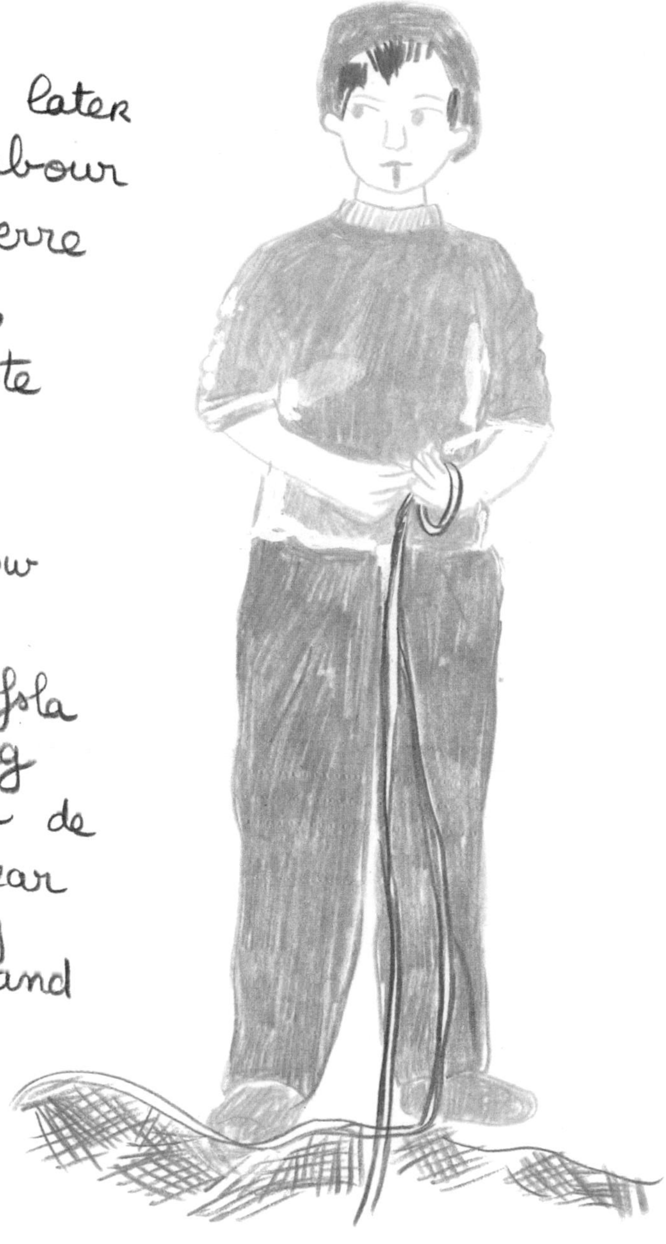

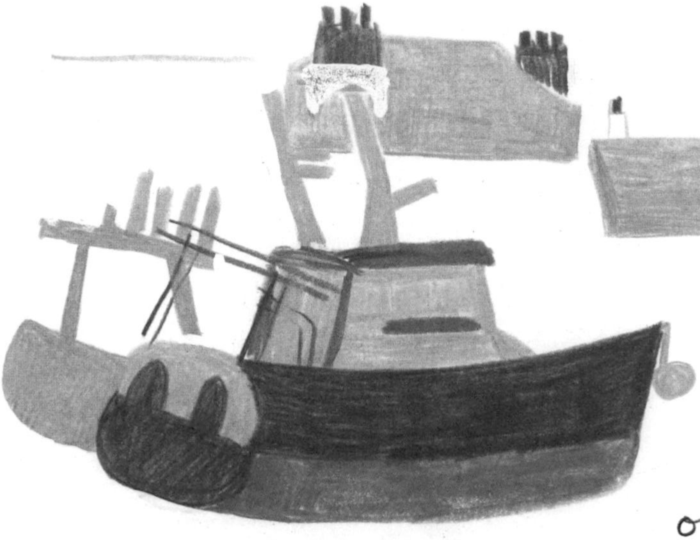

"The other day I missed the bus and walked eight kilometers over the salt flats all the way to my friendly light-house"

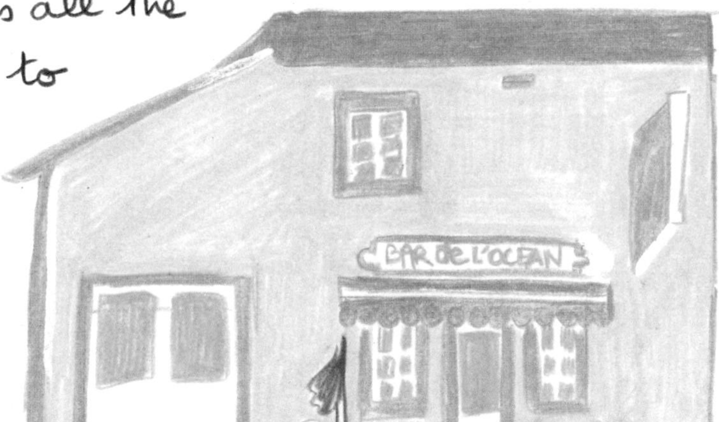
BAR DE L'OCEAN

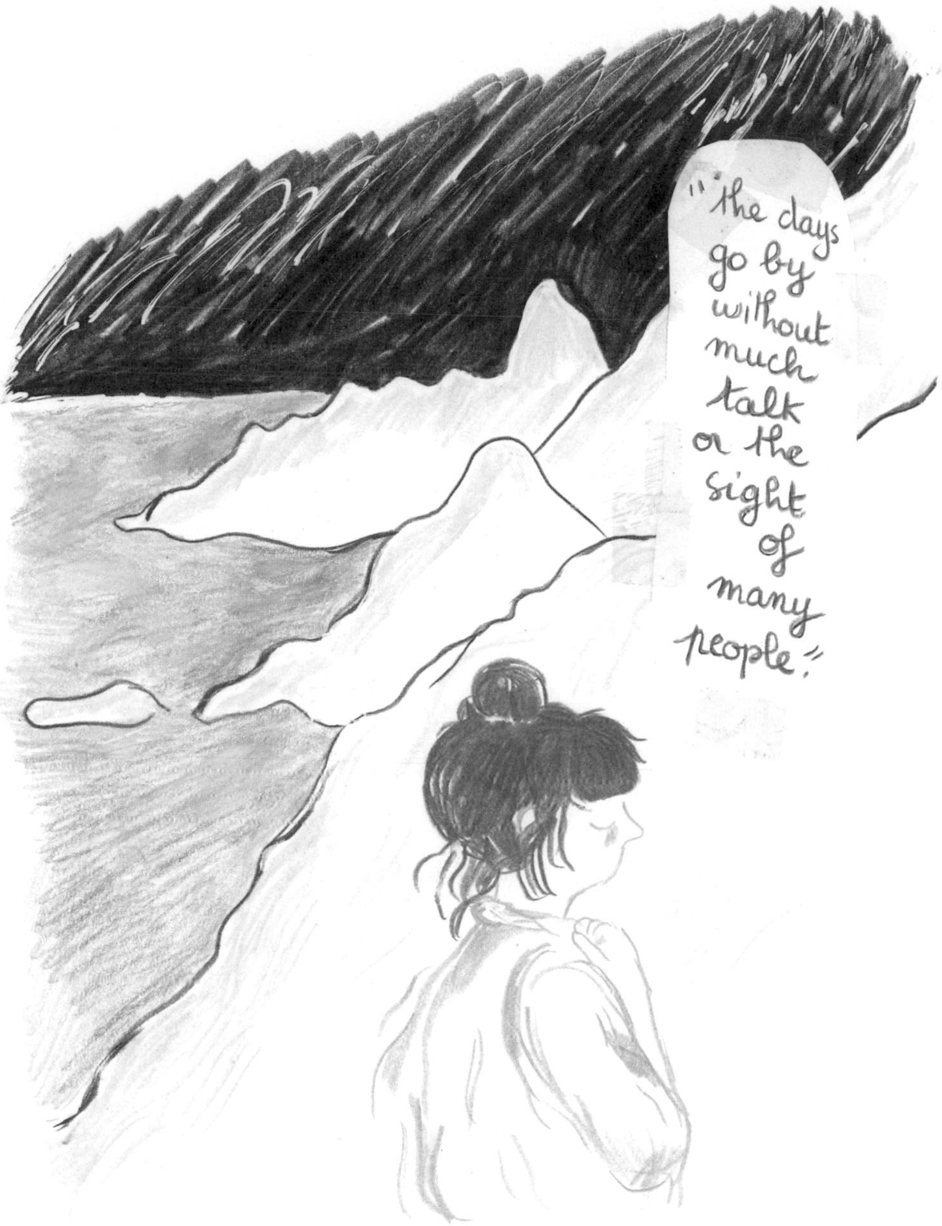
"the days go by without much talk or the sight of many people."

" A wonderful cadmium-yellow moss on the low stone walls,

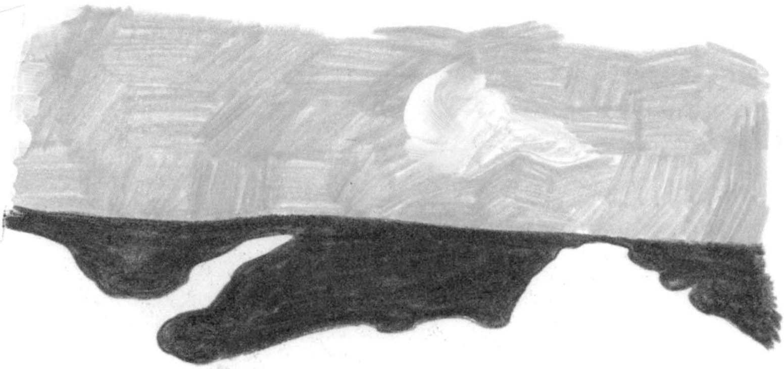

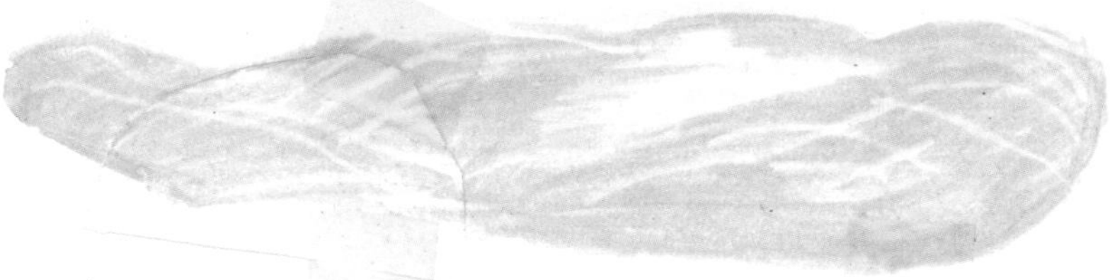

seaweed of every hue between blackish purple and honey-yellow, grey-white sand"

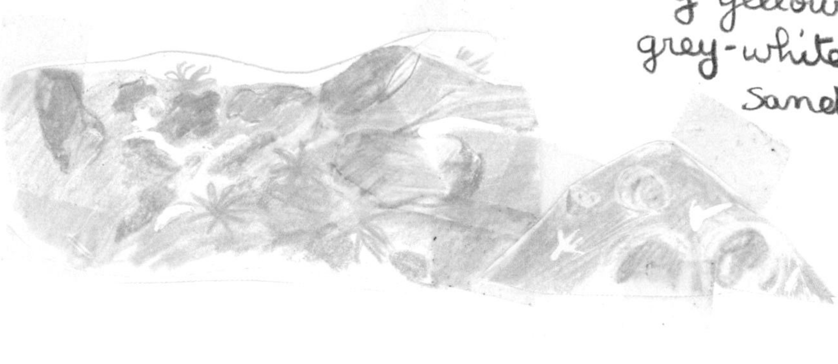

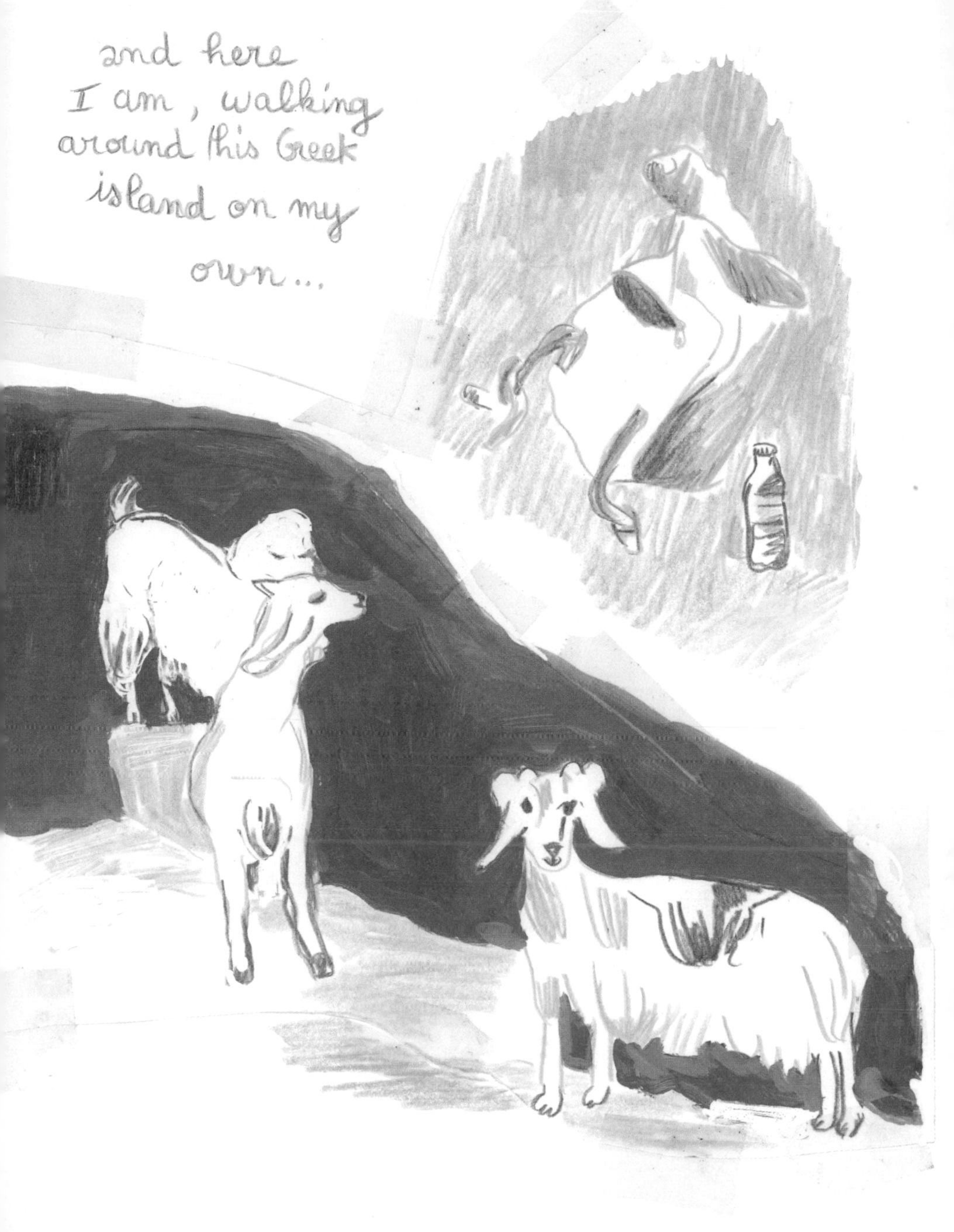
and here I am, walking around this Greek island on my own...

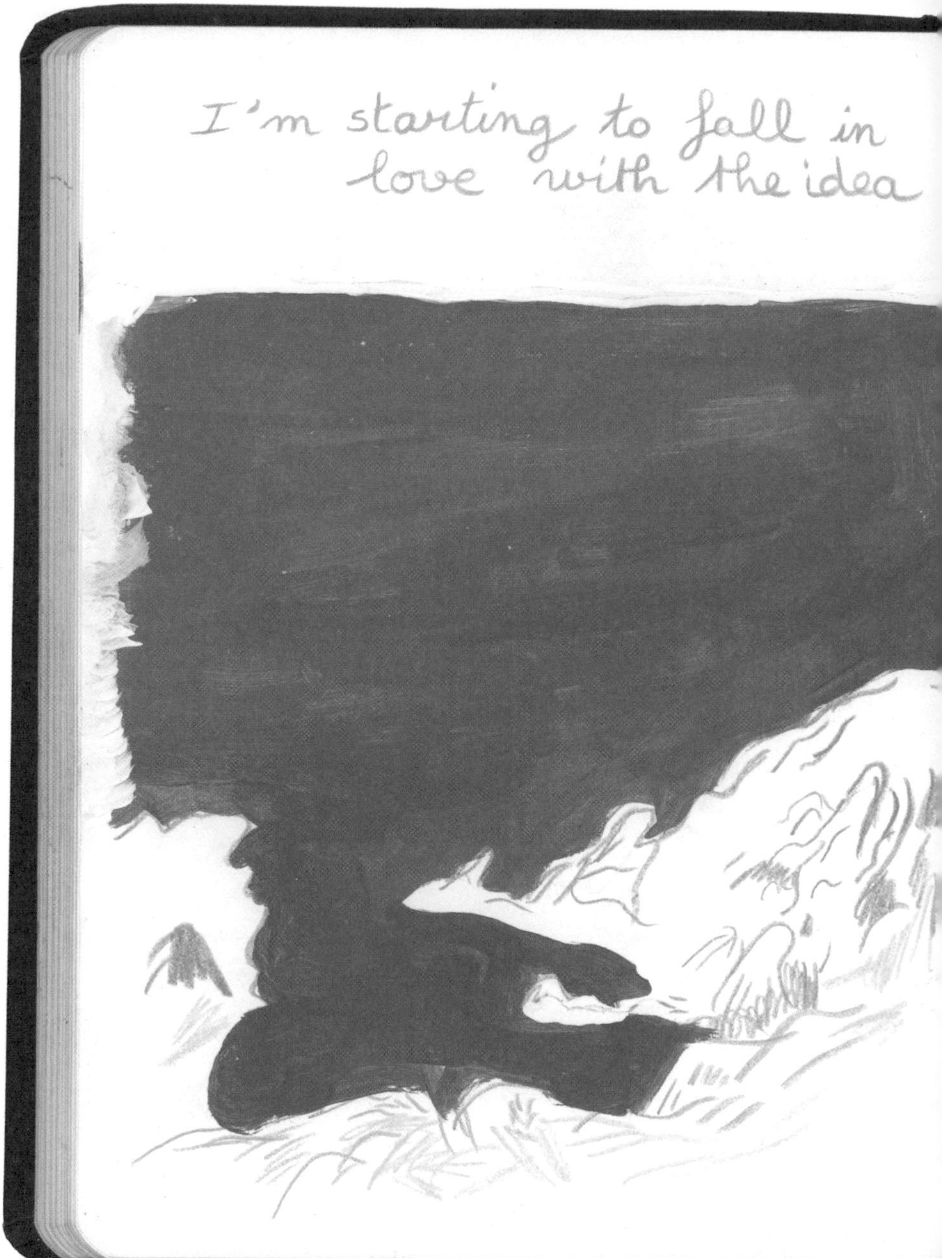
I'm starting to fall in love with the idea

of being a woman.

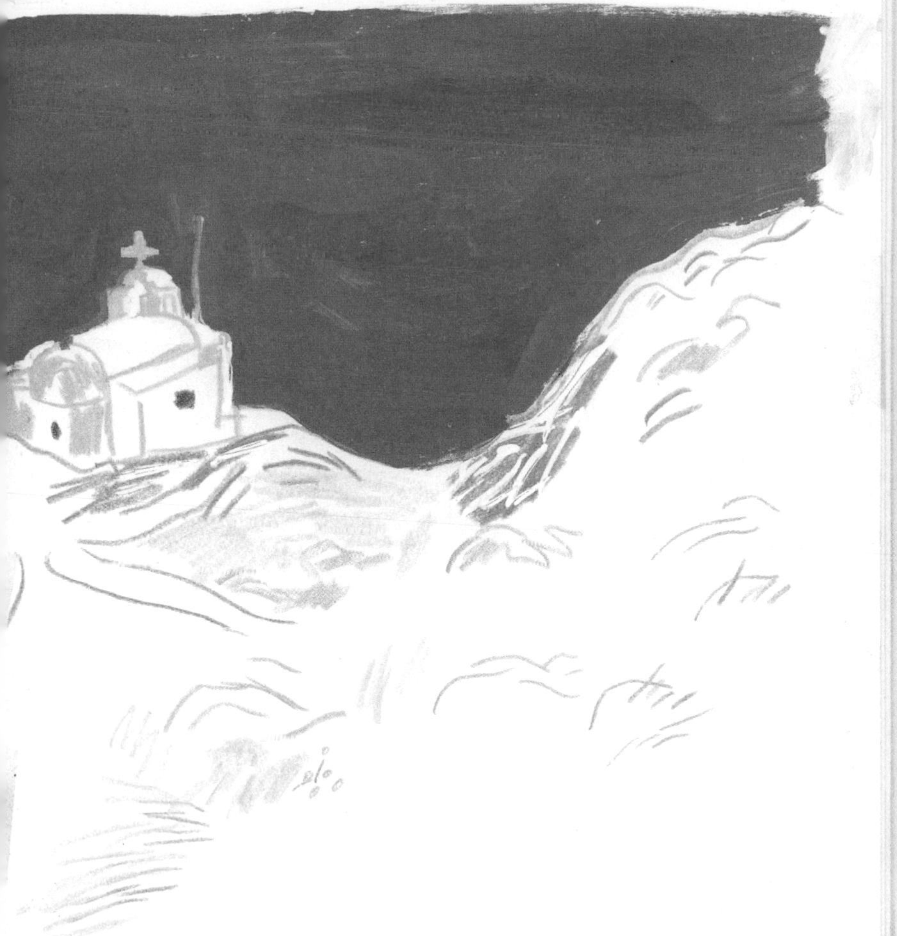

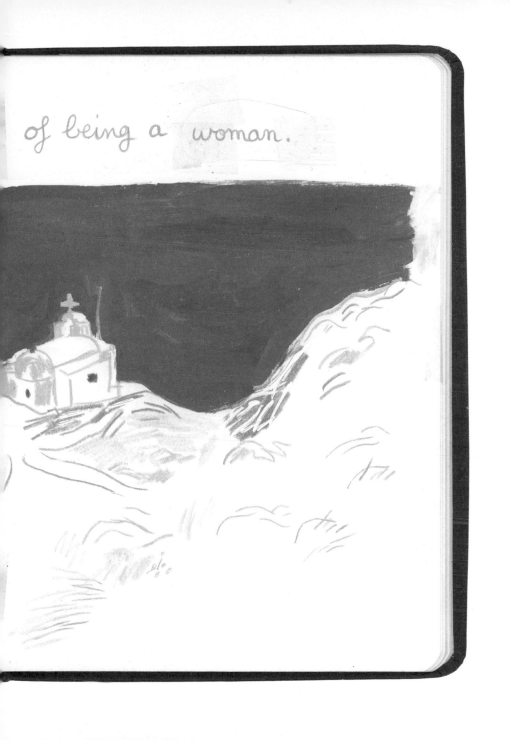

The dream of the béguines

the
women
are poets

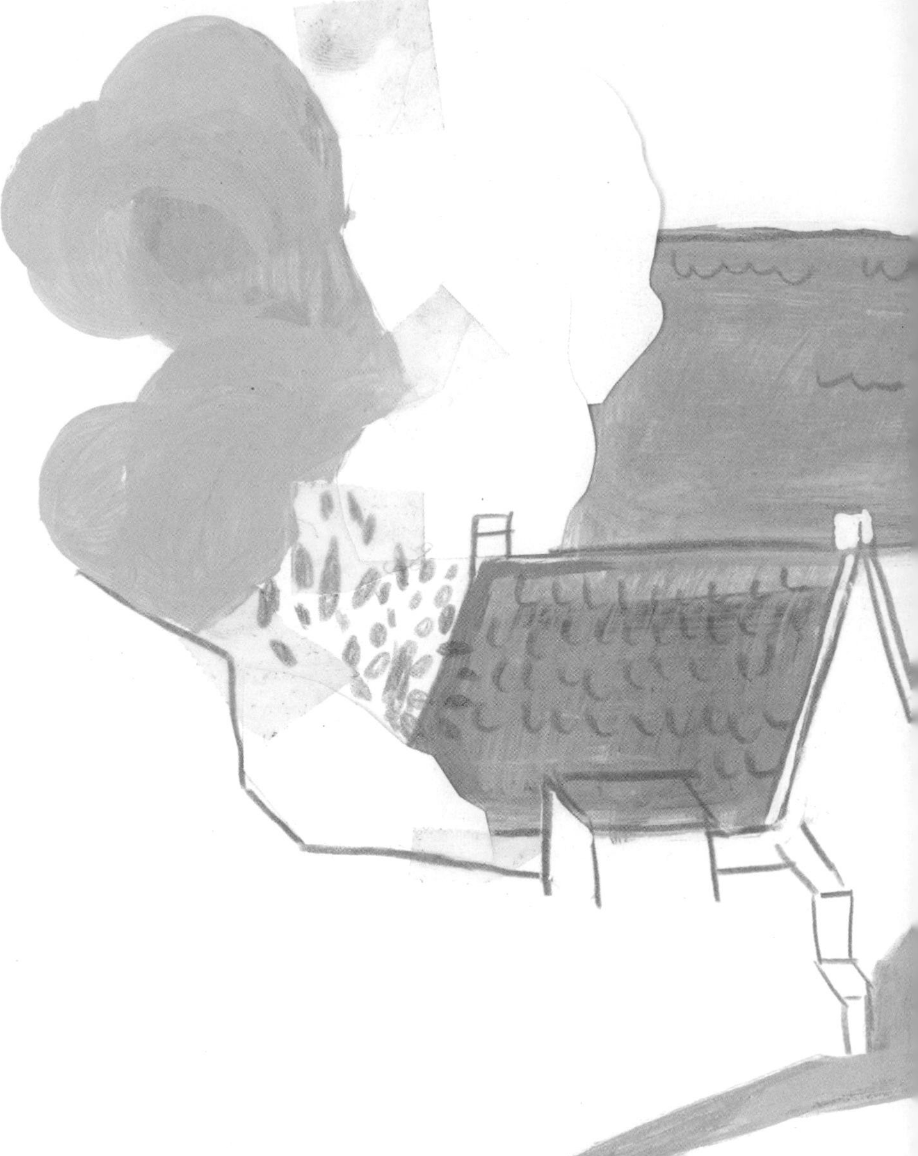

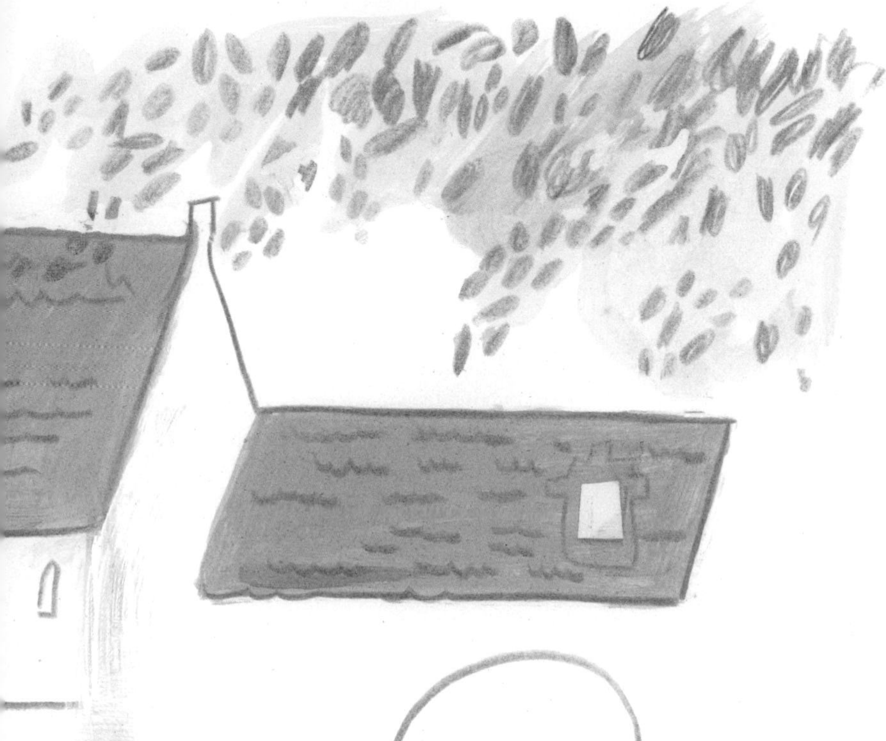

they live in an
old béguinage, in
the middle of a
city.

with orphan girls
they've taken in

they no longer
need to
decide if
they want
children.

they write
and read

all day long

and make
ceramic bowls
for people
in the
neighbourhood

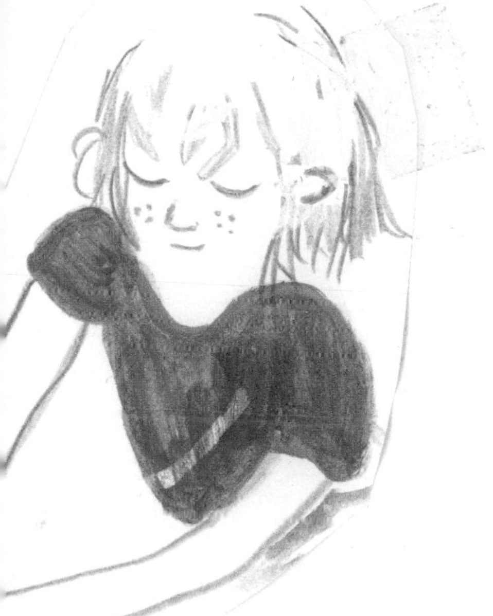

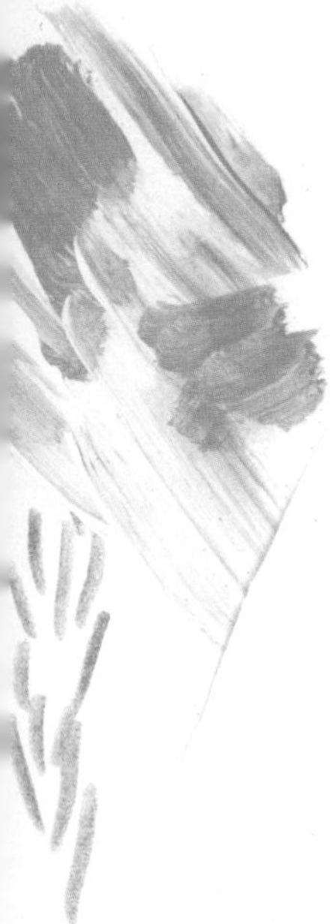

sometimes,
they go off
on their own,
up to

the woods of the north

they come back
older,
with
new
books,

or new children

every night,
they show each
other their
work

and talk about it over
a glass of rum.

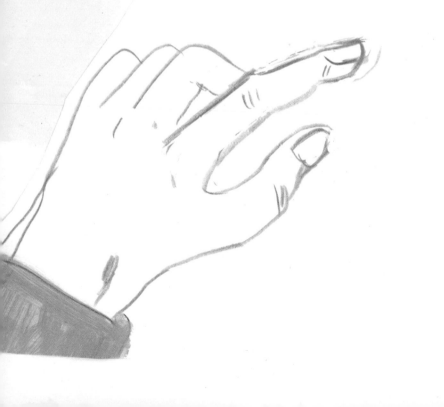

then they fall asleep
thinking of their
poems.

the orphans
grow up
    dreaming
of the outside
        world.
when the
    time comes,
the women
    let them go.

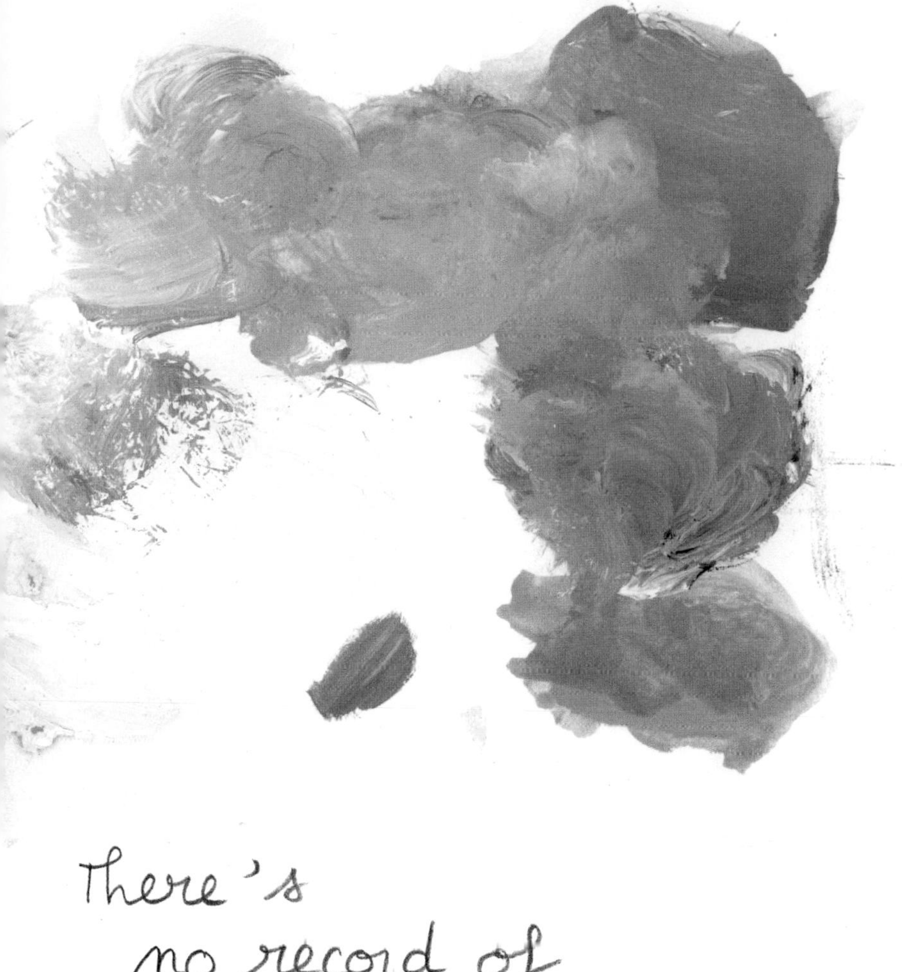

There's
no record of
their intimate
lives.

June 19

I'm alone in J.'s bed, he's sleeping down-stairs, we've just had a fight.

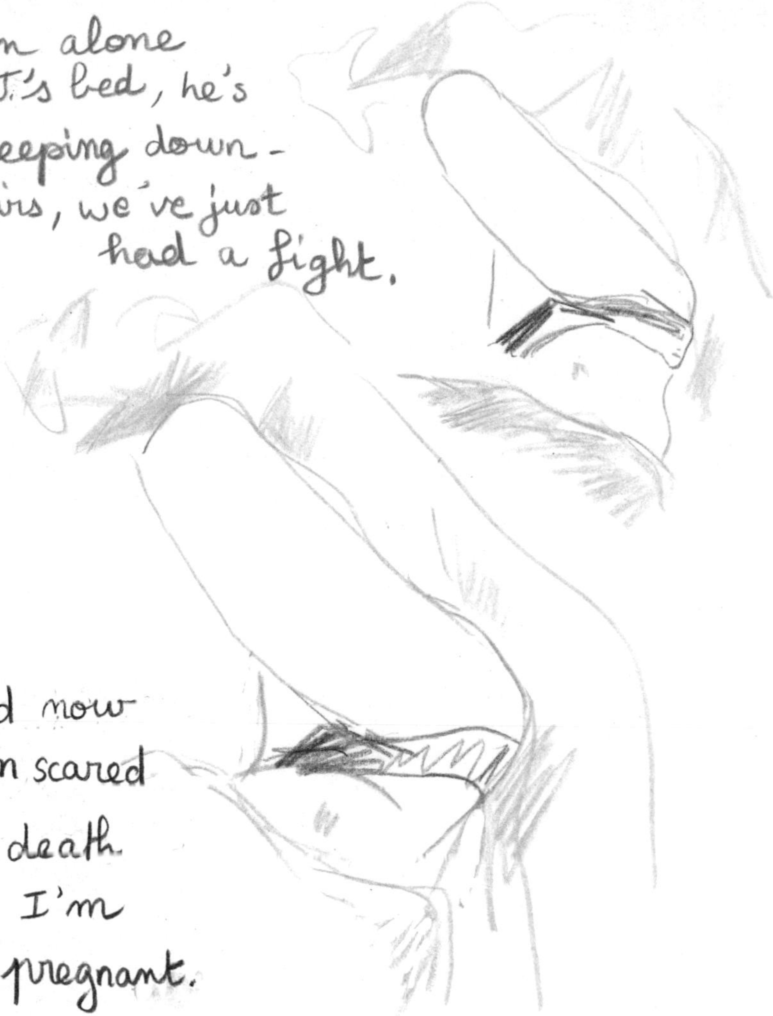

and now I'm scared to death. I'm pregnant.

Thanks to daphné b., catherine ocelot, marcela huerta, aleshia jensen, helge dascher, the d+q team.
And to moomin and the Helsinki Comics center.

Some of the feminaries that proved invaluable while I was writing this book:

King Kong Theory, Virginie Despentes
            translated by Stéphanie Benson
Being Here Is Everything, Marie Darrieussecq
            translated by Penny Hueston
Mémoire de Fille, Annie Ernaux
Choir, Rosalie Lavoie
The Neapolitan Novels by Elena Ferrante
            translated by Ann Goldstein
Suzanne, Anaïs Bardeau-Lavalette,
            translated by Rhonda Mullins
Mettre la hache, Pattie O'Green
Maman Sauvage, Geneviève Elverum
Réflexions autour d'un tabou: l'infanticide
                    (collectif anonyme)
The comics of Liv Strömquist and Mirion Malle
Tender Points, Amy Berkowitz
And all the works of Tove Jansson

The narwhal sweatshirt was made
            by gabrielle laïla Tittley

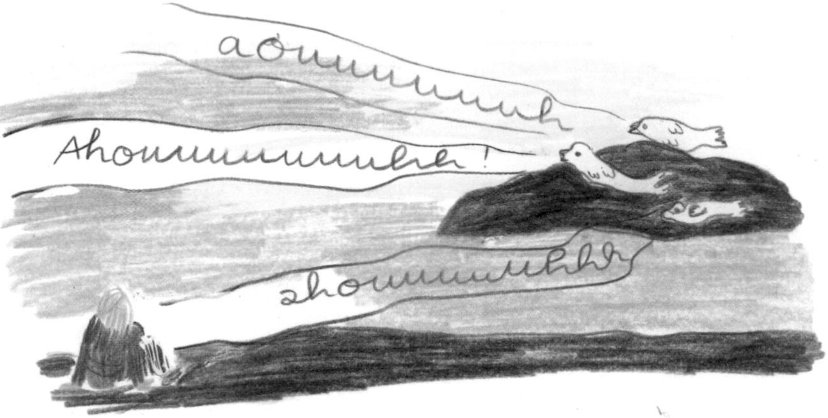
aouuuuuuuuh
Ahouuuuuuuuhh!
ahouuuuuuhhh

julie delporte was born in Saint-Malo, France, in 1983. She presently resides in Montreal, Canada, and *This Woman's Work* is her third graphic novel, after *Journal* (2014) and *Everywhere Antennas* (2015). She holds a degree in cinema studies and was a fellow at the Center for Cartoon Studies in White River Junction, Vermont. When she's not working on comics, she makes ceramics, writes poetry and essays, and works on risograph and silkscreen projects. She loves animals, plants, and sometimes humans.